THE BOOK WHAT I WROTE

THE BOOK WHAT I WROTE

ERIC, ERNIE AND ME

EDDIE BRABEN

Hodder & Stoughton

Copyright © 2004 by Eddie Braben

First published in Great Britain in 2004 by Hodder and Stoughton
A division of Hodder Headline

The right of Eddie Braben to be identified as the Author
of the Work has been asserted by him in accordance with the
Copyright, Designs and Patents Act 1988

A Hodder and Stoughton Book

1 3 5 7 9 10 8 6 4 2

A CIP catalogue record for this title is
available from the British Library

ISBN 0 340 83373 4

Typeset in Monotype Sabon by Hewer Text Limited, Edinburgh
Printed and bound by Mackays of Chatham Ltd, Chatham, Kent

Hodder Headline's policy is to use papers that are natural, renewable
and recyclable products and made from wood grown in sustainable forests.
The logging and manufacturing processes are expected to conform to the
environmental regulations of the country of origin

Hodder and Stoughton Ltd
A division of Hodder Headline
338 Euston Road
London NW1 3BH

To Deidree, for making life beautiful

ACKNOWLEDGEMENTS

I would like to thank the following for their help and advice throughout my career, erm . . .

SERIOUS ACKNOWLEDGEMENTS

Thank you so very much, Graham McCann. Your immaculate biography, *Morecambe and Wise*, proved my lifebelt on the scores of occasions when I went blank trying to remember names, and dates of shows.

My sincere thanks to Norma and Janet, the ladies of the 'Orme Court Comedians and Comedy Writers' Protection Society'.

And thanks also to Helen at Stodder & Houghton for all her superb efforts in giving this work a meaningful shape.

Foreword

This is not a textbook with precise detail, nor is it a powerful novel with a strong storyline. It's the story of my time with two mates who happened to be the funniest and most-loved double-act in the rich and glorious history of British comedy.

It is also about ordinary men and women, people who unknowingly inspired my comedy style, who made me smile and, quite often, laugh out loud. What they said and the things that they did sometimes found their way into my comedy writing. They were the very funny bits.

This book is an autobiographical chocolate box. If it has a theme it is an earnest desire to make you feel good. So, let us begin by giving thanks to the God of laughter. Is there a God of laughter? 'Giggles', perhaps. Yes. I like that: 'Giggles, the God of Laughter.'

My biggest problem when I came to write this chronicle, was me. I was the biggest problem because I was creating problems that weren't there, I was building hurdles I didn't have to jump. How did I manage this? Well, before I placed the very first word on paper, I was thinking: 'I can't spell, I don't know any big words, I haven't been to college or to a university, which makes me as thick as a king-size beef burger.' Ruggish! Ruggish! Ruggish! Writing a book isn't as difficult as those who write them make them out. Go in to any bookshop and you will see thousands and thousands and more thousands of books, millions of them! Do you really think that the people who wrote them were all brilliant scholars with a long line of A levels? Ruggish!

I can't spell, but fortunately there's somebody in the publisher's office who can and he/she will correct all my spelling mistakes and place all the punctuation marks in the correct places. (I have been known to put all the punctuation marks in a matchbox with a note: 'Please put these where they belong.')

All the words you will ever need to use are in the dictionary, all you have to do is pick the right ones, put them on paper in the order you want and you're home on a pig's back. That's what I have done – I think. Anyway, this is the book what I wrote.

THE BOOK WHAT I WROTE

Walk This Way

It's not easy being a legend. Us legends never get a minute to ourselves. Even when I'm out in the street, mothers point at me and say to their children, 'Do you see that man over there? He's a legend.'

'Which man, Mum?'

'That man on the corner; the one selling the balloons.'

That's about right, and it could have been a lot worse.

The day I was leaving school at the age of fourteen I left with these words of encouragement from my teacher: 'I'll see you in a couple of years time when you come to empty my dustbin.'

Huh! Little did he know he was talking to a trainee legend.

I don't think he ever forgave me for the answer I gave to a question he asked in class: 'Where does Demerara sugar come from?' I put my full-of-confidence hand up and said, 'The Co-op, sir.' I really was as thick as the leg of a billiard table. When I look back over my life it's rather like taking the lid off a box of chocolates because there's so much to choose from, some I like more than others. I don't like the hard ones or the dark chocolate ones with nuts in, so they're staying in the box. I'm only going to take out the ones I know I'm going to enjoy.

I was once doing an interview for a very prestigious and much-respected journal on 'How I Became a Legend'. I think it was the *Beano*. The reporter asked me to describe myself and I couldn't do it. I could do it now because the last three videos I bought must prove something. They are *The Thief of Baghdad*, Walt Disney's *Pinocchio* and Steven Spielberg's *E.T.* I also sent off for Will Hay in *Oh, Mr Porter* but that was issued by Virgin trains and hasn't arrived yet. It's quite true about those videos and only now after so many years do I realise it's something that I share with Eric and Ern – we never quite grew up.

It was the very start of our relationship, and I wanted to bring into the writing one of their most endearing characteristics: their innocence. One of the ways in which I established this early on was by having Eric reading either the *Beano* or the *Dandy*. This was particularly effective whenever I wrote a bed sketch.

One of the very early bed sketches had Eric reading the *Beano*. After the recording Eric called me up on the set; they were still pyjama-clad in the bed and the audience hadn't left. I went up to the bed and Eric handed me *The Wind in the Willows* he had been reading in the sketch.

'Open it. I think you might like it.'

I opened it up and inside the cover they had written, 'To Eddie "Stolen" from BBC props. July 1969'.

I treasure that beautiful book.

Since that July night in 1969 many of the guests who appeared in the shows have signed their names.

Des O'Connor wrote, 'What am I doing in this book? Get me out!'

Peter Cushing signed his illustrious name with a request: 'As you appear to be well acquainted with Messrs Morecambe and Wise, might you be able to persuade them to pay me my fee?' Peter appeared in so many scary, bite-your-neck films. Anyway, Peter was a vegetarian: he only ate greengrocers. He was a very gentle gentleman and we became good friends, a friendship that blossomed when we discovered we shared the same hobby, collecting cigarette cards, and he was so very proud of the fact that he was featured in more than one set of cards, the ultimate accolade for the collector.

More than likely, I'll appear in a set of cards. I'm sure to if they ever issue a set called 'Legends of Tarryasson Street School'.

Tarryasson Street featured quite often in our comedy routines, we used it because it had a good Northern, working-class ring to it, but there's no such place, because I made it up. Now, just watch the letters pouring into the publisher's office telling me there are hundreds of Tarryasson Streets. I'll probably get one from the President of the Tarryasson Street Appreciation Society. More than likely, a very angry letter from Lord Tarryasson, giving me stick for deriding the good name of his late grandfather, the Fourth Duke of Tarryasson. I'll probably discover that the Americans have a National Tarryasson Street Day with parades and cheerleaders leaping all over the place and shouting 'T–A–R—' well, you know what they're like over there. The mythical Tarryasson Street is, in fact, the genuine bricks and mortar of Monkswell Street in Liverpool's South End.

Number 24 was the place of my birth on Duck Apple night, 1930. Incidentally, whatever became of Duck Apple night? For some reason that I can't understand we have done away with it in favour of the American Halloween. Why? Now, on what used to be Duck Apple night, children knock at my door and say, 'Trick or Treat?' The first time this happened to me I was puzzled, never come across this one before.

'What do you mean, "Trick or treat"?'

A tiny, bright-eyed and rosie-cheeked spokesman smiled up at me and said, 'You give us fifty quid each or we'll fragment your kneecaps', or some such threat. We're all suffering from Uncle Samitis. We don't have chemist shops anymore: it's 'pharmacy' now. The local garage is a 'petrol station' and the cinema is the 'movies'. Boys and girls are called 'guys'. We don't 'pay attention' we 'listen up'. I'm going to shut up and get off the soap box.

Unfortunately I'm not very good at recalling my childhood, as it all happened when I was very young. My mother did say that when I was born I came as a complete surprise, as she was expecting a roll of lino. She told me that joke when I was old enough to appreciate that type of humour. I was about two and a half at the time. My father once came out with a line that amused me so much that I used it many years later in a flat sketch. It first raised a laugh when my mother was looking through the curtains of our front parlour. I don't know why it was always called the front parlour – it was the only one we had.

She was looking through the window and my father said, 'Come away from there; people outside will think it's a pet shop.' It made me laugh and it made many people laugh thirty years on.

So, that must prove that it's in the genes, and if my father had been a golfer it would have been in the plus fours.

It's rather pleasant for a nice, amiable, grey-headed old gentleman like myself to look back at my childhood, because I really did enjoy it. I'm enjoying the one I'm having now as well.

Cross my heart, I really and truthfully can't remember anything nasty or unpleasant from those early years, except for my father complaining, 'Christ, this bloody house is freezing!' at five thirty in the morning when he reluctantly left my mother's side to begin his twelve-hour day, six days a week job as a butcher in Liverpool's St John's Market for a reward of four pounds ten shillings a week.

The very same workplace in which TV presenter Anne Robinson and award-winning journalist Gillian Reynolds occasionally helped their mums on their respective stalls. It was also the building in which, at the age of twenty, I proved a complete and utter disaster as a vendor of fruit and vegetables.

Without question, the market's greatest gift to the world must have been George. Let's hear it for George! I often passed the time of day with George when he came to fill his bucket at the tap next to my stall. I really was very naive in those days, because I could see nothing unusual about George, even though he was tall, with a willowy figure, long black eyelashes and he talked and walked a bit differently compared to other lads I knew. One day at the tap George told me he was going down to London the following week and might not be coming back. He didn't elaborate. The joke at the time, 1953, was that George had gone to Somerset House to change his name and that he had accidentally gone through the wrong door and changed his sex.

This really did happen, because George went on to make headlines the world over as April Ashley. George became a beautiful woman, dated and fêted by the rich and famous, lots of newspaper and TV interviews. Which all goes to prove that if you lose your bearings it isn't necessarily a bad thing.

Now was St John's Market a hotbed of talent, or what?

You're probably right.

My father was very proud of the wireless set he'd bought; this was in 1938 and was the first wireless we ever had. It cost him five pounds, and was a Marconi, the size of a small shed.

Dad had put a shelf up on the wall for the wireless and my mother was a little apprehensive because he wasn't the best in the world at DIY. If he had to repair something and it couldn't be fixed with a six-inch nail, it stayed broken.

He lifted the wireless up and placed it on the shelf, which collapsed and took with it a large quantity of wallpaper, plaster and four six-inch nails. Fortunately he didn't let go of his beloved Marconi; unfortunately the weight caused him to take a step backwards and his black wavy hair got entangled in the flypaper hanging from the light. I knew what was going to happen next and ran quickly upstairs, closely followed by my sisters, Shirley and Lilian. 'Sod it! Bugger it! Bloody thing!' My mother said, 'Why don't you put the wireless on the table? We can all eat in the backyard.' He saw the funny side after he had washed the sticky mess out of his hair. When he'd sorted himself out he knocked on the wall, and a minute later Mr Charnley came in from next door.

'What's up, Ted?'

Father pointed to the wireless. 'What do you think, Jim?'

Jim was impressed: 'It's a Marconi!'

Dad lovingly polished the top of it with his elbow. 'Best wireless you can buy.' He then delivered a line I shall never forget. He said, 'On a clear night you can get Birkenhead.'

Radio is and always has been my first love, and I would very gladly, very happily give the Nobel Prize for Jolly Biffing Entertainment to the man who invented Radio 4. Wednesday night was the highlight of my week: it was the night I was allowed to stay up late and listen to Arthur Askey in *Band Wagon*. I was seven and he was the first man on the wireless to make me laugh. I liked Arthur Askey because he sang funny songs about bees and moths and called me 'Playmate'.

I was totally captived, enhanced, astonished and amazed at this magical box called the wireless. Even now, all these years on, if I ever have to go to Broadcasting House I pause outside in awe and think, *Is this really happening? Is it me actually going into the BBC?* I even went up to the floor, then on to the roof so that I could boast, to whoever was interested, that I had been to where Arthur lived with his best friend 'Stinker', Lewis the goat, Mrs Bagwash and her daughter, Nausea. The child's wonderment has never left me.

*

Jeffrey Green was my very best friend from when I was seven. We lived in the same street, we went to the same school and sat in the same class, we slept in the same bed when we were evacuated, and when we left school we both started our first jobs at Ogden's Tobacco Factory as well.

I was tall and thin; Jeffrey was short and stocky with close-cropped hair. Whenever he knocked at our back kitchen door to see if I was in, my mother answered and would call out, 'Bullet 'ead wants to know if you're playing out.' Always complimentary.

Jeffrey was ten and I was nine when we were evacuated to the village of Gaerwen on Anglesey. We marched from the station to the school hall on a very wet and cold evening in May 1940. Three hours later two very hungry, and what must have been very pathetic, boys sat side by side. We were the only two left out of the twenty-four children who had entered the hall: the others had been carefully selected and taken off to their new homes by very caring temporary mums.

There was a woman sitting behind a desk in the hall. She had a WI hat on and kept staring at us, when she occasionally smiled it wasn't very convincing. She was probably thinking, 'If these two aren't taken in the next half hour I'll push the little buggers off the Menai Bridge!'

She didn't get the opportunity, because the phone rang. 'Hello . . . Mrs Hughes? . . . No, they haven't all gone . . . I've two left . . . Girls? . . . all the girls have been taken . . . two boys . . . Come and have a look for yourself . . . see you in a bit.'

The WI lady was beaming. 'Mrs Hughes will be here soon. Lovely house, very nice.' Then came the piece of information that made us both look at each other in total disbelief and more than a little terror. 'Mr Hughes is a schoolteacher.'

We'd travelled all the way to get away from Hitler and we were going to live with a schoolteacher! Mrs Hughes arrived.

She looked at us, walked around us, sniffed, poked us in the ribs; then said to the WI lady in Welsh, 'Let's push the little buggers off the Menai Bridge.'

Mrs Hughes was the most gentle lady I have ever met; even better, she was not unlike my mother. She was tiny, slightly built with jet-black hair, a beautiful complexion and merry blue eyes. In complete contrast, Mr Hughes was tall, bony, thin and angry looking, though in fact, he never was. Really, he was delighted to have two boys living in his home. A school teacher without children of his own, he was a Welsh Mr Chips.

He took us for rides in his car (I'd never ridden in a car before), he took us for walks over the hills behind Gaerwen, some of them more than fifty feet high. They both took us to Chapel three times on Sunday. And just in case we were missing God between Sunday School and evening service, Mr Hughes opened up the parlour, which was only ever opened on a Sunday. In we all went and Jeffrey pumped away while Mr Hughes played the harmonium and knocked out half a dozen hymns before Welsh tea and Mrs Hughes' memorable sponge cake and scones.

'Fancy rabbit pie for supper tomorrow, boys?'

Mr Hughes was carrying a gun under his arm, a real gun!

'Come on. Put your wellies on and let's bag a few rabbits.'

We followed Mr Hughes through wet Welsh fields.

'Stop.' He hissed this command and we stopped. He pointed and we saw the rabbit about twenty yards ahead, a happy looking creature nibbling away. But not for long. The noise of the shotgun terrified Jeffrey and me, all of a sudden this wasn't a fun adventure anymore, this was rather nasty, this was real and neither of us liked it.

'Go and collect it,' said Mr Hughes, before marching off into the next field. He looked gladiatorial. I would have said that had I known what it meant then.

We found the rabbit: it wasn't dead. 'Get a brick,' said Jeffrey.

'What for?'

'Can't let it suffer.'

'I can't drop a brick on a rabbit.'

'We'll do it together.'

We found a large stone in the hedge, lifted it up together and after my count of three, dropped it on the rabbit. We had our eyes closed. 'It's not suffering now,' said Jeffrey.

We were both crying.

'We bloody hate you, Mr Hughes.'

If we hadn't dropped a stone on that rabbit it would be sixty eight now.

One winter evening, Mr Hughes was reading his copy of the *Caernarvon and Denbigh Herald*, his favourite newspaper.

He said to me, 'Do you fancy a job, Edwin?'

This surprised me.

'Are you serious, Mr Hughes?'

'Of course I'm serious. Just right for you this job is.'

'What kind of a job? I'm not good at sums.'

'That doesn't matter, Edwin, not for this job.'

'What will I have to do?' For some reason, he always called me Edwin.

'Well, it says here that the donkey has died at the slate quarry.'

He hid behind his newspaper and it shook as he laughed at his joke.

I shall never forget them.

Thank you, Mrs Hughes, thank you for filling those three war years with love and affection.

Thank you, Mr Hughes, thank you for making me the envy of all my city dwelling friends, for it was you who taught me how to say – Llanfairpwllgwyngyllgogerychwyrndrobwll-antysiliogogogoch.

The city of Bangor was only fifteen minutes and a sixpenny return train ride from Gaerwen, and for me it was the most exciting train journey in the world. Once a week I went to the Plaza cinema and then on to Pen-Rhyn Church Hall with my autograph book, for this was the place, much to my delight, that was the new home of the BBC Variety Department, moved up to North Wales because of the bombs in London. I didn't think the programmes were that bad.

Had I been visiting West End Theatres at that time I don't think I would have gathered such a collection of star names in my book. In just one week I got the autographs of all the stars who were appearing in one of the greatest and most successful radio comedy shows of all time, ITMA – *It's That Man Again.*

The star was Tommy Handley, the man who used the medium of sound in a way never heard before. The show went at breakneck speed, with crazy and hilarious characters whizzing on and off, and with very funny lines. It was a show that blazed a trail that we who came later were grateful to follow. It forever changed the face of radio comedy yet it still remained so very British.

As I waited outside with my autograph book, inside the building, a matter of a few yards from me was a very young John Ammonds. John was a sound-effects man, opening and closing doors for the crazy characters to come and go, knocking coconut shells together, making telephones ring. Young John was learning his comedy trade from its very roots. Along with Eric and Ern I gained so much from him, as John had been a part of the best in British comedy for many years. We were always happy when the final credit read, 'Produced by John Ammonds'.

Autograph hunting had been a hobby of mine from a very early age. One Saturday evening I returned home after a name safari at the stage door of the Pavilion Theatre and getting a couple of signatures, and proudly showed them to my father. He looked at one of the names; it was Monte Rey. Didn't mean anything to me. 'What does he do?'

'Monte Rey sings about brown-eyed senoritas and falling in love south of the border down Mexico way, and he's from Glasgow,' explained Dad. He looked at the next autograph and started to chuckle. 'Billy Matchett? You met Billy Matchett?'

'What's wrong with that, Dad?'

'There's nothing wrong with it, it's just that Billy Matchett is my Uncle.'

In reality he was a distant relative of my gran and my father had called him 'Uncle'.

Needless to say, I was delighted to have such a famous relative no matter how distant he was. For the rest of his life he was also my Uncle Billy.

*

Eight o'clock in Lodge Lane outside the Pavilion Theatre and I had never been up so late in my young life. As I held my father's hand I looked open-mouthed at brilliant colours reflecting from the wet pavement like tropical fish. Shops that were bathed in the gold of gas lamps, barrows laden with fruit, a woman wearing a shawl and selling posies from a basket, and there really was a man selling hot chestnuts. My father gave me a packet of crisps, which I ate in the doorway of the pub he'd just nipped into for a pint of Walker's Best bitter.

Now we were sitting in the best seats in the stalls, three and sixpence each, that's about ten thousand pounds in today's currency. Billy Matchett was first on after the interval, first on after the juggler who gave interval drinkers time to get back to their seats before the star turns came on.

Applause for the juggler and the indicators placed at either side of the stage lit up showing the number 12. Billy Matchett was number 12 in the programme I kept until it fell apart. He came on beaming, a well-built man without being fat. 'Jolly' sums him up. He was wearing a grey suit, shirt, tie and trilby hat. I remember him now and think of a toby jug. He began his act with a silly song that started:

> Pull the cork out of the bottle,
> Humpty, Humpty, Hey!
> Throw your cares away and be happy.

He finished with another very silly, very happy song:

> When you're up to your neck in hot water,
> Be like the kettle and sing.

Going backstage after the show was a disappointment: it was dark, dirty and niffed a bit. I've found this with all theatres from the Pavilion in Lodge Lane to the London Palladium and the Olympique in Paris.

Seeing Billy Matchett was not a disappointment; he was everything I wanted him to be and he was delighted to see me. He gave me half a crown and a complimentary ticket to watch Liverpool play their next game at Anfield. Only much later in adult life did I understand what happened next. As we left his dressing room and on the way to the stage door, Billy stopped a man who I'd seen dancing earlier in the show, and said to him, indicating my father, 'This man's a police inspector. He wants to know what you were up to last night at Lime Street station.'

I couldn't understand why the man suddenly looked frightened. He said to my father, 'Honestly, I was waiting for a friend. I give you my word I wasn't up to anything, sir.'

My father said, 'OK, I believe you. Just don't let me catch you next time. On your way.'

Billy laughed, my father laughed and the dancer looked very angry as he called my father something very untoward. I realised then it was a grown-up joke I'd have to wait some years to appreciate. The comedian who had made me laugh that night gave me a hug and told me to visit him at his home in Mossley Hill, very posh. I did visit him many times, and for the rest of my life he remained 'Uncle Billy'.

I still to this day smile when I remember his joke about the man sitting in a café with a piece of blotting paper in his ear: 'So I said to him, "Why have you got a piece of blotting paper in your ear?" He said, "Quiet! I'm listening to the Ink Spots." '

A very close friend of Uncle Billy's was a man called Bruce Williams, who was an undertaker. Imagine my surprise when I discovered he also had another name, Eddie Latter, and that he wrote comic songs for George Formby. I have this picture of Mr Williams the undertaker standing in church next to a client, and as the congregation is singing 'Now the day has ended', Bruce is thinking, *I might write a song about a window cleaner.*

Remembering the stars I saw as a lad, I thought of Wilfred Pickles. I would have binned Wilfred Pickles if it hadn't been for my sister, the ugly one. (Now both sisters are saying, 'He's talking about you.') She said a lot of people still remember Wilfred because of his radio quiz show *Have a Go*. She was right. It ran from 1946 with a final Christmas special edition in 1972. During that time it travelled nearly eighty thousand miles of the UK, Wilfred had asked close on four thousand questions and nine hundred competitors stood to win the weekly jackpot of thirty-four shillings. That's about two and a half pence. Wilfred's *Have a Go* was one of my favourite radio programmes, so you can imagine how excited I was when my father handed me a brown paper parcel tied with string and said, 'Take this chicken to Wilfred Pickles at the Empire.' I thought he was kidding me, but he wasn't.

'Take it to the theatre between houses at about five o'clock, and make sure he gives you the four shillings.'

I was about fourteen when this memorable event took place and couldn't believe I was going to meet one of the most popular radio stars of ever and ever. To this day you can still see the name Wilfred Pickles as it hangs framed on the wall of the bar at The Rovers Return in *Coronation Street*. It's a reproduction variety bill; Wilfred's name is at the top of the bill as it was that week at the Liverpool Empire. Number One dressing room. I'd never been in a Number One dressing room before. I was now, and a famous face was smiling at me.

'You'll be Ted's lad?'

'Yes, Mr Pickles.'

He took the brown paper parcel, thanked me, gave me a complimentary ticket for the Saturday matinee, the door was closed and I was outside without the money. He hadn't given me the four shillings! *Bloody hell! My dad will go hairless!*

He didn't go hairless but he was a long way from being delighted. 'Bloody cheek! He's given you a two and sixpenny complimentary ticket that cost him nothing and he didn't pay for the poultry.'

Nice one, Wilfred. He'd had a go himself and gone off with the star prize – a fresh chicken.

*

Ern. What are you reading?

Eric. Mark Twain.

Ern. Who's it by?

Eric. Huckleberry Finn.

The Eric Morecambe you saw on TV was only a slightly magnified version of the man as he really was. I well remember the time when I was staying with Eric and his wife, Joan, at their Harpenden home. I was making a rare visit south for the recording of one of our shows, and it was obvious he was very much on edge. Like all natural-born funny men he was a natural-born worrier, which is understandable because when twenty million people are watching your work you do tend to worry. It was the day before the recording, and Joan, as caring as ever, suggested it might be relaxing if we both went bird watching, a hobby Eric and I shared.

Off we both went, o'er bush and heath. I had the binoculars and Eric had the notepad and pencil as we set off o'er bush and heath. He loved that 'o'er bush and heath'. He said to me, 'Remember that: we might be able to us it,' and use it we did, many times. Anyway, after a couple of minutes something fluttered into a tree just ahead of us. I raised the binoculars, looked for a couple of seconds and said, 'Good Lord!' Quick as you like, Eric replied, 'They're powerful binoculars.' He said, 'Let me have a go with the binoculars,' took them from me and gave me the notepad. After a couple of yards he looked upwards and said, 'Quick! Write this down.' I was really excited. He said, 'A great big pole tied down with two thick wires. Write it down.'

Before the walk was over he'd sighted David Attenborough with a suitcase strapped to his leg and flying south for the winter. This was closely followed by a rare look at the Ozzlum bird. Eric explained that the Ozzlum bird comes here from the desert regions. He said, 'You can't miss it, because it flies backwards to keep the sand out of its eyes, but that does create another problem.' We had a few laughs and he was relaxed by the time we arrived back home.

That Harpenden day out was so enjoyable it inspired a sketch that did quite well in one of our shows, and Eric did say to Ern:

Eric. I'm off now, Ern. Off o'er bush and heath.
Ern. OK.
Eric. O'er bush and heath. I'm off now.
Ern. Good.

17

Eric. Try not to upset yourself. I'm off now, Ern.

Ern. Just go.

Eric. O'er bush and heath with the Raggle Taggle Gypsies. Perhaps a gypsy poem before I leave?

Ern. No.

Eric. Very well. 'Dance to me my gypsy maid, / Dance as the firelight flickers . . .'

Ern. How dare you! I know what you were going to say.

Eric. I was going to say 'cardigan'.

Ern. I thought you were going o'er bush and heath?

Eric. It's pouring with rain. I'll go tomorrow.

Whenever I was in the company of Eric and Ern I did more observing than talking. It was important for me to know and understand these two characters, their feelings towards each other, how they spoke to one another, any favourite words, gestures, their individual characteristics. The three of us were sitting in Ern's dressing room at the BBC TV Centre; there was a break in rehearsals and we were having a cuppa. I hadn't spoken during the conversation and Eric said to me, 'Are you OK?' Ern knew, because he said, 'He's Morecambe and Wise watching.' And I thought I was being discreet.

When writing their sketches, if I could blend all of their character traits into the comedy they would feel comfortable and the viewers might think they were making it up as they went along. Well, it must have worked, because it was quite astonishing, sometimes dispiriting, the number of people who genuinely thought they did just that. And there's me, drinking gallons of tea, hammering the life out of a typewriter for endless hours, day after day. And everyone thinks, 'They make it up as they go along.' Don't they realise there's a young lad in the background on the way to becoming a legend? Those who did think it was all made up on the spur of the moment are in very good company. In 1999 I was privileged to meet the Duke of Edinburgh at the unveiling of the truly stunning Eric Morecambe statue on the promenade of his home town, at the ceremony performed by Her Majesty the Queen. The Duke of Edinburgh shook hands with Joan Morecambe, Sir Robin Day, Sir Frank Finlay, and I was next in line. The Duke shook my hand and said, 'So you're the writer chappie? I always thought that they made it up as they went along.' That was too much for me to take. 'No, they do not make it up as they go along. When your missus makes her Christmas Day speech to the nation, does she make it up as she goes along?'

I really did say that, but so very quietly. I was the only one who heard it.

*

The year 1945 is well remembered. Not only did I leave school; it was also the year a man in a raincoat asked me if I'd like to earn half a crown. I very much wanted to earn half a crown – it would pay for the best seat at the Carlton Cinema, (our posh cinema). Everywhere had a posh cinema in those days, and another cinema that didn't cost so much to get in, because it was a bit grotty. Our not so posh cinema was the West Derby. Downmarket it might have been, but the manager was always standing and smiling in the foyer as he said 'Good evening' to all his patrons. When the cinema was full and it was a wet and warm night the fireman used to walk slowly down the aisle spraying disinfectant over our heads from a brass cylinder. I used to sniff it and think, *That's nice*. I thought it was perfume.

'Do you want to earn half a crown?'

I noticed the man who asked me that question also had a ginger moustache. I'd been warned about men with ginger moustaches, especially the ones wearing raincoats.

'What do I have to do?'

He handed me a sheaf of papers. 'Shove this lot through letter boxes.'

I looked at one of the leaflets and it had his picture on it, and underneath was printed, 'Vote for Harold Wilson.'

'Is this you? Are you Harold Wilson?'

'I am.'

'My dad says that he's going to vote for you.'

'Your dad's very sensible.'

I tried to get him up to four shillings but he wouldn't budge. He should have become Chancellor of the Exchequer.

Instead he became mine host at 10 Downing Street in 1964. I'll bet he only became Prime Minister so that he could appear in the Morecambe and Wise show in 1978. It was a very funny sketch, and credit where credit is due: it was written by two good friends of mine, Barry Cryer and John Junkin. I think I was suffering from mental fatigue at the time. It would have been nice to have met him: we could have talked about my part in his rise to worldwide political acclaim.

*

Mental sinews were stretched to the limits in order to recall this next episode in as much detail as possible, because it is a very, very special memory.

I was twenty years old and busy at my little fruit and veg stall, turning the oranges around so the rotten bits didn't show, when a voice behind, a very cultured voice, said, 'Could I have a couple of apples, please?'

When I turned around and saw who it was I froze on the spot (and remember, I was an enormous film fan). It was John Mills. John Mills! And standing beside him was the breathtaking Joan Greenwood. John Mills at my stall and he wanted a couple of apples! My first instinct was to spring to attention, salute smartly and say, 'Torpedoes loaded and ready to fire, sir.' Captain Mills would have returned my salute and replied 'Carry on, number two.' Then he would have turned the peak of his cap to the back of his head and snapped, 'Up periscope.'

He didn't say any of these things; he said, 'Could I have a couple of apples, please?'

'Flustered' just about describes the state I was in as I placed the two apples in a bag and handed them over. 'Thank you,' said John Mills, in person to me. 'Thank you so very much,' said Joan Greenwood, in that wonderful plummy voice. This was something I was going to talk about until my dying day, and I needed proof. Quick, before they start to move off. 'Could I have your autograph, please?' John Mills smiled. 'Yes. Of course.' Then a silent panic on my part: I didn't have my autograph book; I didn't have anything respectable for these two illustrious film stars to put their names on, except . . . 'I'm terribly sorry about this but would you mind signing on this brown paper bag.' They both graciously signed on the brown paper bag; then left for the Royal Court Theatre where they were appearing in a play written by John's wife, Mary Haley Bell. I also remember standing as close as I respectfully could to Joan Greenwood, so that I could say to my mother, 'She came up to about here.'

Let's take a massive leap forward to October 1971 and a telephone call from John Ammonds, now the producer on our show.

'We've got John Mills for our next show.'

I couldn't believe this one.

'We've really got John Mills?'

'Yes. If you could come up with an idea for a main sketch. We'll also need a two- or three-minute introduction chat in front of the curtains.'

'That's written, John.'

'I beg your pardon?'

'The bit in front of the curtains; it's written.' Then I explained to him what had happened twenty years earlier.

'Good Lord. That really happened?'

It most definitely really happened.

This is how the fact became comedy fiction in the Morecambe and Wise show, October 1977:

Eric. We have met before. A small grocer's shop next door to a theatre in Manchester.

John. I did appear in a play in Manchester in 1950.

Eric. You came in one day and I asked you for your autograph. You signed it for me on a banana.

Ern. On a banana?

John. I remember that.

Ern. You never forget autographing on a banana.

John. To Eric!

Eric. Yes. On that banana it said, 'To Eric, yours sincerely John Fyffe Mills.'

John. I remember that very well. It was a good few years ago.

Eric. I've still got that banana.

John. After all these years?

Eric. I ate the banana but kept the skin. It's all shrivelled up now.

John. It would be.

Eric. It happens to us all in time. On that banana all you can read is 'JiMills'. Ern, what do I say to you every time I see a banana?

Ern. John Mills.

It wasn't until the show had been recorded that I spoke to John Mills about the reality of that sketch. Very much to my surprise he did remember signing my brown paper bag. Come to think of it, I don't think I gave him his change.

Comedy L Plates

Rarely, if ever, do I recount my life and experiences as a Captain in the Royal Marine Commandos. Active service in various world trouble spots was somewhat hazardous. It was a period of some unpleasant memories best left in the past. For that reason medals are still kept locked away and never displayed, a time in my life I always try to avoid, as I do now, because it's a load of cobblers. The truth is, I spent two years in National Service as a dishwasher in the cookhouse at RAF Kenley in wooded Surrey.

'2424082. AC2 Braben, sir!' Dishwasher, sir! I reached the elevated rank of dishwasher through trying to be funny; I spent a lifetime trying to be funny. It's not something I do to be offensive; it's just the way I am. What happened was, I'd finished my eight weeks basic training at RAF Bridgnorth, which is about ten miles from nowhere in particular, and I was being interviewed by a flight sergeant, a not very nice man. Before I go any further I have to confess I always have a problem spelling 'interview'; it throws me every time it crops up and it must have cropped up ten million times. It's the same with 'barrel' and 'tunnel': reach for the dictionary – and I'm supposed to be a writer? I'm in good company because some of the greats of English literature weren't too hot at spelling. Would you believe, Shakespeare couldn't spell 'microwave'?

Ernie Wise was another great writer who had problems with words. Ern was never sure if it was one or two f's in pharaoh.

Anyway, this not very nice flight sergeant asked me what I wanted to be now I'd done my training. I told him I really was very keen to become an ex-serviceman. I smiled; he didn't – just a scowl. And seven days later I was shoehorned into a tiny white kitchen with a supply of pot scourers and gallons and gallons of washing-up liquid, the equivalent of in those days.

After a couple of weeks I niffed, I really did stink of grease, and, as is usually the case when somebody is a bit ripe, I didn't even notice. Day after day I was washing grease-encrusted pots, pans and trays, hundreds of them, and not surprisingly nobody would come near me because of the overpowering stench of grease. No matter how crowded it was when I went into the canteen at night, I always got a table to myself. I swear, if I'd put a wick on top on my head I would have burned for a year. That tiny kitchen was my kingdom; I ruled it on my own and was glad of the pots and pans and the grease because it meant I was excused all parades and guard duties – my clothing had become too greasy to be seen in open areas, this despite my wearing overalls. I was happy: I never went hungry, and dogs loved me.

It was in that cookhouse that I did my best ever ad-lib. It was as far as I was concerned, because it was aimed at somebody who really deserved it, Flight Lieutenant Alton. On this particular day he was the inspecting officer, lifting lids off pots with his stick, prodding, poking and sniffing everything in sight with a pained expression as we all stood to attention. He poked me in the chest with his stick, as though I was something noxious and said, 'Are there any mice in this kitchen?' I said, 'No, sir; it's chicken today.' Everybody laughed. Everybody, except Flight Lieutenant Alton, who, before his embarrassed exit, put me on a charge. If you are still with us, Flight Lieutenant Alton, and reading this in a Home for Retired Burkes, I forgive you. RAF Kenley was the location for that Epic Kenneth More film *Reach For The Sky*. Whenever I watch it on TV I get so nostalgic and weepy that I have to go into the kitchen and start washing up.

The cinema in Caterham was just fifteen minutes' walk down the hill from the camp and I wonder how many times I've walked past Peter Cushing's house without knowing it.

On my rare afternoon off I could be found in that den of dreams, especially if they were showing a musical film.

On one such afternoon I was sitting at the back of the stalls with my arm around a disgraced vicar, and just as the gorgeous Doris Day started to sing one of my favourite songs of ever and ever, a song called 'Again', the woman in front of me started eating a carrot. That is quite true and something difficult to forget. Can you imagine what it would be like if we had vegetarian cinemas? You'd never hear a note or a word. By the way, the bit about the vicar isn't true; it's a line nobody during my time would use and I just had to get it out of my system.

My two years' National Service were worry free and a joyous romp at the Government's expense. The difficult bit was yet to come.

'Are you serving here, or what?'

A customer was eyeing the tomatoes. The reason I wasn't serving, that I was reluctant to serve, was that I really was terribly shy. It greatly embarrassed me when a customer paused at my stall, looked at the goods and waited for me to do what all greengrocers are supposed to do: sell fruit and veg. I'd look the other way or bend down, pretending to adjust the awful, awful artificial grass that was draped around the base of the stall like a tatty skirt. More often than not the client would snort and march off to another supplier, and there were lots of them. I didn't want to be a member of the Royal and Ancient Guild of Greengrocers, even if there was such an organisation.

I forgot to mention that I wore a brown overall coat, God help me! There's got to be an escape tunnel somewhere!

'Excuse me! Are you serving here, or what?' she demanded, as she methodically squeezed the tomatoes.

'I'll be with you in a sec.'

I might be a bit longer than that because I was writing a joke on the back of a brown paper bag. I'd written about 400 that week.

'Are these tomatoes fresh, lad?'

I wonder if she realises she's talking to someone who is going to be a multi-award-winning and universally acclaimed comedy writer one day?

'Are these tomatoes fresh?'

'They should be, missus. They've been lying on top of one another all night.'

She left in a huff, it's a foreign car.

I had one regular customer, a retired bank clerk. He was quiet, very polite which is why the following dialogue took me by surprise when he asked for five pounds of potatoes. Usually the conversation was about the weather or the previous night's TV. Not only did he take me completely by surprise but he made me laugh out loud. He looked at the potatoes.

'What sort are they?'

'King Edwards.'

'They're very big.'

'Yes.'

'They look more like King Kong's.'

Well said, that customer. I'll remember that when I'm being universally acclaimed.

Four or more hundred jokes a week and not one of them worth a smile. Still, I suppose Rudolf Nureyev had to cock his leg up a few thousand times before he made it. The break-through would have to come soon because I was running out of brown paper bags and all the fruit was going rotten. When it did happen it wasn't so much a breakthrough; it was more of a tiny crack in the comedy wall.

'I like this gag.'

It had happened; it was actually happening! I was in the star dressing room at the Liverpool Empire, standing just a couple of feet from one of my comedy icons, Charlie Chester. Bless you, Charlie. Charlie was dressed as Napoleon as he actually read out loud the joke he liked. In all honesty it wasn't the best joke in the world. There have been millions of much better jokes, but this one was special, quite different from any other joke ever written: it was my joke and as Charlie read it out loud it was as if a doctor was telling me I'd had a beautiful baby boy. This was my joke, as read out by Charlie Chester, in the presence of me and a dresser holding Charlie's bottle of stout. 'When Hopalong Cassidy was a baby, his mother knew that he was going to be a cowboy because he always wore a ten gallon nappy.' I left the Liverpool Empire feeling so proud and overjoyed to have just been given a cheque for thirty shillings. 'When Hopalong was a baby. . . .' Wow!

At that time, in the early 1950s, Charlie was doing an enormous amount of radio work and was being well served for comedy material by Bob Monkhouse and Denis Goodwin. Charlie was still buying the odd thirty shillings worth from me and he must have mentioned this to Bob because his agency office rang me and offered me my first ever commission to write a ten-minute spot for Peter Sellers. For this I was paid the monumental sum of ten pounds. Believe me, after the barren years it was a monumental sum. Try as I might I just cannot recall what it was I wrote for Peter. I do remember that halfway through the routine somebody laughed; I think it must have been a drunk and he was quickly ushered out of the studio, because nobody made a sound after that. Twenty years later I came face to face with Peter when we were both godparents to

Graham and Audrey Stark's son, Christopher. Peter Sellers stepped out of a very impressive car and swept past me without saying a word. I did try to tell him that somebody laughed, but he was unmoved. Being an aged legend, like what I am, I don't remember having to use canned laughter in a comedy routine. If it wasn't funny, it had to be worked on until it was. Tough, as they say.

I was watching a sitcom quite recently and a character opened a door and said, 'It's me.' It got a roar of laughter. The years I've spent grinding away trying to think of funny lines when all I had to write was 'It's me.' If I knew then what I know now, I could write the funniest, the most hilarious Morecambe and Wise show of all time:

Eric. Ern?
Ern. Yes.
Eric. It's me.
      Roar of laughter
Ern. Who?
Eric. It's me.
      Roar of laughter
Ern. It's you?
Eric. That won't get a laugh.
Ern. What will get a laugh?
Eric. It's me.
      Roar of laughter

But there was a time when Eric and Ern would have been more than grateful for canned laughter. I had gone to the Empire Theatre to see and hear that great American singer Lena Horne. Before that rare treat I had to sit through a very young and very inexperienced Morecambe and Wise. They were dire! They were two young Northern comics trying to be like the Americans Abbot and Costello, and it just didn't work. Eric came on with an apple on the end of a fishing line and held it over the orchestra pit. When Ernie asked Eric what he was using for bait:

Eric. A worm.
Ern. Where's the worm?
Eric. Inside the apple.

We often spoke of that stage in their careers, the learning time: 'Do anything, try anything, and just keep going until we get it right.' When they returned to that city twenty-five years later they had got it right. I was again in the theatre and it was memorable. That night, as the band struck up with 'Bring me Sunshine' the audience stood, clapped and cheered. This was before Eric and Ern had even set foot on stage. This had only ever happened once before in my experience and that was for Laurel and Hardy. I think that comparison is a fair one.

*

Before Eric and Ern, I spent fourteen ferocious years writing for Ken Dodd. It was the pace of the comedy that was ferocious. If you've ever been to the theatre and watched Doddy perform live, you will know he makes the London Marathon seem like a casual stroll in a garden.

When the curtain finally comes down, if there's a stage hand still around to bring it down, you will witness tearful reunions on the pavement outside the theatre. Anxious relatives, waiting with blankets and hot drinks, rush to embrace their loved ones and sob, 'Where have you been? Christmas wasn't the same without you. We missed you so much; the grandchildren missed you as well.'

The loved ones look surprised. 'Grandchildren? What grandchildren? We didn't have any grandchildren when we went in. Is Neville Chamberlain back from Munich yet?' Meanwhile a thoughtful Doddy is sitting in his dressing room and thinking, 'I wonder how much I could charge for all-day breakfasts?'

Time and time again I've watched a Doddy audience collapse into total exhaustion under a comedy onslaught that has to be seen to be believed. Red-faced ladies of all ages clutching the seats in front of them with both hands and gasping, 'Oh God! I'll have to go to the toilet.'

I was at the Opera House in Manchester when a man in the audience laughed so loud and long that he cracked a rib and was carried out by two paramedics: 'I'm going to see Ken Dodd tonight; if I'm not home by eleven give intensive care a ring.' Many years later when I was talking comedy with Bob Hope in his suite at the Savoy Hotel in London (Did you get that? When I was talking to Bob Hope in his suite at the Savoy) Bob said he'd seen Doddy at the Palladium; the audience was laughing so loud, he said, nobody could hear him booing.'

In my opinion there can be no debate as to who is the funniest stand-up comedian of all time: it's Doddy.

When I was talking comedy with Morecambe and Wise at the YMCA, Accrington (Did you get that? When I was talking comedy with Morecambe and Wise at the YMCA, Accrington) Eric said to me, 'I'll tell you something. We would never follow Ken Dodd.' Ernie agreed. Very honest and probably true. If Eric and Ernie couldn't follow him then nobody could.

There's the world we live in and there's the other very secret world Doddy inhabits. I shared it with him for fourteen years. It's the planet frenzy at a thousand miles an hour. The ratio was five gags per minute; probably more. I was writing one-liners that didn't even take up one line: 'Literature killed him. He got run over by a mobile library'. Or, 'He's a physicist: he put the bubbles into lemonade.' It was one hell of a lick and well worth an ulcer, a relentless pace.

Ken rang me one night from the Royal Court Theatre in Liverpool; he wanted a topical gag. If I remember correctly it was because a newspaper had written a piece that day about

Cliff Richard earning more than the Prime Minister. I told him the gag and he wrote on the back of his hand, 'Did you know that Cliff Richard earns more money than the Prime Minister? I'm not surprised: have you ever heard Harold Wilson singing "Bachelor Boy"?' Then Doddy said, 'I'm on. Speak to this girl.' He handed the phone quickly to a bewildered young lady who had just come off stage. She told me her name was Deidree; she was one of the George Mitchell Singers and came from Carshalton in Surrey, a place I knew well from my days at RAF Kenley.

Up to that point I hadn't been to see the show. I would go the following night; I had to meet the owner of that warm honey voice. We met the following evening and I asked her if she'd like to go for a meal after the show. She said yes, and she said yes again six months later when I asked her to marry me. It really was the voice that did it.

It was a warm summer evening in 1964, three months after that first brief telephone conversation and, hand in hand, we had twice walked the length of London's Regent Street trying to find the Edmundo Ros club. The previous night, after Edmundo had filled the guest spot on the Doddy radio show, he had invited us to his club in Regent Street. Both of us were overjoyed at the invitation, as it would be our very first visit to a nightclub, and not just any old nightclub. The Edmundo Ros Club was the favourite of British and foreign royalty, dignitaries, the elite of the aristocracy, and now me and her. There was a slight problem – I had only fifteen pounds in my wallet, and those places can be a bit pricey.

Footsore and in need of sustenance, we headed for our favourite watering hole, Lyon's Corner House, and what a wonderful establishment that was. Whoever stopped you trading committed a dreadful crime against humanity, at least those of us humans who loved the clatter, the chatter, the brightness and those delightful waitresses in their uniforms of black dresses with crisp white aprons and caps, if 'caps' they were called.

When I'd visited Lyon's on my own I'd had to wait to be shown to a table, and as I'd waited, I'd wondered, dreamed I'd be shown to a table where there sat a young and beautiful girl who was also waiting and dreaming that someone just like me would be placed opposite her. It never ever happened like that. More often than not, I found myself sharing a table with a couple who were overage, overweight and lacking in sparkling dialogue. And they never raised their eyes from the assassination job on their cod, chips and peas. 'Why does it always rain on me?'

It was getting dark as we left Lyon's after an assassination job on a pot of tea for two and a couple of toasted tea cakes – thirteen pounds left in my wallet and I was secretly hoping we wouldn't find that nightclub. But we did find it, very quickly.

The illuminated sign shone out clearly in the night sky: 'The Edmundo Ros Club'. We hadn't seen it before, as it was only put up when it got dark. The young lady sitting behind the desk in the foyer gave me my first problem of the evening.

'That'll be five pounds.'

'Pardon?'

'Five pounds admission fee.'

I told her who I was and this was met with a 'So What?' expression. I paid the five pounds.

Hand in nervous hand we went down the stairs to be met by another young lady who showed us to a table and asked us what we'd like to drink. Eight quid left, the rest of the night still to go. I quickly scanned the drinks list for Tizer, Dandelion and Burdock or Vimto. They didn't have any. Dee asked for a jug of fruit cup; good thinking, and that should last us until I had to leave to catch the sleeper back to Liverpool. Just when I thought I could sit back, relax and enjoy the Latin American music, a woman popped up from nowhere, called out 'Smile!' and took our picture. Two pounds please. Bloody hell! Was there no end to it? No, there wasn't, because another bloody woman with a tray said, 'Would you care to buy a red rose?' How could I say no? Things were now really desperate and as far as I was concerned you could stuff your West End night-club.

'Hello, hello, hello! How lovely to see you both. Forgive me for not greeting you when you first came in. I'm so pleased that you came.' It was the man himself, Edmundo. A very warm handshake for me and a Latin American kiss on the cheek for Dee. 'Did you have to pay to get in? Did you pay for the photograph? The drink and the rose? No, no, no! You are my guests.' Big genial and generous gentleman that he was, he insisted on giving me my money back.

That evening became unforgettable when he asked me if the band could play a request for us. They could and they did play their signature tune, 'Cuban Love Song'.

Is that romantic or what?

It's still a great shame about Lyon's Corner House.

*

My learning class started in 1945. That was the year I left school at a headlong gallop, started work at Ogden's Tobacco Factory and came face to face with a man who gave me my first lesson in the art of the ad-lib. This man was Ernie Blake and he had an ad-lib for everything. No matter what happened, Ernie had his ad-libs ready, and this is it; listen to it because it's good. 'Whoops. Taxi!' Ernie would stand, watching: he was our charge hand. He would stand, waiting from eight o'clock in the morning until six o'clock at night, eight to five on Fridays and eight to twelve on Saturdays, waiting and watching for an opportunity to get in quick with his famous all-over-the-factory ad-lib. No matter what misfortune happened, Ernie was in like a shot. If somebody dropped something, walked into some-thing, hit a thumb with a hammer, gave birth to quads next to the conveyor belt, or if your head fell off and rolled down the lift shaft and came to rest next to the Thick Twist and Gold Flake, Ernie was ready with, 'Whoops. Taxi!'

I shall remember forever and cherish lovingly the golden memory of the day Harry Turner was pushing a truck loaded with wooden crates of Player's cigarettes, and one of the crates toppled off and landed on Ernie's foot. Being a man of con-siderable resilience and, despite the excruciating pain, Ernie surprised as all by coming out with a brand new ad-lib, 'Jesus Christ all bloody mighty!' Under the circumstances it wasn't a bad effort, but it could never replace, 'Whoops. Taxi!'

Almost every Saturday I treated myself to the luxury of a seat in the balcony of the more than splendid Philharmonic Hall, to listen to the Liverpool Philharmonic Orchestra under its re-sident conductor, Dr Malcolm Sargent (he didn't get his sir-hood until 1947). It was at the Phil that I heard the number one, best ever, the gold medal, award-winning ad-lib of ever and ever anywhere in the world. The only problem was, I couldn't laugh out loud and came quite close to giving myself a hernia. It came about because a couple of my mates at work couldn't understand my interest in classical music, not the norm for a young lad working in a factory, when there were hundreds of gorgeous girls waiting for me at the Grafton Ballroom, a dance hall affectionately known worldwide as 'The Sailor's Home'.

Eventually curiosity got the better of Joe Moore and Frank Edwards and one Saturday night they decided to come with me and find out what the attraction was. It was the second half of the concert and we'd reached the main item in the concert, the Grieg piano concerto (not knowing then that it was to play a part in my life yet to come).

About ten minutes into the concerto Frank put sixpence in

the slot to take out the binoculars housed in the back of the seat in front. Up to then everything was as it should have been. He raised the binoculars, very slowly scanned the entire orchestra and then said to me, 'That's a lovely pair of top bollocks on the one playing the cello.' If I live to be 976 I will never ever hear an ad-lib that comes anywhere near that one. The man sitting in front of me obviously heard it because he clamped both hands over his mouth and almost went into convulsions. I defy any writer past, present or yet to come to top that.

Whenever I hear the Grieg piano concerto I chuckle out loud, not because of Morecambe and Wise and André Previn, but because of my mate from Ogden's. When I first told Eric and Ern this story they laughed loud and long and we were thinking the same thing: 'If only.' But we knew we'd never get away with it. What would the critics have said? I know they would have said, 'Whoops. Taxi!'

To be a part of a show when it isn't a show, just a stack of pristine A4 paper, up to writing the closing line, is quite a lengthy trek. It usually worked out at one show to about three hundred ciggies, four gallons of tea and possibly a few minutes head-butting the wall and asking my wife if she knew any jokes. Let's put a sheet of paper into the typewriter and see what happens. Tip-tap-tip-tap-tip-tap. I type with the forefingers of each hand, have done all my writing life, and they now look like pork sausages. What have I written? 'Good evening Ladies and Gentlemen. Welcome to the show.' Now quite honestly that wasn't too difficult. It's the chunk in between that and 'Goodnight and thank you for watching' that causes all the grief. Every other comedy writer I have ever met agrees totally with me on this and we often talk about it when we meet in the queue for the free soup and the round of bread from the Sally Army chuck wagon.

A little trick I often used in the days when the pressure was on, was to draw with a pencil the outline of a TV screen on the wall above the typewriter and when ideas weren't coming, and that only happened about every day, I'd look at this pretend TV screen, watch two little figures walk into it and let them do whatever they had a comedy mind to.

I have just drawn a pretend TV screen on the wall above my desk (washable crayon if you're trying this at home). I promise you, I give you my solemn word of honour and cross my heart and hope to die in a cellar full of Des O'Connor CDs, the following really did happen:

> *Ern looking very worried as he walks slowly back and forth.*
> *Eric is watching.*

Ern. Eric.

Eric. If you like, I could change it.

Ern. I'm very worried.

Eric. I could see by the way you were walking that you're worried: that is your worried walk. Do you need new batteries?

Ern. Will you listen to me?

Eric. A couple of double A batteries should do it because you've only got little legs. I'll put them in; I'm not proud.

Ern. Please listen.

Eric. After all, I did offer to shave your legs when you had that back problem and you couldn't reach.

Ern. Eric, I am very worried.

Eric. You're upset.

Ern. Very.

Eric. Understandable, and I'm very sorry about your goldfish. I honestly didn't know that the cat could swim.

And off they went in search of the jocular jugular. Where that routine would have gone from that point, I really don't know.

What I do know is that it was something I wanted to develop later on, along with a lot of other Morecambe and Wise routines that had yet to experience their first chuckle. It's many years since I've used that blank screen on the wall device and I'm delighted it still has its uses. It worked exceptionally well for me when it resulted in one of my favourite sketches of ever and ever.

It came about through Eric telling me they loved to work with props, anything they could hold, pick up or carry. 'If it's a good prop we'll get the laughs.' I gave them a prop I'd first seen on the pretend screen over my desk. He was a ten-foot-tall ventriloquist's doll, and his name was Oggie. Eric staggered under the weight and size of Oggie, as he struggled with him through the curtains to meet an astonished Ern.

Ern. What's that thing?
Eric. Ventriloquist doll.
Ern. I've never seen one that big.
Eric. Solid wood.
Ern. Really?
Eric. His mother was a Pole.
Ern. Where did you get him from?
Eric. Do you know that clearing, Epping Forest? That's him.

And it went on for seven or eight laughter-rewarding minutes, and was one of those very rare occasions when a sketch took as long to write as it did to perform. When you're an icon like what I am, you have to get everything spot on; it has to be perfect. If I don't put the right words down in the right order they won't make sense, and there'll be a right cock-up. It must have been the same for other icons like Michael and Angelo when they were painting the Cistern in the Chapel. If they had used that cheap 'Buy one get one free paint' then all that stunning work they did on the ceiling would have looked like a damp patch. I don't intend falling into the trap of finding the easy way out – I'm going to get this right. What I certainly don't want is for you to put this book down and say, 'I've had it with this rubbish. I think I'll watch *Emmerdale*.' Which, I believe, a lot of first-time offenders are having to do now instead of community service.

Fraught

'Fraught': that's just about right, that's the way it was on that day in the office of Bill Cotton, Head of BBC Television Light Entertainment.

The room was fraught with tension and anxiety as I met Morecambe and Wise for the first time in the spring of 1969, and it was a very important meeting for the assembled quartet.

The success of this meeting and its potential was important to Bill Cotton, as he was the person who had come up with the idea of me writing for Eric and Ernie – if it didn't work he had two of the biggest stars in the country with nowhere to go. For Morecambe and Wise it was crucial; their future as the most popular duo on British TV was in the balance. Ernie had said he thought it was the end for both of them, following Eric's health setback and the sudden and unexpected departure of their writers who had served them so well in the past, Hills and Green. The meeting was crucial to me, as I had a wife, three children and a mortgage.

Outside the comedy arena nobody had heard of Eddie Braben, so I had no problems regarding my status. I was a very long way from being a household name, unlike the two stars I was about to meet. And the awful truth is that ever since Bill Cotton had telephoned me and arranged this meeting I had thought it was never going to work, and that I wasn't right for Morecambe and Wise. This thought was based on the fact that I had watched a lot of their shows and they didn't make me laugh; I was not a fan.

In the early stages of the meeting there was a lot of nervous laughter, but gradually, over the next couple of hours, things became relaxed and friendly as we discussed our likes and dislikes. We had quite a lot in common. We were all from the North and, most importantly, we all laughed at the same people: Jimmy James, Dave Morris, Laurel and Hardy, and Tommy Cooper.

When Bill suggested I might be able to write for them Eric was sceptical. 'He writes great lines for Ken Dodd, but we don't work like he does; we have a different approach to comedy.' I also think that it was a scepticism shared by Ernie, but nobody had greater doubts about my ability to write for them than I had. Fortunately Bill Cotton had the faith and belief I so woefully lacked, because he suggested I go back to Liverpool, write something for Eric and Ernie, meet up the following week and see what we had. I was more than happy to do this, but I did say, 'It won't be like anything you've done before,' and both Eric and Ernie reacted with some surprise at this. I was being totally honest when I added, 'I can only write in my style; it will be different, but it's the only way I can make you funny – I hope.' We all went our separate ways, a little anxious as to what the following week might bring.

That week was arguably the most frantic and intense in my writing life. There was very little sleep as I pounded the typewriter relentlessly and reeled off page after page of foolscap comedy, one in every five ripped up and thrown into the waste bin. Deidree pleaded with me in the early hours of the morning to 'Give it a rest.' But I couldn't give it a rest; I had to give it everything, because this was going to be the most important week in my life. And it was.

We met the following week, and I had taken with me an opening spot, a flat sketch and three or four shorter comedy items. I remember Eric and Ernie were surprised, almost astonished at seeing a script fully written out. Eric said, 'You've got "Eric: a line", "Ernie: a line".'

I said, 'It goes like that right through to the end.'

Then it was my turn to be surprised – they told me this was a luxury they'd not had before. 'We used to come in to rehearsal,' said Eric, 'and Hills and Green would have an idea on a piece of paper and we'd all sit around a table and work on it.'

That wasn't my style. They had my style in their hands and they were reading it. I nervously lit my fortieth cigarette. Bill Cotton had a reassuring smile and a gin and tonic as we both awaited the verdict. 'Verdict' says it all, because it was like a courtroom: I was on trial for my future as a comedy writer and the two-men jury were still deliberating, but not for long. They laughed. Bless you both! You two wonderful men! You are laughing! Now you're laughing out loud! Eric Morecambe has taken his glasses off to wipe tears of fun from his eyes. Little Ern, wonderful Little Ern is smiling broadly, and Bill looks so happy. Then they put the scripts down and said they couldn't do it! I was stunned. Bill Cotton pointed out the contradiction of their laughter and the claim they couldn't do it, and it took him just a few minutes to convince them that their own laughter was the answer as to whether they could do it or not.

The first ever Morecambe and Wise show in my reign was recorded on 1 June 1969 and shown on BBC Two on 27 July. As Eric said after that first show, 'I thought that came quite close to being almost not bad.' It must be remembered that this was the first TV show they had done since Eric's heart attack, and any doubts, any anxiety as to his fitness were answered when he walked confidently on, looked inside his jacket, patted his chest and said, 'Keep going, you fool!'

The mirthquake had erupted. I was standing at the side of the studio throughout the recording, listening to that wonderful laughter; then the roars of laughter and the spontaneous applause for lines I prayed would get a reaction. An overjoyed Bill Cotton shook my hand and said, 'Well done.' It was a night I shall never forget if I live to be normal. Little did I know then that something very special had just begun. As I never kept the scripts of any TV or radio shows I have written I don't recall much of the content of that first Morecambe and Wise show. The opening spot was about Eric wanting to change his name:

Eric. I went to Somerset House.
Ern. Is that where you go to change your name?
Eric. Yes. I would have changed my sex, only that door was closed.

After that it was all over. I felt as if my wife had given birth to a beautiful baby girl, that I'd won the lottery and there was sausage, egg and chips for tea.

It was and still is a much treasured friendship. Never at any time, except at our very first meeting, did I feel I was in the company of two megastars: it was always Eric, Ern, always Ern and never Ernie. These were two mates like those I had at Ogden's Tobacco Factory, only with my new mates I was working at a factory in Wood Lane, London W12, and on the night of 1 June 1969 we were trying to produce laughter. It was the most unforgettable of nights.

The three of us walking along the corridor towards Studio 8, it was to be our route to work for many years to come. It was like walking down the yellow brick road to meet the wizard – on this important night we were off to meet six hundred wizards who were waiting for us in the studio; they might make our dreams come true, or not. Over the years I have been in a great many TV studios and theatres all over the country, with all their diverse audiences, but this was something I had never experienced before: a nervous audience. The very second I entered that studio I felt the tension from that audience; I could have torn strips off it. They were quiet, apprehensive, nervously looking around at technicians and stage crew going about their business. Not a toffee paper rustled. I went into the changing room at the side of the studio. 'What are they like?' asked Ern. 'Great,' I lied. The problem was that the audience, because of all the publicity, knew how important this show was. They knew this was Eric's comeback after serious illness; they knew the tried and tested writers had gone and that a new man was responsible. They must also have known just how important they were on this very special night. It was just possible that if the show wasn't funny and they didn't laugh it could well be the beginning of the end for Morecambe and Wise.

They didn't want it to be the end: 'Say something funny and we'll laugh.' And they did laugh. They laughed a great deal, and the applause was spontaneous and generous and, towards the end, had it been possible to do so, that audience would have picked up Eric and Ern and given them a hug. It was the start of something special.

A three-handed act, Morecambe and Wise and audience – the start of TV's greatest love affair.

Bill Cotton came into Eric's room minutes after the show had ended. He had a very large smile and a matching gin and tonic. 'Well?' With that one word he was asking a couple of questions.

'Was I right? Didn't I say at the very beginning that it would work?'

Eric took his hand in both of his and said, 'Who are you, sir?' Ern was beaming, 'It, it really worked.' John Ammonds could hardly contain his delight and enthusiasm when he came down from the production gallery and said, 'Jolly good, chaps.'

I lay wide awake in my sleeping berth back home to Liverpool. Two hours later I still couldn't sleep. I wasn't over-excited at the events of that night; it's just that I'm not very good at travelling sideways.

Whatever else had happened that night I had discovered something quite useless and of no importance – I would always know when the two stars were nervous. This is something they were not aware of until I told them much later. Before the start of a show Ern would stand quite rigid, and with a fixed smile keep asking everyone and anyone if they were 'all right?' He even asked the fireman if he was 'all right?' and he only stood at the back of the studio.

Eric showed his nervous state by pacing in a small circle while clicking his fingers and whistling the signature tune from *Housewives' Choice*. However, what was really causing me some concern as I travelled sideways was that we were doing another show in three weeks' time and I hadn't even written, 'Good evening ladies and gentlemen. Welcome to the show.'

*

When I told my wife I was going to chronicle my doings she must have completely misunderstood me because she put the dog in the next room. The woman who sleeps on my right-hand side, who trims my hair because I haven't got the patience to sit and wait my turn at the barber's, the woman who knows me so well that she quickly switches the radio off when a miserable singer kicks off with that awful dirge, 'Why Does it Always Rain on Me?' – when that woman says she doubts the wisdom of putting my life into words, based on her logic that nobody has ever heard of me, I have to admit: point taken. Also, people much younger than me (you know, 65–70 years old) would never have heard of some of the performers I have worked with. Did I mention I'm writing this with a quill?

You've heard of the Magnificent Hubert? I thought you had. For those of you who possibly haven't heard of this great performer, let me explain exactly what he did to gain international acclaim. The Magnificent Hubert would stand centre stage, remove his purple cloak to reveal sequin-studded green tights. The Magnificent Hubert would then do the splits over a live lobster and sing, 'I who have nothing'. He would acknowledge the thunderous ovation before leaving the stage with a slight limp. The sad reality of that piece of nonsense is that I had wanted to do a 'Magnificent Hubert' routine. Eric would have loved being Hubert with Ern as 'His beautiful assistant, Babette.'

This idea is still racing around my head. I can just see Eric as the Magnificent Hubert, with Ern as his beautiful assistant Babette. Babette would introduce the Magnificent Hubert, who would dramatically explain that he was going to perform an extremely dangerous and death-defying trick: he was going to dive into a tank full of water and containing over one thousand vicious piranha fish. The beautiful Babette would take Hubert's cloak, the curtains would open to reveal one small goldfish in a bowl on a coffee table, Hubert and Babette looking very embarrassed. Hubert looking off and asking if he could have a word with an unseen stage manager and protesting, 'I can't do my dangerous and death-defying trick without a great big tank full of water and over one thousand vicious piranha fish.' The beautiful Babette would be in full agreement. Both protesting as the credits roll. It would have been a different death-defying trick every week.

I know I had it written down in an ideas book, before I'd written the first show. Why I never wrote it up I can't say, because the more I think about it the more certain I am it would have worked. Sometimes you get a good feeling about a piece of comedy. I felt a good tingle about this one. Does anyone fancy being a Magnificent Hubert? The trouble is, I've run this routine through my head so many times that nobody but Eric could ever have been the Magnificent Hubert.

Icons

S how number two saw the emergence of one of our greatest literary icons, little Ern and *The Play What I Wrote*. When I first wrote this line I never thought it would become so popular and associated so much with Ern, even to this day. Ern's plays became an essential ingredient in the shows, part of the British way of life, and as Eric observed, 'We all know how bad that is.'

It was Ern who, and with typical modesty, said of his own place in history as an author, 'I have become part of our hermitage.' Few would argue.

Certainly not multi-award-winning actress Glenda Jackson. Glenda appeared in one of the shows and has since confessed it was the first and only time in her career that words had moved her to tears. This quite rare event occurred when she took a very important and much-coveted role in Ern's magnificent 'Antony and Cleopatra'.

The well-remembered line that brought tears to the eyes of this supreme actress, and she delivered the line with such great dignity, was: 'All men are fools, and what makes them so is having beauty like what I have got.'

The effect speaking these lines had on Glenda's career was quite remarkable – she became an MP.

When Ern read for the first time the sketch in which he was to play the part of a pompous and egotistical author he was pleased. I can see him now as he read the sketch, his face beaming. It's the only way I can describe the look of pleasure as his eyes lapped up the words. He might appear pompous and egotistical, but he was very much aware he would also get a lot of sympathy and a few laughs because he was obviously such a terrible writer. What really pleased Ern was that he now had a definite character to play. He would no longer be saying dreadful lines like, 'What happened next?' or, 'And what did you say?' The standard lines delivered to enable the comic to deliver the tag line. Ern had done a lot of that throughout his career; but not anymore, because this was one of the changes I had spoken about at that first meeting. And it became a very important part of the show for the next twelve years.

The change in Ern brought about a change in Eric that seemed to happen quite naturally in the writing. There was now a new dimension to Eric's comedy as Ern the author gave him something new to bounce off, and it also brought the relationship even closer.

Eric became less of the gormless character I saw him as in his earlier TV shows; he was now more worldly and very protective of Ern and his writing skills. He wouldn't allow anyone to say anything untoward about Ern's plays: 'I've got the concession on that.' He was also very supportive of his friend.

When Ern was suffering with writer's block, 'I've only written four plays this afternoon,' he would be on hand to offer words of comfort, such as:

Words fall from your pen like pearls from a broken necklace.

You are, without doubt, the Yehudi Menuhin of the nib.

You have written more belters than John Wayne has shot Red Indians.

You make *Gone with the Wind* look like a note for the milkman.

And a word of warning: 'I worry about you doing all this writing day in and day out. It's not easy, writing plays: it's not like joining the dots up in the *Beano*. You should take it easy; you're overdoing it. And I'll tell you something for your own good: you're starting to walk like Enid Blyton.'

This show might also have seen the beginning of the assassination job on Des O'Connor. I could write insult gags about Des until the cows came home, in fact when Des sings, the cows run home.

When I met Des for the first time he said, 'At last! So you're the one who's been saying nasty things about my singing.' Being the sort of person he is, Des then smiled and shoved a ferret up the leg of my trousers. Despite all the insult gags, Des, Eric and Ern were in fact the very best of friends. They often visited each other's homes and broke a few windows.

The only guest who ever gave me sleepless nights was one of the most respected and revered actresses in the British Theatre, Dame Flora Robson. As a small boy, I'd gazed open-mouthed at her on the silver screen with no less of a film star than Errol Flynn in *The Sea Hawk*. John Ammonds had told me that Dame Flora would be wearing the actual gown she had worn in that film and that it was insured for about thirty thousand pounds. Today that's about six million pounds and seventy-five pence. She really was going to come through those famous curtains wearing the same breathtaking costume she had worn in the film all those years before.

I typed out her first line, hesitated and then threw it away. No way in the world would an actress of Dame Flora's standing say that line. I laboured over it for days. I thought I was pushing my luck with Eric's line, 'Dame Flora, I always buy your margarine.' Would she do this, her first line in the show? She would, she did and it was a moment to savour. Ern introduced her, she came through the curtains wearing that gorgeous costume of Elizabeth I, and she was carrying a football. I was nervous.

Flora. Sorry I'm late; only, a young man kept asking me if I'll be fit for Saturday.

Eric. And will you?

From that moment Dame Flora could do no wrong. The audience loved her because the great lady herself had pricked the bubble of pomposity. Every actor in the land must have said, 'If it's good enough for that great actress, it's good enough for me.' And the star-spangled queue began to form.

Guest stars all received the same treatment: they were all insulted in the most courteous way. Dozens of international stars can claim with considerable pride that they were courteously insulted by Morecambe and Wise.

Yehudi Menuhin was told that if he wanted to appear on the show he would have to bring his banjo.

Eric told Rudolf Nureyev that if he couldn't make it we could always get Lionel Blair.

Laurence Oliver wouldn't be able to appear, as he was doing panto in Birkenhead: he was Mother Goose.

Alec Guinness didn't have to do or say anything to be very courteously insulted. He just stood centre stage looking very much like a senior civil servant from a John Le Carré novel.

Eric walked on, looked at Alec for a few seconds and then said, 'I'm sorry, but we don't allow members of the audience up on to the stage. We are professionals and we are trying to work.' As Alec Guinness didn't respond to this, Eric tried a different tack.

'Are you the taxi for Mr Wise? Would you mind waiting round the back?' Sir Alec left without saying a word.

Lots of quirky ideas were now creeping into the scripts and I was enjoying playing about with words. Did you know that 'Salisbury' spelt backwards is Y Rub Silas? Not wildly funny,

but interesting. I was enjoying playing about with the names of
guest stars, André Previn became 'Mr Preview'. Taxi drivers
who knew who he was, called him Mr Preview. If Kylie
Minogue had been around at the time she would have become
'Curly Monologue'. The name gimmick went back a long way
to my Ken Dodd days when Cilla Black became 'Swill Her
Back'. Putting an 's' on the end of Christian names was
interesting. Again no belly laughs, but it gave the comedy a
bit of character, and playing around with words and names
became almost like a trademark. Eric liked saying, 'Johns
Wayne, Rogers Moore.' He admitted it wasn't going to get
big laughs, but it was just that little bit different. One rather
odd line he became fond of and used often in different ways
came in a 'Knights of the Round Table' sketch. Peter Cushing
entered as King Arthur to be asked by Eric, 'Whom are you and
whenst came you from it?' And the very next line is now in my
favourite Morecambe and Wise lines of ever and ever:

King. What news of Carlisle?
Eric. When I left they were losing two one.

Dinner break during rehearsals for show number two and
the three of us were heading for the BBC Club for a bite to
eat. The previous evening I'd had an unfortunate encounter
with a jumbo sausage in the BBC Club and we now called it
'The Pharmacy'. Whenever we were going to the club for
something to eat, one of us would ask, 'Who's got the
prescriptions?'

On this particular night we were walking along the corridor.
Eric was walking slightly ahead of Ern and me as a young girl
turned a corner and headed towards us. She was very attractive
and had more curves than a plate of spaghetti hoops. As she got
closer, Ern nudged my arm and said, 'Just watch this.' When
the unsuspecting girl was about a yard from him Eric quickly
reached out his hand. The girl let out a startled 'Ooh!' and took

a very quick backward step. Eric scratched his knee with his outstretched hand and said, 'That girl is a bag of nerves.'

The poor girl wasn't to know he was going to scratch his knee.

Ern filled me in on the background to this incident. 'He takes after his father. If you're walking in front of his dad he'll try and trip you up.'

'Honestly?'

'Yes. He'll trip you up and think it's hilarious. He was always trying to trip me up and I became quite good at dodging the outstretched foot.'

Eric looked over his shoulder and said, 'It's OK, tripping you up – you haven't got far to fall.'

'One of these days you'll come unstuck with that knee gag,' warned Ern.

That silly, harmless little episode was for me a perfect example of the difference between the two men. Eric was forever the rascal; Ern was always respectable. Thinking about Ern's natural respectability now, I'm sure it did help in the creation of his on-screen character as the 'successful' writer. 'Be yourself in front of the camera and you're three-quarters of the way to being accepted.' Whoever said that, never said a truer mouthful – because that's exactly what Ern did. To this day I'm not so sure he knew this, but it fitted him like a favourite cardigan.

✳

When you're eulogised for being a great writer, as I are, it can be a burden, the idolatry is getting a bit much as well. It's got to the stage that I'm now afraid to go out in public. I've lost count of the number of times people have come up to me, people I've never clapped eyes on before. They come up to me and say, 'You're too old to be selling *The Big Issue*.'

This is why I'm going to give writing a rest for a while and try my hand at thinking up ideas for TV game shows: they're enormously popular. In fact I have come up with an idea for a game show and I honestly think it's in with a chance. I've called it *Left or Right*.

What happens is that the contestant has first to answer three questions. If he gets the three questions right in ten seconds he wins five hundred pounds. Next he's asked five questions, and if he gets them all right within twenty seconds he wins five thousand pounds. Now this is the part when *Left or Right* gets really exciting. The contestant is asked ten questions and if he gets those ten questions right in twenty seconds he goes away with a massive one hundred thousand pounds. However, if the contestant gets just one answer wrong he has a leg amputated. Before answering the questions he has to nominate which leg he would prefer to have taken off, left or right? This is where the fun starts, because it gives the audience a chance to join in by shouting out, 'Left! Right! Right! Left!'

If, and we don't really want this to happen, if the contestant gives a wrong answer and does have his leg cut off, that's when the audience shouts out, 'Hop it!' I hate to say this, but the way game shows are going, it wouldn't surprise me if this idea became a reality. There would be a lot of people auditioning for the part of Long John Silver.

Bedtime

I was frustrated, and it's a terrible thing to be frustrated. Have you ever watched a bandy-legged wine waiter trying to pull the cork out of a bottle?

The cause of my frustration was that I had written what I thought were two funny sketches – I always think my sketches are funny, because I'm an icon. Unfortunately, icon or not, Eric and Ern didn't agree, and once they'd made a joint decision about a comedy item I accepted it. When they both said no, I didn't give them an argument because I am by nature a crawler. I didn't argue with them because they had a lot of experience, they'd been in the comedy business longer than I had, and I'd just sneaked outside and let their tyres down.

In fairness I have to confess that in my time I have written a good quantity of rubbish, but thanks to the good taste of Morecambe and Wise it never saw the light of the TV screen. But on this occasion I was quite certain they had got it wrong. What puzzled me was that when they first read these sketches they didn't say, 'Not funny.' So there must have been another reason for both items to be given the elbow. The first sketch was 'The bed'. Two men in bed together: that's what was causing all the doubts. Even when I pointed to the real-life situation when as young men just starting their careers they had shared a bed when on tour because sharing a bed in digs was cheaper than single beds, it didn't work. No matter how hard I tried they were not keen on the idea. What finally convinced them both to appear in a bed together was when I said, 'If it's good enough for Laurel and Hardy, it's good enough for you.' That did it, convinced them. It was very funny and the bed sketch became a feature throughout our years together. One thing Eric insisted on was that he smoked his pipe in bed; he said it gave him some masculinity.

It was in a bed sketch that Eric often said one of his favourite lines. When he was in the changing room putting on pyjamas and dressing gown he said to me, 'I've been waiting all week to say this line.'

Ern was sitting up in bed and Eric was standing by the window as a police car went past with its siren sounding.

Eric. He's not going to sell much ice cream going at that speed.

The next comedy roadblock was placed in front of what is one of my favourite sketches, 'Afternoon in the Garden', inspired, if that's not too grand a word for a comedy sketch, by my own experience on a relaxing day off, as I sat in the garden on a gorgeous afternoon and listened to Delius on a portable radio. Even on my day off I was still iconing and I had a picture of Ern seated in a garden, relaxing and listening to 'On Hearing the First Cuckoo in Spring' coming from a radio on the wicker table, Eric entering wearing a safari suit with long baggy shorts and the inevitable black socks and suspenders. When I wrote this sketch I was very specific with directions, something I hardly ever had to do because both of them knew from experience exactly what they had to do for the best comedy reward. On this occasion I wrote, 'Long pauses between each line for the music to create a hot summer afternoon atmosphere.' No, they didn't fancy it, because they weren't used to working slowly: they were used to working at some pace. I left it for about a month and when the idea was put in front of them again I said, 'Why not just read it while the Delius is playing?' Which they did. Ern was relaxing and the music was playing as Eric entered and sat next to Ern. There was a pause.

Eric. Nice music.
Ern. Delius.
Eric. Who's it by?
Ern. Delius is the man who wrote it.
Eric. Oh.
Long pause as music continues
Eric. Is he British?
Ern. Who?
Eric. Delius.
Ern. Bradford.
Eric. I could have sworn he was British.
Long pause
Eric. What do they call those little black and yellow hairy things?
Ern. No idea. Why?
Eric. There's one just crawled up the leg of your shorts.

Again, here was a comedy sketch that could have been lost. Thankfully Frederick Delius came to our rescue. To be honest, it came as quite a surprise to me when I did a bit of research on Delius and discovered he really was born in Bradford. Hands up all those who thought he was French.

*

Golden rule number one (make it two and three as well, just to be on the safe side): never ever ask anyone what they thought of the show. Ask that question and you deserve everything you get.

My own wife was very obviously frustrated when I asked her that question after the final credits had rolled, because she picked the cat up and placed it on the ironing board. She was uncomfortable with my question and replied, 'It was quite good.' Translated that meant not good at all. A conclusion made more obvious when my daughter answered, 'I didn't see it. I got trapped by Mormons at the front door.' In desperate need of reassurance I rang Ern.

'Ern, it's Eddie. What did you think of the show?'

'Didn't you used to be our writer?'

I know he laughed when he said that, but it did send a shudder.

A classic and true incident illustrated exactly what I mean about the golden rule. The sleeper was pulling out of Euston Station; I'm not certain, but I think it was late in 1968 – it was late every other year as well.

Stan the attendant knocked at the door. 'Pot of tea.'

'Lovely, Stan. Thank you.' As he was unfolding the table I asked, 'What did you think of the last show?'

'I liked it.'

'That's good.'

'I think it was the best in the series.'

'We've only done two, Stan.'

'Oh. That sketch in the ironmonger's shop was very funny.'

'Ironmonger's shop? What ironmonger's shop?'

'When the one with the glasses gave the other one four candles and he wanted fork handles. Very funny.'

'That was the Two Ronnies.'

I waited for the train to pick up speed and pushed him off just outside Watford.

Stan was very apologetic, and when the next pot of tea came at Stafford I also got a plate of chocolate digestives, custard creams and a couple of the ones with jam in, and a slice of fruit cake. Now if there's one thing I really do enjoy it's a slice of fruit cake when I'm travelling sideways.

Question: When the Euston to Lime Street overnight train stops at Stafford, who is the phantom porter who walks up and down the platform outside the sleeping car at two o'clock in the morning whistling? It's the most piercing and penetrating whistle I have ever heard in my life. It guarantees that none shall sleep, and more than likely has frenzied sheepdogs savaging startled shepherds in Cumbria.

*

The pace was blistering in 1968. In the space of seven weeks we did eight forty-five-minute shows and I look at those figures now in total disbelief.

The work Morecambe and Wise did that year was rightly rewarded when they won a BAFTA. A glittering night, stars all over the place, the Royal Albert Hall, royalty present, we were all in evening dress because this was the showbiz event of the year and an evening I shall never forget because of the following conversation I had with Eric during dinner. He was sitting next to me, and as he looked at my plate and the meal of steak, salad and jacket potato he said, 'You're not eating your jacket potato.'

'I am.'

'You're leaving the best bit.'

'Which best bit?'

'The skin. That's the best bit.'

'Eagh! I never eat the skin.'

'It's the best bit, full of goodness. Try this.'

He offered me the slice of potato skin hanging from his fork: 'That's the best bit.'

How could I ever forget that night? A truly glittering, dazzling occasion that I had previously seen only on the TV. It was the sort of showbiz gathering that today would be on the front page of every trendy magazine in the country. This time the difference was, and I could scarcely believe it myself, I was a part of it. Stars all over the place, stars at tables, stars under tables and stars staggering into tables. It was notable because there I was sitting next to a megastar. We were surrounded by TV and press cameramen because this superstar had just been handed a prestigious award by the Queen's daughter, and we were talking about skin on a jacket potato being the best bit.

Later that same year, when I received my award, it didn't make the front page of a trendy magazine, but I'm rather proud of the fact that it did feature halfway down page 38 of the *War Cry*. It certainly was a moment to relish as the lovely Hollywood star, Goldie Hawn, handed me my trophy and gave me a kiss. Not something that's easily forgotten. Do you think Goldie might remember? Probably not.

A Touch of the Rustics

Dee and I, a young married couple, checked and double-checked our finances in 1970 to make sure we could afford the luxury of paying four thousand pounds for a truly delightful three-bedroomed detached house. It was halfway up the twin peaks of the Rivals in the village of Llithfaen on the Welsh Riviera of the Llyn Peninsula. To do justice to the view a whole batch of new superlatives will have to be invented – 'breathtaking' and all those other adjectives just don't describe it. When I first saw the view to the south and west, had I been wearing contact lenses they would have cracked at the overwhelming, sharp intake of breath. The view took in the mountains of Snowdonia to the left, and straight ahead south it sloped away forever to the sweep of Cardigan Bay. If Constable had still been alive I would have called him on his mobile and said, 'John, get up here double quick.'

A week before Deidree, Jane, Clare and Graham were to come down for our first holiday in the new home, I had gone on ahead to tidy up the garden. This I was doing when a man from the village stopped and leant on my first ever five-barred gate – I have always been fascinated by five-barred gates. No matter where you go, no matter how many gates you lean on, they always reach up to your elbows. You don't have to make any adjustments; your elbows just fit amazing.

The local greeted me with a 'Good morning' in Welsh. I can say 'Good morning' in Cantonese, which I did. This threw him, so he settled for English.

'You've got a big job on with that garden.'

'I don't mind.'

'You know who's bought this place, don't you?'

'No. He didn't say!'

'Television writer.'

'Oh?'

'Yes, make sure he pays you well; he's bloody loaded.'

Bob, for that was his name, Bob and I had a few laughs at this first encounter over the years. Every time he came to do the garden I paid him well, because I was bloody loaded.

*

In the dictionary it said, 'Poltergeist. Type of household ghost responsible for otherwise unaccountable noises, given also to shifting objects about.' Is that what it was?

Let me tell you about our first and only encounter with the weird, the spooky, the inexplicable (with the exception of Des O'Connor).

Glanrhyd, the name of our Welsh house, was just across the road from a church that had ceased contacting God some twenty years before this incident took place. Incident? This event has been a major talking point in our family ever since it happened.

Early one evening I suggested to Jane and Clare that we might take a closer look at this derelict once-house-of-worship, and they were both enthusiastic, as it sounded like an Enid Blyton jolly wheeze. I took a stick and went hacking a path through the brambles around to the back of the church. We came to a window long since deprived of its stained glass, leaving an opening big enough for an adventurer to clamber through, which Clare did. Inside it was desolate, a picture of

61

total neglect and decay – one of the corner shops God had forgotten about. (I said this at the time and perhaps I shouldn't have.) Trees on their way to maturity were reaching high up over the pews, it really was a sad sight. I called for Clare to come out, which she did, picking up a very old Welsh hymn book on the way.

When we got back home Deidree was not at all pleased. 'You shouldn't have brought that hymn book out of the church; it goes back first thing in the morning.' We should have taken it back there and then.

It was our habit last thing at night when we were on holiday to set the table for breakfast: it saved time and we could get off to an early start. This was the era when glass coffee cups were considered trendy. I never liked glass coffee cups, because when you were drinking the last few drops the person sitting opposite could see up your nose – put you right off you doughnut.

It's important to know that the kitchen floor was stone, the kitchen was at the foot of the stairs and we always slept with bedroom doors slightly ajar. Early the next sunny morning we skipped 'La, La, La, La' out of bed and down the stairs like a shiny-faced family in a TV commercial, only to be brought to a shuddering halt when we saw all the glass cups and saucers shattered on the stone floor; the other breakfast items were still in place on the table. The really weird bit is that none of us had heard a sound during the night. The hymn book was returned within minutes.

If there are such things as ghosts, and you can see now why I'm slightly dubious, do they have to be scary? Maybe there are such things as jolly ghosts, ghosts who make you smile and play tricks on people. That's what it was, a jolly Welsh ghost. I can hear them now, a male voice choir of jolly Welsh ghosts singing, 'We'll keep a welcome in the cardiac unit.'

Funnyfolk

A rummage through the attic of my memory and I come across Eric, Ern and myself seated at a table in the BBC canteen enjoying a tea-break cuppa with guest to be, Patrick Moore. Patrick, the eccentric, charming and most courteous of gentlemen, is holding us spellbound as he explains about the Milky Way: 'It's about four and a half inches long and covered with thick chocolate.' That's an astronomer's joke.

What wasn't a joke was when Patrick arrived on the first day of rehearsal and, smiling broadly as he did so, said, 'I'm afraid I haven't looked at the script, yet.' The thud of dropping jaws probably caused a slight panic amongst those who have to keep an eye on the Richter scale.

'If you have a script available I could have a look at it now.'

This was a first. Nothing like this had ever happened before – a guest who didn't know the words because he hadn't looked at a script. What happened next was to me quite, quite remarkable. Patrick was given a script, he sat and read it for a matter of minutes, put it to one side and announced, 'I'm ready now.' This was our first ever experience of a man with a photographic memory. Patrick sailed through the sketch without a stumble. On the night of the recording, the sketch with Patrick was memorable for the pay-off that was never intended, far funnier than the one I had written. In the piece of nonsense Eric had bought a telescope to study the stars and fortunately Patrick Moore just happened to call in, as he would if anyone bought a telescope. As I remember, he started to get all excited about Mars, the red planet:

> **Patrick.** You really must have a look at Mars.
> **Eric.** I will.
> **Ern.** Where is the best place to see it from?
> **Patrick.** Let me tell you, musically.

Patrick crossed over to the piano (he really is a very fine pianist), sat down and sang as he played 'Deep in the Heart of Texas' as it had never been sung before.

The audience treated us to very generous laughter and applause because it was so obviously the end of the sketch. Or was it?

Not as far as Patrick was concerned, not by a very long way, and onward he played and sang 'The stars at night are big and bright. . . .' By now the audience knew this wasn't supposed to happen, and how they were loving it. As far as I remember, the unscripted pay-off went like this as Patrick played and sang, merrily oblivious:

> **Ern.** It's finished, Patrick.
> *Patrick was having none of it: 'Reminds me of the one love. . . .'*
> **Eric.** We've finished the sketch, Patrick.
> *Patrick hadn't finished: 'The sage in bloom is like perfume. . . .'*

Now Eric and Ern had given up and along with the audience were enjoying this wonderful Patrick Moore solo performance. That unforgettable gentleman enjoyed being on the show so much that a few days later we each received a signed copy of his most enjoyable book on the universe. Even better for me – in a glass cabinet in my home and resting on a purple cushion I have a signed bar of Milky Way.

At the TV Centre our rooms were next to each other. This gave us quick and easy access to discuss changes in the show we were doing and talk about shows yet to come. Last-minute changes were frowned on. I was once gently reprimanded by John Ammonds for giving Eric a last-minute gag during final dress rehearsal of the 'Napoleon and Josephine' sketch with Vanessa Redgrave. She's a very tall lady, which wasn't lost on Eric at the end of the preamble in front of the curtains when, leaving to get changed for the sketch, she said, 'I'll be right back.'

'Right back? You're big enough to play in goal.'

That wasn't the line that got me in trouble. I'd noticed that in Napoleon's tent there was a bronze eagle on a plinth. I said to Eric as he was standing at the side waiting to make his entrance, 'Just tap the eagle hard a couple of times and say, "You've been giving this budgie too much millet." ' He liked the line, did the line on his entrance and John's voice came over the speaker, 'Hold it. Let's go again without the millet gag.' What I had completely forgotten about in my eagerness to get the line in, was that the cameramen had a script that they follow line by line – an extra gag threw everything out. It was a kindly telling off by John, although he knew I meant well.

The three of us were sitting in Ern's room when I put forward an idea I'd had for the next show. Ern had met a fellow writer, a poet, and had invited him round to the flat to discuss their work as writers. Eric was on to this one very quickly: 'And I don't like him?'

'You dislike him even before you've met him.'

Ern liked the idea because he was revelling in his new character as the pompous writer. They both wanted to know if this poet had a name. I knew it was a name they would go for and delayed naming him by placing 'only' in front of his name.

I was savouring the moment as I said, 'Only. . . . Adrian Fondle.' Ern said, 'That's really good.' Eric showed his delight in his usual way: he rubbed his hands together between his knees and said, 'Great.' They were both so experienced that they were now racing ahead with the idea. Ern chipped in with, 'This Adrian Fondle recites awful modern stuff and Eric doesn't like it?'

'Yes.'

Then Eric: 'I get his back up by doing mucky poems?'

'Yes.'

Which, give or take a few lines, is exactly what happened. Eric, not very impressed with Adrian's modern poetry, gave him a sample of what he considered proper – poetry that rhymed, poetry that common people like himself understood:

> There was a young lady from Preston
> Who ran down the M6 with no vest on
> She was just outside Crewe when a
> Sailor named Lou, grabbed her . . .

Ern brought the poem to a conclusion with 'How dare you!'

But Eric hadn't finished. 'How's this for the caring verse on a "Get well soon" card?' Adrian sat and cringed as his good taste was bruised by Eric's caring 'Get well soon' message:

> I'm sorry to hear that you're not well
> Soon you'll be full of life
> Just take it easy and stay in bed
> Like I am with your wife.

Needless to say, that shredded any hopes Ern had of an erudite conversation with a fellow writer.

What was interesting about this sketch was that even at the time we thought it very old fashioned, yet those silly little rhymes got really good laughs and are still raising a few titters even today. This strengthens a theory I've long held, that good comedy, like good music, can be repeated over and over again. Thank God for videotape.

There was one ditty in that poet sketch that we didn't use. It was a reluctant thumbs down, because it made us laugh, and harked back a very long way to the pre-war golden age of the British music hall:

> Once I was a happy man
> With my old granny, my sister Annie
> And my sweetheart Fanny.
> Now I'm all alone,
> No granny, no Annie, no. . . .

I'm quite sure that had we used that rhyme it would have brought the place down. It was simple, earthy, childishly silly. There was also something about it that was so terribly British, perhaps a verbal seaside postcard. How I wish I had written it.

Take hold of the words as they float by. If you don't they'll be lost forever; that's a shame. I remember my grandfather once telling me that if you can get the words down on paper correctly it can make you very wealthy. He passed on that advice to me just before he started a twelve-year stretch on a forgery charge.

It really is true about holding on to words before they drift away: you might be fortunate and recapture them, but not necessarily in the right order. And what happens then is what you're trying to say loses its original flavour – you might as well open a tin of spam. The words will not be quite as piquant. I like that word – bequiteas.

Floating past me now is a name, Amy. It was Amy who proved so very inspirational when I was desperate for an original comedy idea, something that happens only every twelve minutes. I don't think Amy had a surname: she was always Amy, and she was everything a little old lady should be. Merry blue eyes, plump and rosy cheeks, grey hair tied back in a bun, or, as we used to say, 'She had her hair in a bun and her nose in a crab sandwich.'

Amy always wore wellies. In blistering summer Amy wore wellies because the stone floor of the shop she sold her flowers from was always wet. It's upgrading her workplace by calling it a 'shop' – it was a recess under the marketplace that I earned a crust in. Everyone who knew Amy liked her. Come to think of it, you might well have seen a lady who could have been her twin sitting on the church steps in *Mary Poppins* as Julie Andrews sang, 'Feed the Birds'. It's a wonder Amy's twin didn't run into the church shouting, 'Sanctuary!'

Amy was a kindly lady and merits a mention in these despatches for what she gave me in later years: her unique way of getting words wrong, all the more appealing as she didn't know she was getting them wrong.

It was time to close up shop and Amy was counting her Saturday takings, twelve pounds and some shillings. It was the busiest day of the week. She took a pinch of snuff before telling me the sad story of the young couple who lived in her street. Why not? It was Saturday, time to relax and have a bit of a chat.

Amy settled herself on an empty orange box. 'They can't have any children: the doctor says her husband's "impertinent." '

Then the saga of a relative's son who had brought disgrace on the family by deserting from the army. 'He'd been on the run for a week, but the police caught him at two o'clock in the morning. They threw an accordion around the house.' It got worse. 'I think his wife's had enough of him because she says she might desecrate to Australia.'

It was Amy's birthday that Saturday and she and her friend, who sold fresh mint and parsley, were both going to the Philharmonic pub opposite the Philharmonic Hall in Hope Street, the street of hope with its two magnificent cathedrals. It was a long way from Amy's house, and when I asked her how she would get home after her night out she replied, 'It is my birthday: I'll probably inhale a taxi.'

Twenty years later the name 'Amy' floated by and I caught it as if it were a rare butterfly. I placed her with affection in my radio series *The Worst Show on the Wireless*. She became my favourite radio character as 'Mrs Turpin', and was played to perfection by Alison Steadman. That oh so reliable comedy actor Bill Pertwee, of *Dad's Amy* fame, also graced that radio series. He was present in just about everything I ever wrote for that friend in the corner, the wireless.

Bill remembers with some shame the character of Mrs Turpin, for she caused him to laugh so much that producer Jim Casey had to halt the recording for twenty minutes (fortunately we did this series without an audience). He sent a note to say he had a bad cough.

It wasn't that the lines were very funny. It was the voice Alison had found to portray Amy/Mrs Turpin. What destroyed Bill during this particular recording was that Mrs Turpin had brought her son, Precious, to the BBC for an audition. Precious, played by the stuttering Eli Woods, said he was going to climb inside an empty milk bottle. When Bill pointed out that this was impossible, Precious came back with, 'I sing that when I'm inside the milk bottle.' Then Mrs Turpin reminds her son that if he wants to get inside the milk bottle he'll have to take his skis off first. This was too much for Bill and he finally snapped, totally.

Many times I have watched seasoned performers try to fight back the giggles. Glenda Jackson fought a valiant battle against them in the 'Antony and Cleopatra' sketch when Eric worked the bust of a Roman emperor like a ventriloquist's doll. Bill's was a master class in how to get the giggles when you're performing. He agrees it was all so very unprofessional, but what pleases me greatly is that he also said it was one of the most enjoyable times in his career. I value that.

Mrs Turpin also told us about her daughter, Bianca.

'She's desecrated to Australia.'

'Is she happy in Australia?'

'She hates it.'

'Why?'

'What do you call them things that hop up and down all over the place?'

'Kangaroos.'

'Our Bianca says that the beds are full of them. She says in her letter that she can't have any children.'

'What's the problem?'

'It's her husband. The doctor thinks it's his didgeridoo.'

Thank you, thank you so very much, dear Amy. How fortunate to have met such good people.

*

Bill Pertwee tells me this story about probably my favourite character actor of all time, and he wouldn't thank me for calling him a character actor, because he was the finest King Lear ever, John Laurie. Who said he was the finest King Lear? John Laurie did. When John made a statement like that it wasn't the ego bit; he meant it; he was being totally honest; and from what other actors tell me he probably was the best ever King Lear. From our first meeting, when I was writing and he was appearing on radio in the Ken Dodd show, I got on extremely well with this gnarled old Scot: probably one near recluse recognised another.

John was an actor like no other I have ever met. On radio, when he didn't have a line of dialogue for a couple of pages he would be standing in the background and he'd be acting with his eyes, a movement of the head or arms. He'd be reacting to what others were saying even though he wasn't involved – when John Laurie was involved you knew it. There was such enormous strength and power in everything he said, in every movement he made. Many years after the Ken Dodd radio shows John was a guest on the Morecambe and Wise show. I wondered if he'd remember me, this man who captivated me with tales of Alfred Hitchcock, Robert Donat and the original and finest screen version of *The 39 Steps*. He was a rather scary Highland crofter in that film. He made me laugh when he appeared with Will Hay in the very funny film *The Ghost of St Michael's*. That was the very first time I shivered as he boomed out his now famous 'Doomed!', heard to such good effect when he played Private Frazer in Jimmy Perry and David Croft's glorious *Dad's Army*. Just seeing that title on paper makes me smile. I've never met Jimmy Perry or David Croft. Come to think of it, there are so many other interesting and gifted people I haven't met: Spike Milligan – I always seemed to miss him by seconds at BBC TV Centre. The list of talented people I have never met is a long one. It includes: John Sullivan, Denis Norden, Roy Clarke and much missed Jim Hitchmough, writer of one of my favourite TV sitcoms of ever and ever: *Watching*, 1987 and onwards. However, back to John Laurie. Would this now quite elderly man remember me? We didn't meet in the studio, I was walking down the corridor when I heard the lift door opening behind me and that wonderful voice calling, 'Dear Eddie!' John threw his arms around me. 'Wonderful! Lovely to see you again.' No, he hadn't forgotten and it was like being hugged by a very friendly orang-utang.

I'd almost forgotten Bill Pertwee's John Laurie story. He was sitting in a car with John and writer Jimmy Perry; they were sheltering from the rain during a break in filming *Dad's Army* in Thetford. Jimmy asked John if he was OK. 'Aye, aye, I'm fine,' replied John, and then added, 'Did you know that I am the finest verse reader in the country? And I finish up doing this crap.' He got that wrong. That was John. Totally honest he was, a luvvie he wasn't.

At the very summit of his popularity John could be found

outside his Buckinghamshire home sitting next to a notice reading 'Manure for Sale – 2s.6d a bag'. Surely no doubts now as to why John Laurie is my most unforgettable character.

In the same Ken Dodd shows was a lady who was and still is my favourite actress of ever and ever, also one of my favourite people, Patrica Hayes. It astonished me that such a tiny and quietly spoken lady could act with such ferocity – no other word for it. There was a passion and intensity in every word she spoke. If there was meat on the comedy bone there wasn't any left when Pat Hayes had finished with it.

The passion and the intensity showed clearly in the weekly meetings in the shows of Will and Nell. Will was played by Ken, Nell by Pat. They were an impoverished married couple living in a Northern mill town in the early 1930s. By the 'eck, times was 'ard. A brass band would set the scene as a door opened. This was surely inspired by *Love on the Dole*.

Pat. Will, lad.
Ken. Nell, lass.
Pat. You look wore out, Will.
Ken. Aye, lass.
Pat. I'll take your boots off, Will.
Ken. They're too big for you anyway, lass.
Pat. Your dinner's in the oven, Will.
Ken. Can I have it on the table? It gets a bit hot inside that oven.

Every time Pat said, 'Will, lad . . .' you could see the strain on her face, you could feel the anguish, even though it was radio. It is still one of my favourite comedy moments.

I can say of Patrica Hayes the same as I have said of Eric and Ern: give her an ordinary script and she would make it good. Give her a good script and she would make it brilliant. If I'd have written one that was brilliant I think we might have had something quite special.

She had a mole on her neck. It kept jumping up and swinging on her earrings. I'll keep slipping these one-liners in occasionally. Pity to let them go to waste, isn't it?

*

John banged the console with his fist in frustration in the gallery as he watched the final dress rehearsal taking place in Studio 8: 'The silly woman has forgotten her next line.' I squirmed in my seat at the back of the gallery as he said this of the actress who had forgotten her line, Diane Cilento. The reason why I was feeling more than a little anxious was that, unseen by John, Diane's husband had walked noiselessly into the gallery and was sitting just a yard behind him. The husband was Sean Connery. *Double O blimey*, I thought to myself. *Trouble, trouble, trouble, right here in River City.* Thankfully Sean Connery is a very big man with a very big talent and a matching sense of humour. When John made his little outburst Sean smiled a big *I've seen this all before* smile. Not that he would have turned nasty and tried anything while I was around – he knew better. He must have known I've got a black belt: it was holding up my navy-blue trousers.

Diane Cilento was the reason why I had to have a premature eye test – she had knocked my eyeballs off-centre. No question, she was the most glamorous of all the women who had ever appeared in our shows. Sorry, Cilla.

Diane's figure would knock you back a couple of steps – she had more curves than a bag of Hula Hoops. I had spoken to her a few weeks before the show, when my phone rang at home and a female voice said, 'I'm Miss Cilento's maid. . . .'

'Pardon?'

'I'm Miss Cilento's maid.'

I stubbed my cigarette out (I felt I had to do something subservient). I didn't reply, 'Yes, maid,' although I very nearly did, I'd never spoken to a maid before. That's not true; I often spoke to my dad's maid, but I called her 'Mum'.

'Miss Cilento would like to speak to you,' said maid.

Diane didn't speak; she purred. After she had said sorry for disturbing me, she asked me a question no guest had ever asked me before and she really did catch me on the hop. It was a beauty! 'What came first, the part or me?'

In those days nobody had thought of asking the audience or phoning a friend, and there was a mini panic in Liverpool 12. What should I say? If I said the wrong thing I could lose a star guest! Should I joke my way out of it and say, 'Well, originally I wrote the part for Old Mother Riley, but she couldn't do it, as she was dancing *Swan Lake.' Don't be silly. You've got a fifty-fifty chance. Just go with one of them.* I did.

So I said, trying to sound all suave and writer-wearing-a-cravat type, 'When I was told that you were going to be the guest, Miss Cilento, I wrote the sketch hoping it would be right for you and I hope you like it.' *Yes, Miss Cilento, I am a crawler but I do have a wife, ten children and a slight limp*. Whatever I said I can't fully remember, but I do know that Diane liked what she read and the audience liked what she did.

I remember what Eric said to me after the show when I remarked on what a very tall man Sean Connery was. Eric said, 'Yes, he is a big lad. If you melted him down you could make six Ernies!'

From one lady who graced our show to one who turned us down, the only time this happened, to my knowledge, in the fourteen years I was the writer. The guest who never was, the lady who showed us the door and the red card was Sarah Miles.

John, Eric and Ern took Sarah out for lunch – perhaps that's what did it? Maybe she didn't like sitting on a bench at Shepherd's Bush Green eating Ern's corned beef sarnies. I wasn't present but I do know that Ern makes a rather tasty corned beef sandwich, and excellent value at twenty-five pence.

John tells me that they really did have a most enjoyable meal, after which they all went their separate ways looking forward to meeting again in seven day's time for the first rehearsal. There was no meeting a week later, no first or any rehearsal. Sarah had changed her mind.

It all fell apart when Sarah took the script home and showed it to her husband. 'What do you think of this, Robert?' Robert was only Robert Bolt, a proper writer who wrote *Ryan's Daughter* and *Lawrence of Arabia*. What chance did I stand? Showing one of my scripts to him would be like asking Luciano Pavarotti what he thought of Des O'Connor's latest album.

Too late now, but I should have had a clause written into my contract with the BBC stating quite clearly that no female guests would be allowed to take scripts home with them and show them to their husbands. I can just imagine what Robert said to wife Sarah when he read my offering: 'Er. . . . right. Well, sweetheart . . . do you want to sit down? I, er. . . . I don't think that this work has been properly researched; it's not very accurate. I mean, you're supposed to be Anne Hathaway, right? In the opening scene, and this is about the year 1580, you're in the kitchen and William says, "What's for tea, Anne?" And this is the bit I'm not too happy about. You reply, "I've got you a pizza from Tesco's.' Quite honestly Sarah, I don't think you should do this.'

Sarah didn't do it.

We're all entitled to an opinion, right or not. What annoyed me was that I had seen both *Ryan's Daughter* and *Lawrence of Arabia*, and there wasn't a laugh in either of them. This was one of those very rare times, probably the only time, that John failed in his search for a star. It was quite amazing how he got the really big names to appear in the show. He'd say, 'I'll try and get. . . .' Then he'd mention the name and we three would say, 'No chance, John.' But invariably John did capture the star. How he did it we hadn't a clue, except that we thought he might have a stash of photographs locked away in his office that nobody knew about. If John Ammonds was a stick of rock he would have *The Morecambe and Wise Show* running all the way through him.

I doubt very much if we would have got half the big names we did get if it hadn't been for his enthusiasm and relentless determination to find the biggest and best.

In 1972 – and this a story that has never been told before – John went after the biggest name we had ever had on the show; in fact it was the biggest name that had ever appeared in any variety show. Yet again the three of us looked in disbelief when John said quite casually. 'By the way, I'm hoping to get Prince Charles for the Christmas Show. I have written to him and it's just a question now of keeping our fingers crossed.' Everything was crossed. I think John even had his eyes crossed, because in the canteen he kept eating off my plate.

It was a truly valiant effort on his part. At one stage it really did look as though it was going to happen; however, a letter from a Mr Equerry informed us that it wasn't to be, even though His Royal Highness was flattered to have received the invitation. Understandable because on Christmas Day the Prince would have his hands full holding up the cue cards for his mum's speech to the nation. Fortunately we were able to get Vera Lynn, and you can't get much closer to royalty than that.

He had an heir apparent – you could see it just behind his left ear. I told you I didn't want to waste the one-liners . . .

※

What's in a name? A lot of laughs if the name is a famous one and the owner of that name happens to be a guest on the Morecambe and Wise show.

French singing heart throb Sacha Distell would have hung on to his proper name had it not been for this little incident. I was sitting in the audience seats during rehearsal and making notes on lines that weren't getting laughs, about two hundred lines. Sacha was sitting about four rows in front of me and whispering to his manager, who got up and clambered over the seats to where I was parked and said, 'Mr Distel would like a few lines before he does his song.'

I said, 'Tell Mr Distel that as soon as I get a manager I'll let him know.'

That was when he became Slasher Distillery. Des (What would I have done without him?) was short for desperate. Although Julio Iglesias never guested on the show we still spoke of him as Julio Double Glazing.

Elton John, when he was misdirected at the TV Centre, read a note left for him by Eric and Ern, which began, 'Dear Elephant . . .' Poor Elephant finished in the river.

Vanessa Redgrave towered over Ern. As he stood very close to her, Eric put a restraining hand on his shoulder and said, 'Come away, Ern, you won't know what to get up to next.' Vanessa became Vanilla, while Susan Hampshire was every county in England until Eric got the right one. Ern really did have a problem during rehearsal when he was introducing star guest, Edward Woodward.

'Would you please welcome one very special guest, Mr Wood. . . Mr Wedwoo. . .' This wasn't intended and when he said, quite unintentionally, 'Woodwood Woodwood,' it stayed 'Woodwood' throughout the show.

There wasn't a lot we could do with John Mills except to tell him his performance would go like a bomb. Eric then apologised for this near joke, saying that someone was going to do it sooner or later.

It was a charming, inexplicable fact: Ern could not get Hannah Gordon's name right. He really did try not to do it, but every time he introduced her it was always 'Annah Gordon'. He didn't know why, he knew what he was saying, but he could not sound the aitch. I watched him standing alone at the side of the set struggling to say, 'Hannah.' But it kept coming out as 'Annah'. That was Ern. That's what made him such a warm and genuine character that I could build on. They both knew what it was like to have names confused. When they were in America and appearing on *The Ed Sullivan Show* they were introduced as 'Moreton and White'. Even worse was 'Morrie Cambie and Wise' – now they were a trio!

However, of all the name changes in all the world the number one spot has got to go to André Previn. André had been booked for the show by John, who had been told by André's agent that he would not be available for rehearsals, as he was fully committed to conducting dates in New York, Chicago, Los Angeles and some parts of Birkenhead. Neither Eric nor Ern was very happy with this, as they always had at the very least ten days' rehearsal with a guest star. Eric, always the worrier, was a little agitated at the thought of a guest and no rehearsal time: 'How is he going to learn the words?' John tried to reassure him, 'There'll be a script waiting for him when he lands at Heathrow.' It didn't work.

'Golly Gosh!' said Eric, or the adult equivalent. 'It will be a biffing wheeze if he can learn a fifteen-minute sketch during that journey.'

Ern wasn't exactly overjoyed either: 'Oh sticks, Eric old fellow. I concur. I think you are jolly well right. The fellow will never do it.'

'My hat! This is all a bit much, John,' exclaimed Eric.

Now it was John's turn. 'Granny's knickers to both of you chaps! I think you're both being beastly.' What John said next was a great line and so very true.

'If André Previn can learn every note of Beethoven's Ninth Symphony, he's not going to have much trouble with a fifteen-minute comedy sketch.' André didn't have any trouble at all with the words. He learned them to perfection in the time it took to travel from Heathrow to the TV Centre – about six weeks. No! He really did learn the words in less than forty-five minutes.

The fact that he is such a brilliant conductor and pianist accounts for his comedy timing in that sketch. It was immaculate.

There was for me one unforgettable line in front of the curtains with Eric and Ern when André rightly suspected that with Eric as the soloist, the whole thing was going to be a total disaster and he was now looking for a way out. He said, 'I'll fetch my baton.' Then, and this wasn't in the script and he wasn't asked to do it, he did a half-turn before delivering the rest of the line: 'It's in Chicago.'

It made the line far, far funnier then it deserved.

That night as the sketch was being played, I knew something special was happening and I was getting a tingle I had never experienced before – today it's called a 'buzz'. I was listening to the reaction to what was taking place and thinking, *Just listen to that audience – and we haven't got to the really funny bits yet*. Eric looked at the orchestra with some disdain as he asked, 'Which one is the fixer?' When the introduction finished before he could get to the piano he complained, 'It's too short. If you could lengthen it by about a yard.' Ern as Eric's manager could see nothing at all wrong with this request. He suggested they 'Get in touch with Grieg.' André could now see his career disintegrating . . .

André.	[*In disbelief*] You mean – call him on the phone?
Ern.	Why not?
André.	What a shame – I didn't bring his phone number.
Eric.	Well, it's Norway, something or other.
Ern.	What's the code?
Eric.	Fingal's Cave, isn't it. Mind you, you might not get him – he might be out skiing.

It all ends joyously when André plays all the right notes in the right order.

Every piece of comedy I have ever written I would like to have back so I can rewrite and make it funnier. Not so the 'Grieg piano concerto' – I wouldn't change a word.

That was as close to perfection all those involved ever got. I have never helped to generate so much laughter before or since. That was it – we'd done it. That is what in future we will be judged by.

Hooray for the Wireless!

Whenever there was a decent break in the Morecambe and Wise shows, it meant I could devote more time to my favourite medium, radio, that box in the corner of the room on top of the table with the candy-stick legs that brought me so much pleasure all of my life. What makes radio so magical is that it is talking and singing to me, nobody else, just the two of us. If it irritates me or says something I don't like I can switch it off, shut it up, and that's something you can't do in the unmagical real life.

Dave Morris was one of my comedy heroes, his weekly radio show *Club Night* was a must. Dave was a know-all character in that show and a terrible liar. One week in the club they were talking about a cure for one older member who had lumbago. 'I'll cure that for you,' boasted Dave.

'How? My doctor can't cure it.'

'This is what you must do. Get up at half past five in the morning, get a twenty-foot pole, go down to the beach at Blackpool, take a thirty-yard run; then jump in the air as high as you can.'

'Will that cure lumbago?'

'No, but it will get you into Wembley without a ticket to see the Cup Final.'

I couldn't believe it when he walked past my fruit and veg

stall in St John's Market. It really was Dave Morris – I'd know those spectacles anywhere. 'Hello, Mr Morris.' He replied with this gem: 'Don't take any wooden money, son.'

*

I enjoyed writing and taking part in *The Worst Show on the Wireless*. It was 1973 and I was writing the sort of comedy I enjoyed. I was writing for me. I wasn't writing 'under orders': I was writing to please me, and I did please me and never once did I say that something I had written was rubbish. I never, never asked for rewrites, and always told me to finish promptly at five o'clock and always to take the weekends off. It was a glorious, glorious luxury.

The Worst Show on the Wireless was a cosy little show, a family show. I know this for a fact because the family that listened to it often wrote to me from Scarborough. Bill Pertwee, Alison Steadman, David Casey and Eli Woods provided all the voices and got all the laughs as well as the Writers' Guild Award for Best Radio Comedy of the year, 1973, which was why I was mystified when I was told the BBC didn't like the title *The Worst Show on the Wireless*. No reason why; just didn't like it.

This is a show that had just won a prestigious award and the BBC didn't like the title. Now as I understand it, the BBC is a building. Did a building say it didn't like the title, or was it somebody inside the building who was as thick as the legs of the billiard table when it came to comedy and just wanted to be known as 'BBC'? I don't know. What I do know is that I reluctantly agreed to change the name to something more acceptable, something more sensible, so I called it *The Show With Ten Legs*. Just one week before recording the first show I had a phone call from a man who said he was from the BBC (he may well have given a name; if he did I can't remember what it was but I do know he said he was from the BBC), and could I please explain to him why I had called the programme *The Show With Ten Legs*. In an assured voice and with much logic I explained to BBC, 'Because there's three of us in it.' There was a long pause and I'll swear I could hear 'thinking noise' – you can sometimes. Then BBC said, 'Ah, yes. I'm with you now.' Off he went. It was a genuine call because I had been told that questions would be asked. Who the official was I haven't a clue, probably the same man who famously asked Spike Milligan why he was calling his programme *The Go On Show*. It's a bit scary when you realise there are such people involved in comedy.

With free time away from the demands of television I really was enjoying writing for radio, in particular *The Show With Ten Legs*. The shows were recorded in Manchester and pro-duced by James Casey, a man who knew what he was doing when it came to comedy. Not surprising, as he's the son of one of our comic treasures – Jimmy James.

I took part in all of these shows. I contributed little as a performer, as I don't have a style or radio personality. Why then was I in the shows? Self-indulgence and fulfilling that childhood dream of wanting to be 'on the wireless'.

My conscience was eased by the fact that the fee matched my performing talents. As Eric used to say, 'I see you're wearing your BBC suit, small checks.'

The music of Elgar's 'Chanson de matin' played as Bill Pertwee narrated his weekly tour of *This Beautiful Britain*. This regular item had its origins in a well-remembered holiday spent in the Cotswolds, and the astonishingly glorious view from the summit of the Malverns. As I stood and slowly scanned that wondrous landscape I found it inspirational and in a way rather moving. I well remembered thinking, *This is what England's all about. This really is the true England.* It was wet, windy and bloody freezing!

Bill narrated, 'You are invited to join me as we sample and

enjoy the many and varied delights to be found in *This Beautiful Britain*. Here we see the home of one our greatest composers, Sir Edward Elgar. It was here in 1899 that he first tried out his variations and did his back in.

'We come now to the delightful village of Grippen-next-the-well. This was a favourite haunt of Charles I, who often said, "I'm going to Grippen-next-the-well over the weekend." This he did quite frequently; hence Charles II.

'The village green is steeped in history and many other things that can ruin your shoes.

'Just a few miles to the west we find the charming hamlet of Grerrem Down, also favoured by royalty. When Prince Albert was overheard say "I'm going to Gerrem Down next week" Queen Victoria said, "I don't think so, matey," and landed him one.

'Here we see the magnificent manor house, famous for its great chamber. It is said that it took twelve men to empty it.

'Join me at the same time next week when we shall be going to Oldham Knightly.'

One of the golden radio moments for me was the unexpected visit during rehearsal of comedy legend Max Wall. Why he took the trouble on a damp and frosty Sunday afternoon in Manchester, I couldn't say. The pleasing thing was that he stayed for the rehearsal. Even more pleasing was that he laughed often. Such an original comic who made me laugh so much as a youngster when I listened to his very popular radio series *Our Shed*. Max would say, in a soppy kid's voice, 'It's ever so nice in our shed. I've got a little green apple in there, and when I tap it a little worm pops its 'ead out of the 'ole! Coo, it ain't 'arf good!'

Is that an age of comedy innocence, or what.

Before he left, Max autographed my script and shook my hand as well as the hands of the other cast members – Bill Pertwee, Alison Steadman, David Casey, Eli Woods, Richard

Gere, Al Pacino, Julia Roberts, Placido Domingo (comedy songs) Michael Douglas. No! Put a full stop after Eli Woods.

You can't have a love of radio comedy without being an admirer of Spike Milligan. I'm not going to call him a genius, as that now is applied too freely to so many who aren't. Spike was rather special: I prefer that.

I was still trying to earn a crust by selling apples and 'taters, when I was introduced to Spike's 'Eccles', the funniest radio character I'd ever heard. So, inspired, I sent off a couple of pages of Eccles material to Spike Milligan, care of BBC, London, just outside Great Britain, near England. Included in my offering was a song for Eccles, a parody of 'I Talk to the Trees'. What I'd written was 'I talk to the trees; that's why they put me away.' A week or so later a reply came telling me he didn't accept outside material. The signature was rubber stamped and I doubt if Spike ever saw my letter. Had he read it he would have said, 'This boy has great talent.' I think he would have said that. Three weeks later I was listening to *The Goon Show*, and guess what Eccles was singing? And went on singing for quite a while? I should have written a letter saying I accepted outside money.

Rural

The break from writing almost fifty shows during 1992–3 was most welcome. It meant more family time could be spent at our home in Wales, such peace and tranquillity on the Welsh Riviera. Some days it's so still you can hear the thud of a butterfly as it lands on a daisy – almost. You can certainly hear Mrs Parry using the Hoover, and her house is two hundred yards away. I know it's not to everyone's taste, but I love it and one day when I'm written out, clapped out, and nobody wants me I'm coming to live here – next week probably.

Lots of time to go o'er bush and heath with the stout boots, haversack, trusty stick and twenty quid in my back pocket in case I feel knackered and have to get a taxi back home.

A couple of hundred yards down the lane and I met Griff, a local farmer and the most laid-back man I have ever met – so laid back that I've christened him 'Lino'.

'What do you grow in that field, Griff?'

'Tired.'

We talked for about twenty minutes about nothing in particular, and believe me it really is a joy to have the time to talk for twenty minutes about nothing in particular. I remembered that 'tired' line and it didn't go to waste, nor did this next one when we got talking about holidaymakers using his footpath.

'They're welcome to use the footpath; they have a right to use it. I just wish they'd close gates after them – it keeps the draught off the cow's bums.'

On another of my mini-treks I stopped to lean on a five-barred gate (it was another one that just reached up to my elbows). I was eating a cheese and tomato butty and watching those most docile and placid of animals, cows, a recommended pastime and far better than valium. It never ceases to amaze me the way cows all line up at the gate when it's milking time, like a coach outing outside the toilets after a four-hour journey.

If you are one of those citizens who suffers from that millennium malady, stress, I urge you, I beg you to get into your car and drive off to your nearest field full of cows. Simply lean on a gate, and I'll bet it's another one that just reaches up to your elbows. Just lean on a gate and watch those oh so calm creatures for an hour. I promise it will work wonders for your nervous system.

It was while I was cow-watching that I was inspired to write one of my best ever poems, and that's saying something, because I've written some belters:

> Two cows chewing grass
> On a warm sunny hillock.
> I thought, 'This time tomorrow
> That grass will be millock.'

How's that for a bovine-inspired potty poem? I jotted that down on the back of a sandwich wrapper and it was used in a Morecambe and Wise show when Eric and Ern appeared as Byron and Keats. There's an outside chance I could become the next Poet Lariat – money for old rope.

Here's something I could never do in the city – as I write

these words the front door is wide open, as it is for most of the daylight hours. Neighbours can and do trot in and out to say 'Hello' or 'Hiya', depending on their age group, and it really is a very pleasant, reassuring way to live a life.

John Edwards has brought a tin of paint for me to agree on for the shed, Mrs Thomas wants a recipe for chicken lasagne, Joyce has dropped in to ask if we need anything from the shops, and a rather big man wearing a balaclava helmet is pointing a gun at me head and saying, 'You silly old bugger – leaving your front door wide open,' while two of his associates ransack the house.

When you are rejoiced as one of the foremost writers in the country as I are it does carry with it a heavy responsibility. However, it does bring with it certain bonuses, little perks of the profession that I find most acceptable. Not least of these is the very high regard in which I am quite proud to be held at our local bakery with adjoining cake shop, famous for a great many miles around for its steak pie 'with rich gravy'. As a lifelong and incurable pieoholic I just can't speak too highly of this prince of pies 'with rich gravy'. If you hold one of these glorious, 'irresistible' pies you will Billy Bunter it within minutes. The most palatable pie I have ever laid a tooth on.

Such is the appeal of this steak pie 'with rich gravy' that a considerable queue forms outside the shop long before its nine o'clock morning opening. On Saturdays there are even small tailbacks as outsiders try to purchase the quite famous steak pie 'with rich gravy'. It hasn't quite got to the police making baton charges stage, but it wouldn't surprise me if it did come to that.

Before the two very nice ladies who have the good fortune to work in the shop knew I was a foremost writer I very often didn't get a steak pie 'with rich gravy', because they sold out very early. Now I'm so much a foremost writer I can call in the mid-afternoon and still collect my steak pie 'with rich gravy'. One minor moan, one small grumble – I do wish they'd remove the sticky flypaper from the window: it's right above the Eccles cakes.

Parkinson Interview
to Plug This Book – *Take Two*

Parky. Let's see if we can get it right this time. OK?

Me. Thank you.

Parky. How long have you been writing comedy?

Me. All day.

Parky. Are you married?

Me. No. I've always been round-shouldered.

Parky. I'll tell you something: I wouldn't buy your rotten book.

Me. You've had Elton John on your show and I bet you didn't buy his CD.

Parky. He gave me one.

Me. There's no answer to that.

Parky. I've had a bellyfull of you.

Me. You wouldn't talk to me like that if I was Frank Sinatra. If I was Frank Sinatra you'd be all over me like a collapsed tent.

Parky. But you're not Frank Sinatra.

Me. That's not my fault.

Parky. Gerroff.

Me. Next time I'll bring my emu.

Parky. Just go!

Me. Thank you.

Dennis and Menace,
Budget and Budgie

It was VIP night in Studio 8. Denis Healey, Chancellor of the Exchequer, was the VIP guest who had come to see the show. But for me there was an even more important guest: my father. Now I must be honest, my dad's presence worried me just a little bit because there was to be a reception in the hospitality suite after the show with nibbles and drinkies, and my dad, God bless him, rather liked a drop of the falling-down water – and why not? Get up there, Dad, and down a few, for you deserve it after putting up with me for all these years.

All that day Dad had been having the time of his life; he had a permanent smile because he'd met Eric and Ern, and he was talking to anyone who would stand still for thirty seconds, and made sure they knew that his lad wrote the scripts for Morecambe and Wise. I told him before the show that he would have to make his own way up to the hospitality suite, as we usually had a small inquest after the recording. 'Just tell them who you are.' He was very happy that day and I was glad to be able to give just a little something back for his life of hard work and love of his children. I owed him so much – especially when I remembered the episode with the budgie.

It all began when I was aged twelve and strolling around Woolworths. I stopped when I saw a blue, green and yellow plaster bird on display.

'How much is that bird, please?'

'It's a budgie. Be a collector's item in a couple of years.'

'How much is it?'

'Sixpence.' (That's about seven hundred pounds in today's money.)

I counted my pocket money and to my joy discovered I had seven pence: that's about—. No, it doesn't matter. I bought the budgie and still had a penny left for my bus fare, or was it a tram? Might even have been the chariot. Anyway, I had my fare home and wouldn't have to walk the four miles from the city centre. It was a tram! I remember because my uncle Walter, the one who always sobbed his heart out when anyone sang, 'My Mother's Eyes', was the conductor on the tram and I didn't have to pay.

Incidentally, Uncle Walter's and my Aunt Agnes's house was right next door to the house used by the BBC to film Carla Lane's popular sitcom, *Bread*. It was a very steep road – you couldn't run down it or you'd finish up in the Mersey.

The plaster budgie was intended as a birthday present for my mother, but when I arrived home and saw that my dad was having his tea I had another use for the bird. I went quietly to the bottom of the garden and stood it up in the soil, I stepped back and it looked quite real.

'Dad.'

'What?' He was having his favourite: rice pudding with lots of horrible brown skin. He loved the skin off the rice pudding, said it was 'good for you and the best bit'.

'There's a blue, yellow and green bird in our garden.' He put the spoon down quickly. 'Are you joking?'

'No, Dad.'

'I'll come and have a look.'

He stood in the back kitchen door and looked.

'Bugger me! It's a budgie! It's a bloody budgie. Somebody's left the cage door open and it's flown out. That's a good budgie. Get my coat.'

This was Dad at his best, head of the family in complete control and knew what he was doing. I handed him his coat and he crouched like a matador. 'Just stand back.'

My mother wanted to help, but he wouldn't have it. 'Just get out of the bloody road and keep quiet, you're a bloody menace.'

He tiptoed the twelve yards to the bottom of the garden. He was about six feet from the little plaster beauty when he hurled himself full length, throwing the jacket over the bird and shouting in triumph, 'I've got the bugger!' He very, very slowly removed his jacket and found the plaster head and tail separated from the plaster bird, and I was slowly walking backwards getting ready to leg it, when my father started to laugh and his laughter grew. 'You cheeky sod! You little bugger!' My mother was laughing, as were sisters Shirley and Lilian. We laughed ever after when we remembered the budgie incident. (If ever I misbehaved as a child my father never raised a hand to me – he used to kneel on my neck).

I needn't have worried about Dad getting into the hospitality suite. When I arrived he was doing rather nicely: he had a glass of the falling-down water and was talking to Bill Cotton. He was probably telling him of the time when he and my mother took me to see Billy Cotton and his band at the Empire. On that occasion during the interval, when Dad had returned to his seat, he handed me a bag of sweets. 'I've just been to have a word with Billy Cotton and he asked me to give you these sweets.'

I really did believe him – I was only seven or eight at the time. 'Billy Cotton gave you these sweets for me?'

'Yes. He said, "Give these to your Eddie." '

I could not believe that the famous Billy Cotton, the man I had heard so many times on the wireless had given my dad a bag of sweets – just for me. They remained untouched in the bag for so long that they solidified and had to be thrown away.

Dennis Healey was a very big man; I had to look up to him, and I'm five foot thirteen. As I was talking to this amiable Cabinet minister I spotted my father swaying towards us. I thought, 'This should be fun.' And it was, because he hadn't been neglecting the falling-down water – noticeable when he took hold of Mr Healey's hand and said, 'Mr Heelum. . . . Mr Heelum.' Eric Morecambe was with a group just a couple of yards away and was enjoying this. He'd met my father earlier that day and said what a character he was. My father, still holding the Chancellor's hand, I shall never forget what he said next: 'Mr Hellum. . . . I'm the son of the scriptwriter.' Mr Healey smiled a more than friendly smile and replied, 'How very nice to meet you. I was just telling your father how much I enjoyed the show tonight.'

Thanks, Dad.

Meeting the Chancellor of the Exchequer had been a very pleasant experience. I knew what 'Chancellor' meant but I wasn't sure about 'Exchequer', so I looked it up and found that it comes from the Latin 'scaccarium', the practice of keeping accounts on a chequered cloth. Would you believe that?

It proved that it is true and there was such a thing as a BBC suit – small checks.

New Lines What I Wrote

More funny thoughts have been racing round my head. I've got to get them down on paper . . .

'He was caught trying to readjust his priorities and got six months.'

What a pity that line didn't arrive a long time ago; I know it would have worked. Even more certain when I put it on paper, because the rest just happened.

Eric. At the age of eighteen you were caught trying to readjust your priorities and you got six months.

Ern. That's not true! I'll have you know that I worked very hard.

Eric. You went to a high school.

Ern. Yes.

Eric. Up steps?

Ern. No! I worked very hard and became a physicist.

Eric. You put the bubbles into lemonade.

Ern. You know what I mean. I had a BA.

Eric. You still have.

Ern. Are you trying to wind me up?

Eric. I wouldn't know where to put the key. Tell me about your childhood, or haven't you finished with it yet?

Ern. You're deliberately trying to ridicule me.

Eric. That's true. You got your first professional engagement in pantomime.

Ern. I was very good in that pantomime.

Eric. Few would argue with that. You were the finest pumpkin that Cinderella ever had. Let's hear it for little Ern the Pumpkin King.

Ern. How dare you! I wasn't a pumpkin.

Eric. Do you still keep in touch with the other six dwarfs?

It really did happen like that when I wrote down the readjusting priorities line. If you smiled it's because you know there's no malice in what Eric's saying and you feel warmly sorry for Ern, especially when he says, 'I was very good in that pantomime.' Self-praise and you know he's going to get clobbered. In a routine like this when Eric is having a go at Ern he delivers every insult with a smile. I'll tell you something: it was a joy to write.

Northern Rocks

Ern. What would you do without me?

Eric. I'd probably buy a hamster.

The relationship between Eric and Ern was there long before my arrival. It was cemented and they were bonded closer together than any two brothers I had ever met. I wanted to highlight the genuine affection that existed between the two, and one of the ways I did this was by placing them as close to each other as possible, in the flat, in the bed. In these situations they could speak as they felt; like being in a pantomime horse skin, there was no escape and we viewed them as through a microscope. Ern proudly reading his latest play to Eric:

Ern. Rocky felt a tingle of excitement as his executive jet touched down in Amsterdam. It was his first visit to Italy.

You would think after saying something so silly that Eric would ridicule Ern – he doesn't.

Eric. That's knockout, that, Ern.

Ern. Yes. Another mammoth spectaculor.

Eric. Aren't they all.

You smiled with affection and warmth at his own self-esteem. Cliff Richard had been the guest.

Ern. Cliff surprised me in that play.
Eric. I told him to be careful with that umbrella.
Ern. I meant he could really act. Just a little more style, a little more sophistication and he could well be another me.
Eric. Never!
Ern. No. I suppose you're right.

Always praise for Ern's writing, despite the fact he isn't too sure just how many e's there are in skiing. Their relationship could not be written or in any way contrived – it was quite simply a fact. Morecambe without Wise is unthinkable: like Blackpool without the Tower.

In his own way Ern was every bit as talented as Eric, he underlined his comedy greatness. Even at their peak I don't believe Ern's contribution was fully acknowledged. Eric was probably his greatest admirer; he knew how important he was: 'Ern doesn't know just how good he is.' This to me after Ern's greatest ever performance in the 'Antony and Cleopatra' sketch with Glenda Jackson. Eric added (and the more I think about this the more I understand what he meant), 'If Ern knew how good he was he'd go to pieces.' The truth is, I don't think Ern did know how good he was. His wife Doreen tells this story of humility. 'We were coming out of the stage door after a show when a lady comes up to Ern and says, "Thank you for all the pleasure you've given us." When she'd gone Ern said, "Why are people saying things like that? It's only a job." That's not true, Ern. That's like Stradivarius saying, 'It's only a violin.'

He never behaved like the star he was; he was the most under-showbiz performer I had ever met. One evening after rehearsal I was seated next to him in his Rolls as we made our way to his home in Harrow on the Hill, when he said, 'I'm going to have to take this car in so they can have a look at it.' When I asked what the problem was he said, 'I went out for a takeaway the other night and I accidentally knocked the curry and it went right down inside the gear lever. It's sticking a bit.'

If I didn't know who he was or what he did for a living, I would say he was 'that rather nice man from the next street who I sometimes meet when he's taking his book back to the library. I think he works for the Prudential.'

Eric. Do you remember our first meeting?
Ern. I do. We decided to team up and have a go at comedy.
Eric. We should have done that.

I'm so very grateful they did. Had they not teamed up and had a go at comedy I might well have been the librarian Ern was returning his book to.

The guest in the first show of that year was Cliff Richard, duly insulted when Ern brought him back to the flat to meet Eric. When Ern started playing Cliff's record 'Livin' Doll' Eric shouted, 'Take it off! You know I can't stand him.' He then tied a piece of string to a banana for Cliff to use as a hand mic, which he did; then all three went in to Ernest Maxin's brilliantly choreographed 'The Fleet's In'.

A lifetime later I met Cliff when he was one of the guests on *Des O'Connor Tonight* and I was supplying Des with a weekly joke (should that be weakly?). Cliff shook my hand and said, 'Being on that show with Eric and Ern is one of my warmest memories.' He also said he felt that he had been a part of something special.

What viewers didn't see during the 'Fleet's In' number was when three mops were thrown from offstage to be caught by Cliff, Eric and Ern while they were dancing. Unfortunately Eric missed his mop and there was an audible crack as it hit his nose. We all thought it was broken – it really was a nasty clout on

Eric's nose – and we had to stop recording for half an hour while we had a good laugh. There's no business like it. When we had John Ammonds producing the comedy and Ernest Maxin creating and directing the musical numbers we had quality. Those two gifted gentlemen were the best in the business.

The year 1971 was, in my opinion (and I was very close to what had happened and what came after) the year we reached the summit of Everest in comedy. It was certainly the year I reached higher than I ever had before or would in the years to come.

Bill Cotton recalls, 'Probably the most exciting time that I ever had in light entertainment. Everywhere you went, people were talking about Morecambe and Wise, "Who have they got on their Christmas show this year?" It really was mind-blowing.'

The Christmas show people were asking about was the 1971 edition with, amongst a galaxy of others, Shirley Bassey. That was the year when Shirley really put her foot in it – to be precise, she had her foot put in a size 10 army boot. There was a line in that routine that was never used; I can't remember why it wasn't used, as they both liked it. It was when Shirley was struggling to walk with the boot on and Eric should have said to her, 'If you can't get it off by the time we get to your number, you'll have to sink down and sing through the lace holes.' I think we missed a good line.

By the mid-1970s the Morecambe and Wise Christmas show had become the most important television event of the year with more viewers than the Queen gets for her Christmas Day Speech to the Nation. This doesn't surprise me. Have you ever heard Her Royal Highness singing, 'Bring Me Sunshine?' And the final dance around the desk with Prince Phillip doesn't look right.

Morecambe and Wise at Christmas were becoming more

important than Christmas itself and that was ridiculous. All we were doing was putting on a light entertainment show to the best of our combined talents, and it was being blown up by the tabloids.

'He'd been blown up by the tabloids.'

'The poor man must have been in agony!'

The Christmas show was now taking on more significance than the religious event we should have been observing. It really was crazy – 28 million people watched the show on December 1977. I wonder if that many people went to church that day? It became a massive talking point with the press becoming more and more desperate for news, anything to do with the Morecambe and Wise Christmas show.

Who were the guests going to be? Would there be a big Hollywood-style dance routine? Money was being surreptitiously offered by the media for 'inside information'. I was deeply offended when such an offer was made to me, and I lost my temper and told the Editor of the *Beano* that he could keep his £1.75.

Such was the pressure on all of us leading up to the 1977 Christmas show that all the programmes we should have done that year were put on hold so that all our efforts, all our time could be concentrated on that one programme. This did not appeal to me one little bit and I wrote sixteen radio shows. The whole thing had gone mad! It was absurd, ludicrous. I lost count of the number of people, people of all ages who kept coming up to me and pestering me, 'What's going to happen in the Christmas show?' I'd get very angry and say, 'Get out of this bathroom.' The whole thing really had got out of all proportion. Ern was right: 'It's just a job.'

Let's be honest, if we hadn't had this enormous interest in what we were doing we would have had something to complain about. No complaints from me, except to say that I wish I had paid more attention to Miss Arkinstall at Matthew Arnold Primary School.

She got it right when she said I was a bit thick. 'Say your nine times table, Braben.' How I hated that nine times table with all its horrible odd numbers. 'Once nine is nine . . .' I was always spot on with that one. 'Two nines are. . . . eighteen; three nines are. . . . finish.' A lot thick, Miss Arkinstall. There's lots I could tell you about Miss Arkinstall, but I'm not going to, as I may meet her again one day and she might give me a hard time. I really should have paid more attention to Miss Arkinstall.

Even now I have to reach for the dictionary whenever I have to spell 'pharaoh' (I've just done it again) not that I have to spell 'pharaoh' all that often, as there aren't many of them about in North Wales. It's the bad weather that puts them off – or else they're allergic to sheep. Not many pharaohs. Rather like trying to find a deckchair attendant in Wolverhampton.

*

Eric asked me what I'd been doing following the break of 1972, and he was interested when I told him I'd been playing around with words that might be suitable for a children's book: 'Have you written anything?' I told him that what little I'd put on paper I'd bring with me the following week.

There wasn't a great deal of children's material that I could show to Eric, just a potty poem and a couple of short stories. He didn't object when I asked him if I could read them out, explaining that they weren't written with him in mind and that they might sound better coming from me – and I told him that if he wouldn't let me read them I'd break his nose properly. I read him the potty poem about Ella and the tooth fairy:

> My loose tooth came out last night,
> I placed it under the pillow on my bed.
> When I woke up this morning there was
> No pound coin there!
> My daddy said the fairy was dead.

At this point Eric was wanted in the studio. What might possibly have been an interesting new venture for both of us never happened – other demands were all-consuming. A pity, because writing for children had always interested me, and Eric had mentioned that he would have loved having a tiny slot in a children's programme. Sorry, but we've got to make the grown-ups laugh. So tell them the one about the couple who moved into a beach hut so they could boast they'd made love in every room in the house.

Foundations

I've heard a lot and read a lot about writer's cramp: it must be an author's nightmare. Fortunately it's something I never . . .

Three Days Later...

Hello again! I'm full of words! If you prick me I'll explode into twenty volumes. Now I don't want to bore you into watching *Eastenders* with gloom-laden tales of my North Country childhood, cobblestones and stuff like that, sixteen of us sleeping in the one bed – four to a nightshirt. Much better for me to tell you about the fun foundations, the happy beginnings that made me the writer who I are.

Me, Jeffrey and Vinno being chucked out of the Salvation Army Citadel for singing our own words to 'Jesus Bids Us Shine'.

When I was about two my mother took me with her to Brown's fish and chip shop to get my dad's tea. 'A nice piece of cod please, Edna. It's for he's tea.' She sat me on the counter while she got her purse out, and I fell backwards into the batter. A little old lady said, 'I'll have him with peas.' It's true about falling into the batter, but I made the little old lady up.

Our mother darning our socks with the lid of a tea caddy, and whoever explains that one to you must be at least 120. I wish I could remember the next character's name, because he deserves recognition. Whoever he was, he often sat on the front doorstep of his house in Monkswell Street and played the accordion. Played it? He was a musical magician.

Imagine this next scene happening now. He's playing popular songs on the box, as the accordion used to be called, because it would be packed into a box, hung over the shoulder by a strap and carried to the Saturday night do. 'Good, he's brought his box with him.'

He's sat on his doorstep playing away, and in minutes mums, dads and children are crowding on to the pavement, listening and singing. Sometimes twenty or thirty people congregated; they'd come from Longford Street and Kinnaird Street just to listen or join in singing to his accordion. My dad doing a bit of a tap dance in the road and my mother telling him, 'Stop making a holy show of yourself.' For the first time since I've been putting these words down I feel sad, but it's a nice sad because that is a truly beautiful memory and it can't ever happen again.

My mother complaining to the landlord about the damp patch in the bedroom. 'Not much of a damp patch,' he said. 'Not much.' Kate was angry. 'Not much?' It looks like the River Mersey's making a detour.'

Mr Towes, as in one and one makes, was our insurance man. I know I've likened Ern to an insurance man, but he wasn't like Mr Towes. Mr Towes was short, tubby, red-faced, had a walrus moustache, bowler hat and leather gaiters, and he rode the most enormous pushbike I'd ever seen. It was a Hercules, and it would have taken Hercules and a couple of his Greek mates to lift it. Mr Towes was also as Welsh as a pack of corgis, and that was his weakness – at least as far as my mother was concerned. Kate, as we fondly called her, was tiny, slight of build, blue-eyed with jet-black hair. She had an impish sense of humour that surfaced every Friday night. You only had to mention Lloyd George to Mr Towes and the tears of Celtic pride would begin to build before starting to trickle down his red cheeks like a small Welsh mountain stream, to be lost in his whiskers. Each Friday night, when Mr Towes called for his sixpence, taken from a pillar of copper coins kept on the mantelpiece in the parlour, my mother always made sure she turned the conversation to accommodate Lloyd George. She really was a devil. 'There was a bit on the wireless this afternoon about Lloyd George, Mr Towes. It said that if it wasn't for him we wouldn't have the old age pension.' Mr Towes sniffed. 'He was a good man, Mrs B, a good man. He did a lot for the working class.' He'd go on to embellish Lloyd George's CV, and the tears would flow. One Friday night he got so emotional he gave Kate too much change. She gave it back to him the following week – I think.

Ross Hodgson! That was the name of the man who played the accordion sitting on his front doorstep in Monkswell Street. I feel much better now. I've done it, Ross! You are forever etched in ink on quality paper.

*

It was Ern who caused Eric and me to react with some surprise when he produced this little gem: 'You know, the truth is that we make a living by telling lies.' (We were in his dressing room during a break, and talking comedy.) 'Think about it,' Ern was having a chuckle now. 'You write the lies and we go on and tell them.'

I'd never thought about what we did in that way before.

'It's true,' I admitted. 'But you're both such very good liars. You tell the lies; people laugh, applaud, sometimes shout for more, and we give them more lies.'

Eric was smiling at all of this. 'We're like politicians: we get paid for telling lies.' Ern had taken us down this road and was enjoying it.

'We live a life of lies. You, pointing at me, you come down here with scripts in your briefcase and I think, "What lies has he got for us this week?" '

Eric took his pipe from his mouth. 'That's a stupid thing to say. Where else would he take it from? It's all lies,' he said. 'We go home that night and say to our wives, "You look beautiful." ' He stood up, rubbed his hands together vigorously and said, 'Shall we go up to the club for a drink? Ern will get them in, and that's the biggest lie of the week.'

As I don't drink, it was John who went to the club with Eric and Ern, and he tells of what happened in the lift.

'We got in the lift and we were followed by a woman carrying a toddler, aged about two; three at the very most. The lift started its upward journey and Eric and the toddler were staring at each other for what seemed ages; in fact it was about ten seconds. Mum was looking a bit apprehensive as Eric very slowly leaned a bit closer to the child and said, "How's the wife?"

'Mum clasped the child close and got out at the next floor – whether she wanted that floor or not I'll never know.'

These formal conversations were well worth having: they did sometimes lead to quite useful comedy situations. Ern once spoke casually about a visit he'd made to a supermarket and this aroused Eric's interest: 'We've never done a supermarket sketch.' We hadn't, and I can't think why, because it's a good place for comedy. So I wrote one. I'm glad I did, because two lines from it leap to mind whenever I go to the supermarket, which is every day, as I am an assistant trolley stacker.

These are the lines I remember fondly.

They are both looking at some tinned goods when Eric picks up a tin, looks at the label and asks, 'What's this stuff?

Sugarapsa.' Ern takes the tin, turns it the right way up and explains, 'Asparagus.'

Then the delightful Hannah Gordon enters. She sees Ern and starts to plead with him to let her appear in one of the plays what he wrote. As she begs for a part, she places her hand on his basket of shopping. Eric is mildly shocked and says, 'You've got your hand on his pilchards.'

Eric told me that when he knew I had written the sketch he paid a visit to a supermarket to observe and get the feel of things. He said, 'It really does help to get first-hand experience. By the way, when are you going to write the one about a nudist camp?' And do a sketch for Ern while you're at it. One where he's locked in a bank overnight. He'll love that.'

I was never very keen on writing anything that took them out of doors away from the television studio. I didn't like it when they had to do location work. They more than once asked me to write something that would have to be filmed somewhere warm and exotic. I did suggest Filey but they didn't seem very enthusiastic. New Brighton? No.

I had to explain why I was always reluctant to write anything that took them out of doors. Once they went outside they were in the cold, harsh world, not the cosy, warm world of the TV studio.

The real world isn't always cold and harsh, but it isn't a 'Once upon a time' world, a place full of laughter and a magic. The real world is a place I never felt comfortable in.

*

Eric was escorting me from room to room at his home and proudly showing me his individual collection of clocks, a hobby we both shared. He told me about a clock that sounded rather special. I could tell it was special because he told me very quietly, very slowly, 'I went into an antique shop in Harpenden the other day; I'd never been inside it before.'

Now he's got my full attention, because the antique shop's becoming something of an Aladdin's cave.

'I walked into the shop and the owner knew straight away who I was, because he locked the till.'

I said, 'Are you trying out a routine on me?'

'No, no. This really did happen. I went to the back of the shop and saw this carriage clock on the shelf. It was over a hundred years old and as black as the ace of spades. I bought it. How much do you think?'

'Seventy five, a hundred?'

'A fiver.'

'That wasn't bad for a clock that old.'

'Black it was. I brought it home and I've been cleaning it up for half an hour every night. You should see it now.'

'What colour is it?'

'Black.'

He did laugh. It was that laugh he tries to hold back. I laughed at my own gullibility: he'd led me on beautifully.

That same day we had a short walk o'er bush and heath. It was during this walk that the idea came to me about a bird box. We were bird-watching and were talking about the merits of bird books (we both had quite a collection). I said, 'How about going into a bookshop and asking for a book about bird songs and the way that birds communicate?'

'What do you mean?' He had his serious face on now because we were talking comedy. He always looked serious when we talked shop.

'Ern owns the bookshop and you ask him for a book called *The Language of Birds*.

'Instead of words you whistle, like bird calls.'

He liked the idea.

'Great! I like that, using whistles instead of words.'

We spent the next half an hour talking to each other in whistles.

Eric started laughing.

'Wouldn't it be hilarious if a couple of blackbirds saw us, actually spoke and said, 'Look at those two silly sods.'

In fact it was a pity we let that line go because it would have been a very good pay-off to the sketch, with two prop birds in a cage watching what was going on in the shop.

The sketch was done in the show, without a couple of pretend birds calling Eric and Ern 'two silly sods'.

The pay-off to the sketch was Eric paying for the book with two very large eggs and Ern giving him these very small eggs in change.

That afternoon we drove to the home of Gordon Benningfield, a wonderfully gifted naturalist painter. Eric had shown me a couple of watercolours of Gordon's that he had and they were quite stunning.

'So you think he'd do a couple of bird paintings for me?'

'Let's go and ask him; he only lives a couple of miles away.'

As we turned into the drive of the Benningfield home I really did gasp with delight.

What a higgledy-piggledy home: it was a glorious shambles, and I mean that in the nicest possible way, the sort of home that wouldn't look out of place if it was illustrated in *The Wind in the Willows*.

It was like driving on to the set of *The Darling Buds of May*.

It was surrounded by an assortment of dogs. Shaggy-haired dogs, short-haired dogs, chickens, sheep and laughing children, the sights and sounds of that afternoon will remain with me eternally.

Gordon was one of the most self-effacing men I have ever met, often the case with men who are blessed with great talent, as are I am. I was delighted when he said he would be able to paint a pair for me, a goldfinch and a jay.

Six months later Gordon came to the TV Centre with the paintings, and they were quite superb.

'How much do I owe you, Gordon?'

This oh-so-very-shy man did not like talking about money: his embarrassment at my question was almost painful to watch.

'Come on, Gordon. Nobody works for nothing. How much do I owe you? These paintings are quite beautiful.'

His cheeks flushed; he shuffled his feet.

'Is seventy pounds too much?'

'No, Gordon. It most certainly is not.'

I wrote out a cheque for one hundred and forty pounds and handed it to him. He looked at it and said, 'Not seventy pounds *each*; seventy pounds for the *pair*.'

The goldfinch and the jay are still gloriously beautiful in our home, and whenever I look at them I can hear a chorus of dogs, chickens sheep and laughing children.

*

'I'm not really a very nice person, am I?' This was Ern talking about his TV character. 'I'm a pompous, semi-literate author who is also a bit of a scrooge.'

Ern. How dare you! I'm not mean.

Eric. Oh. Then how is it that when you took a fiver out of you wallet six years ago it was no longer legal tender.

Ern. It was legal tender! You're making this all up. I'm not mean and nasty. I'm a nice man!

Eric. You took that fiver out and George III had sunglasses on.

(This dialogue has never been heard before, except in my head.)

Ern was a long way from being mean; however, the meaner, more pompous and semi-literate I made his character, the more he enjoyed it.

When I drove with him to TV Centre once, after an overnight stay at his home, he handed me a slip of paper. I unfolded it and read, 'Early morning tea and three digestive biscuits – £1.25p.' He laughed and said, 'You've only yourself to blame.'

Robert Morley was the celebrity guest in the show being recorded that day. I'm told that when he arrived at the outside rehearsal room two weeks earlier he was appalled at the arrangements for lunch – pea and ham soup from a flask, and sandwiches. We had always been quite happy with this menu, but Robert was not impressed. 'This will never do. I think we deserve much better.' It certainly was much better the following day when his chauffeur opened the boot of the car and carried in an enormous Fortnum and Mason hamper. Sadly I wasn't present at this banquet: I was working on the next show. In no way do I wish to be offensive to such a reputable actor, but every time I see a tin of pea and ham soup I think of Robert Morley.

> **Eric.** I don't like pizza.
> **Ern.** Why not?
> **Eric.** It looks like a pancake with acne.

I was as much in awe of Robert Morley as I had been when Flora Robson was our guest, but probably more nervous because he really was an actor with an enormous presence, and a Hollywood star when I was a child. You would never cast Robert as a binman or a carpark attendant – a king or a pope would be about right. Or perhaps as a world-famous architect; then you could call him Bob the Builder. Not that I would even contemplate doing such a thing.

Robert was appearing in a sketch about Tutankhamen's Tomb, and for some reason I wasn't one hundred per cent happy with it. I watched it being rehearsed on camera and still felt unsure, so I left the studio for the nearest tea machine. I got my cup of BBC tea, which also makes an excellent wood preserver, and went and sat with Johnny Ball, who I'd known as a good stand-up comic on radio: *Blackpool Night* and

Workers' Playtime (excellent grounding if you want an ulcer). I asked him what he was doing.

'A new children's programme.'

'That should keep you busy.'

'I hope so.'

'What's it called?'

Play School.

It did keep Johnny busy, and quite right too. Johnny Ball must be the best children's TV presenter of them all, with due respect to Anne Robinson. Anne would make a good TV presenter, if you wanted your kiddies to volunteer to go to bed early.

'Robert Morley would like to see you in his dressing room.'

This from a young lady carrying a clipboard, and I'm always nervous of people who carry clipboards because it means they're important. She was also the first punk I can remember seeing. She had metal rings through her ears, eyebrows, nose and lips – she looked like she'd been making love to a curtain rail.

'He wants to see me?'

'Now.'

I almost choked on what was left of my tea.

'Just say you couldn't find me.'

'I have, and he's waiting.'

The sketch must be the problem: it isn't working, he's not happy with it and he wants to see me. The curse of Tutankhamen had followed me to the Television Centre.

I knocked on his dressing-room door.

'Come in.'

It was the first time I had ever heard anyone say 'Come in' imperiously.

When I entered the room I felt there was something missing – like a fanfare for a royal occasion by William Walton. From the expression on his face there could have been something rancid in the room, like my script. I very nearly said, 'You sent for me, my liege.' I didn't; just, 'You wanted to see me?'

He indicated for me to sit down. When I say 'indicated', he sort of twirled his hand regally. I sat down.

'So, dear boy, you are not a recluse after all. How very nice to meet you. This,' he was holding the script aloft, 'this is great fun. I particularly like this line when I say to Eric, "Can you hire a camel?", and he replies, "Yes, there's a little screw underneath the saddle." Very funny.'

This from a man who was a Hollywood star when I was a child. This from a man who had starred with Humphrey Bogart and Katherine Hepburn in one of my favourite films of ever and ever, *The African Queen*.

The curse of Tutankhamen didn't follow us into Studio 8, and Robert Morley was majestically glorious.

Liver Girls

The sun was shining. Rain wasn't invented until I was about fourteen. My face was turned smilingly upward in admiration in Liverpool's Duke Street. I was smilingly upward in admiration at a plaque on the wall of a once residence, one of those blue plaques that commemorates a famous person who lived there. When my budgie falls of its perch they'll probably put one up to commemorate me on the wall of the Home for Vagrants.

The plaque I was gazing at with great affection read, 'Felicia Hemans was born here 1793.' There was no line across the leg of the 7 – they didn't do stupid things like that in 1793.

Felicia Hemans was a famous lady poetess. She wrote, 'The Landing of the Pilgrim Fathers', which is traditionally recited in America on Thanksgiving Day. Wait. Before you say, 'So what? I've never heard of the woman,' let me tell you that the lovely, lovely Felicia wrote that epic poem 'Casabianca'. Still doesn't ring any bells? Then how about the opening line of that poem, the one beloved by all comedians, comedy writers, rugby players, drunks and naughty schoolboys who write things on playground walls. Felicia's famous line is, 'The boy stood on the burning deck'. As far as I'm concerned, they're the seven most inspirational words in English literature. That line has led to some of the best laughs I've ever had,

though I freely admit I did plagiarise Felicia's poem just a little
bit. This is what it led to:

> The boy stood on the burning deck,
> The flames they drove him crackers.
> A spark shot up his trouser leg
> And set fire to his . . .

I actually recited that one as I was looking at the plaque, not with
any disrespect – it was a thank you. And I haven't finished yet:

> The boy stood on the burning deck,
> He waved to all the dockers.
> He waved to his girl,
> She was known as Shirl,
> The one with the great big . . .

That was one of Eric's favourites, he loved reciting potty
poetry; and there's more, and, if I remember, this next version
was waiting for Jimmy Cricket and in one of the shows in the
series *Jimmy's Cricket Team*, what I wrote. That was jolly fun
and Felicia Hemans helped the fun along, like this:

> The boy stood on the burning deck,
> As all around him did wilt.
> But it didn't bother this brave Scottish lad,
> He was wearing his asbestos kilt.

Finally, and this is my favourite. Honesty insists I lay no claim
to the following, except the first couple of lines. The original
potty poem harks back to the pre-war days of the variety
theatre. Even then Felicia was not being neglected.

> The boy stood on the burning deck,
> His body was all a quiver.
> He gave a cough, his leg fell off
> And floated down the river.

Thank you so very much, Felicia. Those of us who crease our brows, put our brains through the mincer, drink gallons of tea, pace the floor, kick the dog and turn viciously on our wives, children and neighbours in our never-ending struggle to find the next funny line, thank you, thank you.

I was so proud of Felicia's inspirational line that I featured her birthplace in Duke Street in a film I made for BBC's *Nationwide* in the early eighties.

The day after the programme was transmitted I'm told there were more visitors to her home in one day than there were in a whole year! All of them burning deck fans. Give that lady another plaque.

Just ten minutes' walk from Felicia's birthplace and you are in 'Lil's Kingdom'. More about yet another inspirational lady shortly. Clayton Square, at the heart of the city centre, is a glorious mixture of colour, sounds and smells. Heaving with buses, taxis, multicoloured flower sellers, multicoloured people, buskers, barrows loaded with fruit and veg and the little old lady with a shawl wrapped around her slender shoulders. She stands at the entrance to St John's Market with a wicker basket at her feet and tells the world of her goods as she cries, 'Sage-a-mint-a-parsley! Sage-a-mint-a-parsley!'

Whenever my mother was in town shopping she always bought from her a bunch of mint and a bunch of parsley and said every time, 'The poor old devil probably hasn't got two ha'pennies to rub together.'

The herb seller died when she was 89 and left sixty million pounds.

She didn't really leave sixty million pounds. It's just that when half-starved little old ladies die they usually surprise us.

Then there was Bonny. He sold dogs out of cardboard boxes, when the police weren't watching. If the pup had a lot of hair he told potential buyers it was 'one of them Eskimo dogs'; short haired, and it was 'one of them hound dogs'.

'How much are the dogs?'

'Ten shillings and five shillings.'

'What's the difference?'

'The ten shilling ones have got four legs.'

I knew Bonny quite well and on a busy Saturday afternoon he would ask me to keep an eye out for scuffers.

If you're one of those people who doesn't sell three-legged dogs illegally, a 'scuffer' is a constable.

A customer would buy one of Bonny's puppies. There was also an extra service.

Bonny would ask, 'Do you want the dog's tail docked?'

'Yes.'

Bonny would pick up the puppy and bite the tail off with his teeth.

'That'll be a tanner,' he said, spitting the tail out.

At the hub of all this delightful activity was Lilly Benson's kiosk, like a small wooden cathedral dispensing the good word of all the national daily newspapers, as well as a range of magazines, sweets and tobacco. It was a time when a Mars Bar was as thick as a brick and you could buy a loosie (one cigarette) and a match for twopence – that's about 320 pounds in today's currency, I think.

Lil is fixed in my memory with superglue, a lady who wouldn't have been out of place in a Damon Runyon novel. She had the knack of being able to look you in the face without raising her head, this trick learned from a lifetime of looking down to make sure nobody nicked a *Daily Mail*, *Girls Crystal* or the *Wizard* (given the choice I would have nicked the *Wizard*).

Lil knew everyone and everything that was happening in that square. She said little, except 'Thank you' or 'It won't be out until Tuesday' or 'Are you trying to memorise that magazine? Come back at six o'clock and I'll read it to you.'

She was razor sharp and had the best collection of one-liners I'd ever heard outside the comedy business.

I visited Lil's kiosk every night after work for my cigarettes. Cigarettes were good for you then. What went wrong? If you bought a packet of Craven A the doctor in the advert said that smoking was good for your throat and chest – certainly the thing to do was flash your cigarette case at your girlfriend. I remember watching Paul Henreid placing two cigarettes into his mouth, lighting both of them and handing one to Bette Davis in *Now Voyager*. That was quite sensational at the time and I had to do it to impress my girlfriend, the only trouble was when I tried to do it the cigarette got stuck to my bottom lip and when I tried to hand it to Joan Pye I pulled a piece of skin off and cried, 'Jesus!' Ruined the evening.

If Lil was in the mood when I visited her kiosk at night the dialogue could be memorable. To this day I still don't know, can't think of any reason, why she should call me 'Dirty Heels'.

'Hello, Lil.'

'Hello, Dirty Heels.'

'Got any Swedish magazines in a plain wrapper for adults only?'

'I've sold them all to the chief of the Vice Squad. Here's your cigarettes. Now sod off.'

If Lil didn't tell me to sod off at least twice during a conversation I'd think we were out of friends.

'Have you been busy, Lil?'

'Busy? There's more action in a nun's knickers.'

I wasn't expecting what came next. When it did I was left totally speechless.

'You'll never guess who was here ten minutes ago.'

'Flash Gordon.' (Me trying to be smart.)

'I'm serious.'

Lil was serious. Whoever was here, was here ten minutes ago. She had my interest and she knew it. Typical.

'I've no idea.'

'You'll go hairless when I tell you.'

'Tell me.'

'Sarah Vaughan.'

'Here?'

'Honest to God. She stood where you are now, bought a *Melody Maker* and a packet of Churchman and she signed her autograph for me.'

And that great singer *had* signed her autograph, across the top of the *Woman's Own*. 'And I've missed her.'

'She's on at the Empire all this week.'

'I know. I'm going on Friday, second house. Wish I'd been here, though. Erm . . . Lil, I'll buy that *Women's Own* off you.'

'Are you changing your sex or just out of your mind? Sod off.'

I sodded off, very disappointed at having missed the divine Sarah.

I wonder if I could persuade the local council to put up a blue plaque with Lil's name on it. In gold, if you don't mind.

Leafy Lines

I must put this next little episode down on paper because it happened not ten minutes ago as I was putting words on paper. The phone rang and when I answered it a young man, I think his name was Simon, said, 'This is PPP Healthcare. Would it be possible to speak to Mr Braben?' I said, 'He's in hospital.'

Pity to waste it.

Another favourite is answering a call like this, 'I can't talk to you now; we're not on the phone.'

Which flat sketch that line came from, I can't remember. I'm told that Eric caused embarrassment at home by using it.

*

The press had caught hold of the picture of me as a recluse. I told one journalist I lived in a home with sixty-five other recluses. Another spoke of my home as being remote, and I told him I lived in a cottage at the bottom of a valley and the daylight had to be wheeled in on a handcart. If a TV or newspaper reporter was coming to my home to do an interview and asked directions I told him to 'turn left at the fourth shepherd, the one with the beard'.

Hikers climbing the stile next to our front gate often pause for a chat, not always a wise thing to do.

'Beautiful spot.'

'Very.'

'Have you been here long?'

'It's about half past two.'

The hiker now speaks a little more slowly, a little bit louder. 'It must be, it must be dreadful here, dreadful in the winter.'

'Yes. We stock up with supplies early in November.'

'Really?'

'She's very well thank you.'

'Right ho, then.'

'Water, flour, candles. Basic survival stuff, you know. Flares are important.'

The hiker is now taking a step down into the field and civilisation, the real world.

'Nice talking to you. Must be off.'

'How much are they?'

'Bye!'

Well, us recluses we have to make our own fun.

The battle with the mole wasn't fun, it was deadly serious. War was declared on the May morning when I walked out to greet the spring and saw six enormous mole hills in the lawn. It wasn't a *Homes and Garden* lawn; just a nice piece of ground I was rather proud of. I was told it was the work of one randy mole in search of a mate and that it could be eliminated by a local who supplemented his income as leader of the London Symphony Orchestra by catching moles. He wasn't really leader of the LSO. If you gave Tom a violin he probably wouldn't know which end to blow down.

Here was a man who made his living following the ancient skills handed on from generations long gone, and I had to get in touch with him by ringing his mobile number. He told me he could rid me of the mole by placing live worms dipped in cyanide. I've seen that at the pictures and the next day somebody is found dead up at the big house. As Ern would say, 'That is very Agatha Crispy.'

No poison. There was another way to catch the mole and it would have worked if it hadn't been for the book I was reading at the time.

To catch the rogue mole I had to stand stock still over the mole hill with a spade poised to strike, and not move a muscle – not difficult, as I've only got about three.

This method would work only when the mole became active again and the hill moved. I must have stood stock still with the spade raised for fully five minutes, and my body ached. The mole started digging and the earth moved once. I was told to go in as quickly as possible on the third movement, and I did. Whoosh! There to my horror, not to my joy but to my horror, there was the rascal mole in amongst the soil on my spade. I tipped it on to the grass, raised the spade to end the problem once and for all. . . . I couldn't do it. I lowered the spade and watched as the little black and very beautiful creature waddled quickly into the hedgerow. I looked at the awful mess this tiny creature had caused and would go on causing for the best part of his life, as would his offspring when he'd caught up with his mate. I could have ended this there and then, but it's not easy to kill a mole when you're reading *The Wind in the Willows*.

What If?

Ern. It's not easy for us authors to find new words.
Eric. Have you got a thesaurus?
Ern. No, I don't like motorbikes.

They would read that dialogue and laugh. But what if only one of them laughed?

Morecambe and Wise had a golden rule that served them well throughout their careers: if one of them didn't like an idea they didn't do it. Couldn't argue, it worked for them even if it did break my heart on many occasions. They never read something I had written, and then said, 'Rubbish.' They wouldn't and couldn't be so insensitive. What would happen if they didn't like something I had given them was I'd get a phone call from John Ammonds, and how he hated doing this: 'Eddie, the boys feel . . .' Once John began the conversation with, 'The boys feel', he was really saying they thought it was rubbish. Hands up. I have to confess it was rubbish on many occasions. It's very strange, very odd but true, that when something I had written really was rubbish, that was the one that was the most difficult to write, the piece of comedy that had to be a gallon of tea and fifty cigarettes.

Some of the best comedy took only minutes. The sketch in

front of the curtains when Eric was showing Ern his enormous dog, holding a lead that went up and through the curtains to a height of fifteen feet:

Eric. He's a guard dog.
Ern. What does he guard?
Eric. High-rise flats.

That big-dog routine, as with the enormous ventriloquist's doll, took as long to write as it did to perform, give or take half an hour. The only time their golden rule was broken, to my knowledge, was over the now legendary Ernest Maxin musical routine from *South Pacific*, when a small army of TV news readers sang and showed what great acrobatic dancers they were in *There Is Nothing Like a Dame*. Eric told Ernest Maxin, 'This isn't going to work. It just won't happen.' However, Ern (little Ern) was so enthusiastic about the project, so excited with the idea, that he finally persuaded Eric, 'Let's do it, look at it when it's finished and edited, and if you still don't like it, then we won't let it go out.' Eric looked at the finished number, and liked it with enthusiasm. It went out and was one of the best musical numbers Ernest Maxin ever produced.

That golden rule had me sulking in the corner on many occasion, and threatening to take my ball in. Eric always knew when I was upset – I threw Ern at him.

The idea was to try something different. Pinky and Bunny were two retired military gents who were always found in reminiscent mood:

Pinky. Do you remember young Carruthers?
Bunny. I remember him very well – he lost his pips at the frontier.
Pinky. They were found the next morning on the barbed wire.

Bunny.   Whatever became of him?
Pinky.   He joined the Luton Girls Choir.

There was something about this comedy, though, that wasn't right, not Morecambe and Wise. This was an idea on a sheet of foolscap that never made it. The gags were used in other comedy situations, but Pinky and Bunny never made it out of their leather armchairs.

Looking at it now I can see that it's more of a Two Ronnies situation; it wasn't Eric and Ern. Had I pushed for this one I know it would have been a phone call and the familiar 'Eddie, the boys feel . . .'

On rare occasions ideas I put into a script, just to see if they'd work, really caught on. A good example of this was Eric saying, 'I'd love a cup of tea, Ern,' and then laughing at the realisation of what he'd said. 'Tea urn . . .' He would double up with laughter, often holding on to the door for support. 'Tea urn. I love that one,' and he really did. When he read it the first time, though, he didn't give it his usual seal of approval with, 'Now that's funny.' The tea-urn line got, 'That is a belter.' In fact it became so popular that guest stars often asked if they could say the line. Every week we did it and every week it got a big, big laugh.

Almost the same thing happened when I thought it might work if Ern were to undermine, albeit unknowingly, his stature as an 'author' by boasting of his latest work as *The Play What I Wrote*, a throwaway line that is now forever Ern.

Sometimes when Ern was trying to convince a doubting guest that the play what he wrote was a classic and every bit as good as 'Henry the Ninth' the guest might use a word Ern didn't understand and he would look to Eric for help (not the best person to turn to for help, but he was his friend). Ern would look rather puzzled when asked by the guest, who was in need of convincing, 'Do you have a rough synopsis?' This would be followed by an embarrassed pause before Eric stepped in on the defensive and said, 'No, not since he's been using the pink ointment.' Ern would be very relieved at this timely explanation and would smilingly agree, 'That's perfectly true.'

As a matter of interest, when talking about ointment in comedy, it always has to be pink, any other colour and the gag won't work – neither will the ointment. Speaking from experience, I can assure you that British audiences like their ointment pink.

Eric was always the protective shield against all doubters of Ern's work; as far as Eric was concerned, he could do no wrong and would stand by him always. This was the case when Arthur Lowe had misgivings about 'Mutiny on the Bounty':

Arthur. I think there's been a typing error in the title.
Ern. Typing Error? 'That's "Mutiny on the Bounty".
Arthur. But you've got 'Monty on the Bonty'.

Ern looking very uncomfortable at a guest finding a mistake in his work, so Eric stepped in:

Eric. That's not Ern's fault. That's a typing error because his typewriter is made out of his old bike.
Arthur. Made a typewriter out of his bike?
Eric. That's true. Now every time he cocks his leg over the ribbon he knocks the keys with his saddle bag.

How very fortuitous that turned out to be; it really was a genuine typing error on my part. As I was typing out that dialogue I quite accidentally did hit the wrong key and printed 'Monty' instead of 'Mutiny'. It looked good, sounded good, so I changed 'Bounty' to 'Bonty'. How I wish I could have made a few more mistakes like that.

Arthur Lowe was the first and only guest in my experience to leave Eric Morecambe speechless – it didn't happen very often. This collector's item happened during a rehearsal for 'Mutiny on the Bounty'. Eric and Arthur were playing out a scene on deck; Eric warned him there was unrest amongst the men and that there was talk of 'mutiny, Cap'n'. Arthur completely ignored the written line, whatever it was. He mimed taking a cigarette out of his mouth, crushed it underfoot and said, and it was the best Humphrey Bogart impression I'd ever heard, 'If that's the way it's gonna be, sweetheart.'

It was the first and only time I had ever heard a guest get applause during a rehearsal.

After Eric and those of us who were present had got over the initial surprise at this quite brilliant ad-lib, Eric said, 'Hell Fire! He's brought his own jokes!'

It was, as far as I can remember, the only time a guest ever altered or added a word to a script with such stunning effect.

It shouldn't have come as a surprise to any of us, as Arthur Lowe was surely one of our greatest comedy and character actors.

*

Ern always managed to undermine himself and we would see the true character of the man. He was what I called 'a frock man'. It was never a 'pretty dress'; it was a 'nice frock'. He didn't do mathematics at school; he did 'sums, adding up and takeaways'. During the rough and tumble of a ventriloquist sketch with Eric he said, 'You're sat on me 'and' – echoes of a dozen or more North Country funny men.

How Many Jokes on a Typewriter Ribbon?

I still have the same typewriter I have played the *Anvil Chorus* on for more than forty years with forefingers that now resemble small toffee hammers. The same typewriter that serenaded our children to sleep: 'Mum, I can't sleep if I can't hear Dad's typewriter.' A very thirsty typewriter – it must have guzzled at least sixty gallons of Tipp-Ex. It's seen better days; so have some of the jokes.

If it could have been fitted with a gagometer I wonder how many would be on the clock now? That's a staggering thought, because it's been rattling merrily from 'First of all, ladies and gentlemen, I would like to say how tickled I ham' to 'Good evening, ladies and gentlemen. Welcome to the show.'

A very long way back to probably the first gag in 1959 when the hula hoop was all the rage: 'My wife's taken her hula hoop back to the shop: it was too tight.'

Then 1964 when Harold Wilson became Prime Minister: 'I see Harold Wilson's at number 10. Is he? I didn't even know he'd made a record.'

How many jokes on the gagometer, I wonder? Thousands. It's got to be more: tens and tens of thousands. Ah, but there are jokes and there are jokes. Awful jokes, like the hula hoop and the Harold Wilson. The not-so-bad jokes, the good jokes and the platinum ones I reach for with my toffee-hammer fingers – the woofer. It doesn't happen often, but when it does it's worth the self-inflicted hardships. The joke that makes you laugh so much it improves your complexion to bright red, brings tears to your eyes, doubles you up. The 'Stop it! I'll have to go to the toilet' joke. The collector's-item joke. The speeding police car with siren sounding – 'He's not going to sell much ice cream going at that speed.' Imagine if all of that laughter could be played back – what a splendid and glorious eruption of sound that would be, the best explosion ever.

It must also be said that if it were possible to play back the reaction to a great many of my jokes there would be a very long period of silence. I was spared that embarrassment, probably because John Ammonds telephoned me and said, 'Eddie, the boys feel . . .'

As for my typewriter, desk and chair (all part of TV history, the golden age), when word got around that anyone who was interested could see these relics of a time long gone, I was surprised at the reaction. In the first week more than five hundred people walked straight past and didn't take a blind bit of notice.

I once sold a couple of my scripts for charity and gave the money to the RSPCA. They sent me a nice letter of thanks which said that the flea collar would come in very handy. That old age pensioner of a typewriter is now clapped out and enjoying a well-earned rest under a sheet at the back of the garage next to my wife.

Friends who own and spend a lot of time on their computers are horrified and almost gasp in disbelief when they learn I'm writing this book in longhand, which I am, and I'm on to my fourth biro. I know that sounds like a load of ballpoints, but it doesn't take into account the many pages that have been torn up and binned, enough to make a small woodland. Lots of those pages wasted on happenings I regard to be dull, to everyone but me. It was not dull when I was offered a trial with Liverpool football club, though; it was very exciting, but turned to embarrassment when I was taken off after just ten minutes. I'd touched the ball twice and fallen over three times. As I walked off the pitch a man in the crowd of half a dozen shouted, 'I've seen better legs on a card table.' Nothing more to say about that episode.

Anyway, 'Writing it in longhand?' they say. 'I don't know how you can do it. What a tedious way to write, it must take forever. I'd be lost without my computer.' They all say, 'I'd be lost without my computer.' I'm lost *with* it.

When computer buffs start talking to me about computers and using computer jargon, they might as well be talking to me in Chinese, because it doesn't mean a thing to me. What beats me is how anyone can say, 'Forward slash' and still keep a straight face.

The truth is, computers frighten me. I once had a very unpleasant experience with a computer when I was using one for the first time. It was also the first book I had attempted and I was printing it out word for word on the monster, when I pressed the wrong key. The screen went blank and the first ten pages of my book went out into space. Despite reassurances that it was nothing to worry about, I never used it again. I have this awful fear that if I hit the wrong key I'll black out the intensive care unit at the hospital and all the hearing aids in the surrounding villages. Incidentally that first book attempt was a disaster. It was all about a boy who goes to a mysterious school to learn how to be a wizard. Have you ever heard of such a ridiculous idea for a book? I knew it was rubbish and would never have worked anyway.

Laugh Lines

Writing for Ronnie Corbett and his Saturday night shows on BBC TV was a lot of fun. A very placid man, polite, courteous and uncomplaining, but give him a joke that wasn't funny and he'd jump up and bite you on the fleshy part of the thigh.

A terrible worrier, he got extremely nervous before a show. I often went into his dressing room before a recording and he was pacing up and down under the table. After a show there was nothing he enjoyed more than having a nice soak in an eye bath.

In the list of comedians what I have written for, Ronnie is in top spot, because he is a 24-carat person.

Were it at all possible to go back and make changes to my writing career, I would have rearranged my commitments – not a pretty sight. I would have done everything possible to have left time to enable me to write for the *Two Ronnies*, a show that was quality from first to last. I did on occasion contribute to this quite brilliant series but not as much as I would have liked to.

Eric and Ern were great admirers of their work, particularly Ronnie Barker's dazzling manipulation of words. Often the morning after a *Two Ronnies* show they would come in and say, 'I wish we could have done that.' I just smiled and set fire to their overcoats.

*

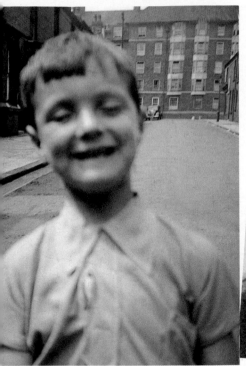

1 my first adventure playground.
Monkswell Street, 1938.

Reach for the sky?
No, reach for the dishcloth.

Our first ever visit to a West End nightclub. When Edmundo Ros found out
I'd paid a fiver to get in to his club, he gave me my money back. 1964.

Checking the 'Magic Box' props with Jimm[y] Cricket. 1988.

The Writers' Guild of Great Britain Awards 1969. Goldie Hawn presents the award tha[t] was followed by a kiss. Which do I remember most clearly?

's been a long day ... *The Ken Dodd Show* Left to right:
atricia Hayes, Ken Dodd, Bill Worsley, Judith Chalmers, John Laurie, and self. 1966.

ace to face with Eli Woods. I defy anyone to go face to face with Eli and
ot smile. 1975.

(*Above*) 'Hellfire!' He wants to rehearse with us! Even worse, Des sang on this show. 1975.
(*Above right*) I've got the best seat in the house to listen to the Syd Lawrence Orchestra. 1975.
(*Right*) This Morecambe and Wise script from a Thames production was found in a cardboard box in my shed. No disrespect to those who took part. October 1980.

With Ern and André Previn. This was taken just hours before Grieg started to get laughs. Sorry Edward! Christmas 1971.

Top) Left to
right: Ernie Wise,
John Ammonds,
self, Eric
Morecombe,
circa 1971.

(*Above*) 'The Small Back Room' as journalists liked to call it. This is where I wrote most of the shows. The typewriter is now at the back of the garage. 1980.
(*Left*) My daughter kept this *Show With Ten Legs* script, *circa* 1983.

'Have a doughnut.'
'I'm not hungry.'
'Just eat the hole.'

NO.2

29·12 (half/frad.)
+23 /
(NOW-27·31+23)

"THE SHOW WITH TEN LEGS"

EDDIE BRABEN
BILL PERTWEE
ELI WOODS
DAVID CASEY
ALISON STEADMAN

Written by: EDDIE BRABEN

Produced by: JAMES CASEY

EMIGRATING - P. 4-5-6.

REST of SCRIPT NOT CHECKED

2.30 Playhouse Theatre
8.00 - 9.00 p.m.

REHEARSE: 27.2.77
RECORD: 27.2.77
PROD. NO: LLD0940940
TAPE NO: BMR9/0940940
TRANSMISSION:

'Do you come here often, Bruce?'
'Only when I've got concussion.'
1992.

The most exciting footballer I have ever
seen. I was proud to stand beside my soccer
idol, the irreplaceable Billy Liddell. 1988.

It didn't have an open top until Santa stood up . . . 1987.

ith Peter Cushing. A dear friend
d the most gentle of gentlemen.
91.

An affectionate moment with my
favourite comedy actress, Patricia Hayes.
1990.

Sharing a joke with wife Deidree and Glenda Jackson after *This is Your Life*. 1991.

Monkswell Street revisited 50 years on. 1982.

Amazing the way all five-bar gates always reach the elbows . . . 2003.

He was well dressed (you never read of anyone being unwell dressed, do you?), middle aged, a musician and he was Alexander Cohan, a very famous Broadway producer – not very famous to me, as I'm not well up on most aspects of show business and as far as I was concerned he could have been Jake the Peg. He didn't have three legs, but you know what I mean.

'How would you like to write for Jerry Lewis?'

'I've got to be honest. I'm not a Jerry Lewis fan.' What I didn't mention was that a few weeks earlier I had seen Jerry Lewis and Dean Martin in a film called *Pardners* and I'd switched over to *Crackerjack*.

'Have you ever seen Jerry live on stage?'

I hadn't.

'He's over here in Europe. Why not come and see him?'

'But what is it you want me to do?'

'I'm doing a stage version of the 1942 film *Hellzapoppin* on Broadway. I think you would be right for Jerry in the show.'

I was open-mouthed flattered. *Hellzapoppin* was a quite sensational comedy film for that time, and Jerry Lewis was a Hollywood star.

'Yes, I'd like to see him on stage.'

The first surprise came when I found that Jerry was appearing at the Olympique in Paris, which is just outside France. Paris! I thought when he said he was appearing in Europe he meant Batley! Paris? I have to take a tablet if I'm going on the ferry to Birkenhead.

My wife and children were as horrified as I was at the thought of me going all that way on my own. They were so concerned about me getting lost that I thought they were going to stitch my name inside my underpants.

I went to the Olympique, watched Jerry live on stage for the best part of an hour and didn't smile once. I hate saying this, because Jerry Lewis was a real charmer. When it came to writing for him, and I did try to, it sadly didn't work. I wish I'd gone to Batley – Tommy Cooper was on that week.

My one and only meeting with the gloriously funny Tommy Cooper only lasted about ten seconds. Eric, Ernie and me were in Eric's room when this huge funny man came in. Eric introduced us and Tommy shook my hand, with the other hand he took his fez off and half a pound of Smarties cascaded to the floor. Tommy looked down at them, gave that famous laugh of his, said, 'I must do something about this dandruff,' and then walked out. It was Ern who said, 'How about that for an exit line?'

*

The bed sketch, with its long pauses, had now become an important part of the show. When I was writing one of these sketches, I had my golden rule: long pauses.

Eventually, after the pauses proved their value, Eric and Ern became so adept, liked the device so much, that their pauses in the dialogue were much longer than mine.

The following bed-sketch dialogue is only hours old and I don't want to leave it in my head with nowhere to go.

Sometimes I felt I could hear the audience anticipating the next line.

> *Ern is sitting up in bed writing a play. Eric enters wearing a dressing gown over his pyjamas.*

Eric. Ern?

Ern. Yes.

Eric. Good. It's just that I don't like sleeping with strangers. I've put the cat out.

Ern. Why?

Eric. It was on fire.

> *Eric climbs in. Makes noise with newspaper*

Ern. Must you rustle it.

Eric. Pardon?

    Pause

Eric. How many today?

Ern. How many?

Eric. How many sagas have you written today?

Ern. Erm . . . Twenty-five . . . Twenty-six

Eric. Amazing. You could be another Brontë sister.

Ern. I can't sing.

Eric. True.

    Pause

Ern. How do you spell 'Phoebe'?

Eric. P . . . H . . .

Ern. I can never get a sensible answer out of you.

    Pause

Eric. Listen to this:

    Reads aloud from newspaper

    Surrey woman had keyhole surgery to remove Lloyd
    Grossman.

Ern. That's enough for one night.

Eric. She might have said that as well.

    Ern closes exercise book and places it on
    Bedside table with pen

Eric. Finished?

Ern. Not yet. Just got to the bit where her Ladyship is
looking for her lost youth.

Eric. Has she looked under the stairs. He might be hiding
under the stairs, Ern.

Ern. Goodnight. [*Starts to settle down. Then sits up
quickly*] You've put the cat out? We haven't got a
cat.

Eric. Oh. In that case, in the morning if you can't find
your wig, have a look on the front step.
Goodnight.

The pauses were vital. I tried to justify them in the first bed sketch by saying it was like drinking a glass of wine – you didn't gulp it all down in one go. Or, in my case, Tizer.

They were both meticulous with every word of dialogue. Eric was reading for the first time a line in a flat sketch about Ern's enigmatic wig. He did the line and Ern said, 'That's not right. It's a good line but you're not saying it right.' Eric agreed it was a very awkward line. In the scene Ern was telling Eric that it wasn't a wig, and Eric said, 'Then how is it that sometimes on a windy day it moves up and down like badly fitted lino in a draughty kitchen.' Ern asked Eric to do the line again, which he did, and I had to agree that it wasn't right. 'Please don't lose it,' Eric said. 'No, I won't lose it. It's a good line and I'll get it right. This line is like a one-act play.' He stood up and paced up and down for quite a long time. His hands going from side to side as he juggled with the words. I was still fearful this one gag was using up so much rehearsal time that it would have to go. He said to Ern, 'Give me your line.' Ern's line was something like 'You're always having a go at my hair. It's not a wig.' Then it was Eric with the much-worked-on line. 'Oh?' then 'Oh?' again. I hadn't written any 'Oh' but I knew what he was trying to do: he really was acting the gag out. He spoke very slowly and very deliberately: 'If it's not a wig – look at me when I'm talking to you. If, if it's not a wig, how is it that sometimes on a windy day it moves; it moves up and down?' Now he was using his hands to illustrate: 'It moves up and down like badly fitted lino in a draughty kitchen?'

They had both worked for almost twenty minutes on one line that had been proving so difficult that I gave them an alternative gag – Ern saying, 'It's my own hair,' with Eric replying, 'I know that – I've seen the receipt.' No, they wanted the original line. They always wanted to get as near to perfect as it was possible to get, and it was this attitude to their work that made them the Rolls-Royce of comedy.

There was a real enthusiasm that ran right from the stars, the production team, the crew, to the tea ladies. Everyone, however remotely connected with the show, wanted it to be a success. They all wanted to contribute to a show now being watched by 20 million viewers a week. If at the end of the show I could ask those 20 million viewers, 'What do you think of it so far?' you would probably hear the answer on Mars.

*

John Lennon was sitting next to me, or was I sitting next to him? I can't remember exactly. Anyway, we were sitting side by side and he was waiting to go through a Beatles number with Paul, George and Ringo. They were the guests on a Ken Dodd radio show that was being recorded at the BBC studios in Lower Regent Street, London, England, which is not far from Barnsley.

We were discussing one of the things we had in common – words – and how we pursued them. Doddy, Pat Hayes and John Laurie were rehearsing a sketch on stage and I laughed at one of the lines. John Lennon looked at me and said, 'Do you always laugh at your own jokes?' I replied, 'Why not? I laugh at your songs.' He looked at me for about three seconds. He didn't smile, didn't laugh but there was something in his eyes when he said, 'I like that.'

Meeting such a richly gifted man if only for a very short time is something that will always be rather special to me.

Word had leaked out about who was in the building and hundreds of screaming, shouting, sobbing and frenzied teenage girls tried to gain entry. The police arrived to try to restore order, but that wasn't easy, because those girls were very excited – they went berserk.

What puzzles me to this day is, how did they know I was there?

*

Jimmy Cricket was and still is a comic character, a stand-up comedian in the best Irish tradition. I had a lot in common with the gentle comic who didn't know his left from his right – why else would he have the initials L and R printed on the front of his wellies?

The letter he received from his mammy in Ireland was a popular feature in the radio series what I wrote for him, *Jimmy's Cricket Team*. I particularly liked the Irishness of this PS: 'Don't forget that it's your father's birthday last week.'

There was also a policeman who wouldn't tell people the time or the way to the railway station because, and he said this with a laugh, 'I'm in one of me moods.' A not-very-good magician who invited a member of the audience up on to the stage to help with a card trick: 'We haven't met before, have we Uncle George? Now I want you to take a card; don't look at it, and place it back in the pack. Thank you. I can tell you that the card you didn't look at and placed in the pack was [*drum roll*] the fourteen of clubs. Thank you.' It was a happy and very silly show and I had enormous fun writing this harmless, very gentle comedy. As did the rest of the cast: Bill Pertwee, Peter Goodwright, who had a most astonishing range of voices, and Noreen Kershaw. As well as being a very fine actress, Noreen also produces episodes of *Coronation Street* and *Heartbeat*.

*

I've often wondered why radio shows were so well received. In my experience radio audiences are far more relaxed than a TV audience. TV audiences always seemed to be in awe of the surroundings and of the occasion, a bit tensed up. Eric and Ernie were also aware of this and this is why they always did a ten-minute routine to warm the audience up before the actual recordings. Even though Barry Cryer and Felix Bowness were excellent at getting the audience in the right mood prior to a recording, Eric and Ern would still do their ten-minute spot. One week neither Barry or Felix was available to do the warm-up and John asked me to do it. I wasn't overkeen, because I don't like appearing in public – ask any magistrate. What I said when I faced that audience I can't recall, but I do remember when I came off, Eric said something that surprised me: 'I could never do that. I'm OK for a few minutes on my own; after that I start looking round for Ern.' He never made a secret of the fact that he didn't like going it alone.

The audience was never in awe or tensed up after the warm-up with Eric's ventriloquist's doll. They did a condensed version of the vent (ventriloquist) routine prior to the show for the audience. To see the full and glorious routine on stage was a joy. I would say it was one of the funniest pieces of comedy I have ever seen on stage. I can pay it no higher compliment than to place it alongside Jimmy James and his 'box routine'.

Audiences were never tense, never in awe of the hi-tech surroundings of the TV studio, not after the vent doll warm-up. Eric would ask for a chair and it would be thrown from offstage to clatter at his feet. It was a show of disrespect that played a large part in everything we did. Ern would look at the doll:

Ern. Has he got a good finish?
Eric. He's French-polished he is, and you can't get better than that.
Ern. Is he lacquered?
Eric. He's bound to be – he's worked hard.

The warm-up was just as much for Eric and Ern as it was for the audience: the two comedians also needed to warm up. As Ern said, 'We don't want to go on cold. We hear that laughter and it makes us want to go out and get more of it.'

Studio 8 sat four hundred friendly people, eight hundred if they were very friendly. As a thank you to the many thousands who gave us their laughter in that studio, I would like to have the following words done in pokerwork and hung over the entrance: 'They came, they watched and they laughed with unbridled glee.'

*

There was little glee from me when I lay semi-conscious in a Nottinghamshire field – did somebody cheer? We were on location filming a fairground sequence for a Jimmy Cricket special for Central TV, as it was known two hundred years ago. The gag was that Jimmy was in charge of the coconut shy: 'Knock one down and win a prize.' Within seconds of this invitation there was a distant rumble that grew to a quite frightening roar as a real, genuine Sherman tank ripped through a couple of tents before coming to a halt at the coconut shy and firing – it was deafening. The sky turned black as terrified crowds departed in their hundreds above a demolished and smoking fairground.

They didn't do things by halves at Central in those days. As the last tent toppled, the hatch of the tank opened and a little old lady popped her grey head out and asked, 'Have I won a prize?'

'Cut!' shouted the director. Cut? There was nothing left to cut. It was like a scene from a First World War film. As is usually the way after filming something like this, producers, directors, soundmen, the whole crew, were delighted: 'Well done, chaps! Good show!' All that kind of stuff. In the meantime Jimmy was two fields away, his clothes in shreds and he was caked in cow dung.

I was surveying this carnage and wondering why I'd ever stopped selling King Edwards, when some silly gentleman inside the tank, sat at the controls and thought, *I wonder what this button is for?* Just out of curiosity he pressed it, the gun turret swung, the, barrel hit me on the head and I fell in a heap – curse those cows. If you've ever been hit on the head by the gun barrel of a Sherman tank you won't need me to tell you that it rattles your fillings – and one or two other things as well. The producer, who had been standing next to me throughout this fiasco, saw exactly what had happened and was very concerned about my condition. When he saw me lying there he didn't waste a second in writing off for an ambulance. It wasn't too serious, as fortunately the barrel hit me on the fleshy part of the head.

A doctor was sent for, nothing to worry about, but he thought it wise if I went home and rested for a week. When my wife was told what had happened to me she had to be given tablets to stop her from laughing.

More New Lines What I Wrote

I t was quarter past one in the morning and silly thoughts were busy inside my head, making sleep impossible – one of those nights when I just couldn't get comfortable. I felt as though I had three legs, my arms were far too long and the pillowcase was full of small, empty cardboard boxes. Apart from the silly thoughts, the excess of limbs and the cardboard boxes, I was also fancying a corned-beef sandwich. Now if you start fancying something like a corned-beef sandwich or a bowl of tomato soup at a quarter past one in the morning, you'd best get up and treat yourself, otherwise you'll be awake all night thinking about it. A 'Pardon?' after that and I know someone who would have got a laugh with it.

I tiptoed my way to the kitchen, put the kettle on and started constructing a corned-beef sandwich. That done, I need pen and paper to put my silly thoughts on – my wife's shopping list for much later that day was on the kitchen table. It included 'best mince for lasagne'. How times have changed. There was a time when I would have thought 'lasagne' was somewhere you went to on holiday: 'Would you like a pasta?' 'I can't dance.'

As I was demolishing the corned-beef sandwich I put these other silly thoughts on my wife's notepad:

Eric. Think of a number.

Ern. What for?

Eric. It's a trick. Think of a number.

Ern. Right. I've thought of a number.

Eric. The number that you have thought of is. . . . 74.

Ern. No.

Eric. 962.

Ern. No.

Eric. Twenty seven million four hundred thousand and eleven!

Ern. No.

Eric. You keep changing it so I won't guess it!

Ern. No I don't.

Eric. What number were you thinking of, then?

Ern. Begin the beguine.

Eric. Rotten devil!

It's very true what they say about old habits; those words had to be written down.

Inspiration

Another early hours of the morning 'silly idea' came when I was returning home on the sleeper from Euston. Stan, Stan the sleeping berth man, came in with a pot of welcome tea and an unexpected sausage roll – I'm rather partial to unexpected sausage rolls. 'I thought you might fancy a sausage roll for a change,' said Stan, Stan. 'It's not from the buffet, God forbid. You can eat this one: my wife made it. She makes a very good sausage roll.'

I thought I'd better eat it straightaway because when he saw the show we'd done hours earlier he might ask for it back – at the very least I'd never get another Mrs Stan sausage roll.

He placed the tea and sausage roll on the tiny shelf that folds down over the bed and looks as though it was designed to take one finger of a Kit Kat. The sausage roll began to wobble as the train went over some points, and a silly idea was happening. 'What was the show like tonight?' Stan, Stan asked me this question whenever his shift put him on this train; only this time I lied.

'It was quite good, Stan.' If I was being truthful, Stan, I'd have to tell you it wasn't very good at all.

'Who was the guest star tonight?'

I told him we had two guests on the show, George A. Cooper, and Margery Mason.

'Never heard of them. I'd probably know them when I see them.'

And, I thought, *you'll never hear of me again if I write many more shows like the one we did tonight.*

The main sketch (and we always judged a show on the main sketch, even though what might have gone before it got good laughs) was about Eric going home to see his mum and dad, but it didn't work. It doesn't take long to find out if a sketch is going to work or not. If the first hoped-for funny line doesn't get a laugh, then it's trouble, trouble with a big D, three big Ds: 'disaster', 'dire' and 'dreadful', which I thought this sketch was. Believe me, few things are more painful to me than watching something I have written being greeted with an indifferent silence. I've had my gall bladder removed, a cartilage removed and an operation to try to cure a sinus problem (this was attempted by shoving metal spikes up my nose). It didn't cure the sinus problem but I'm told it got laughs. Watching a laughless comedy sketch is a different sort of pain, like your stomach is full of butterflies wearing clogs. It's even worse when your two best mates are having to say the words and you know they're suffering.

Splendid performances from George A. Cooper and Margery Mason wouldn't save this one from being, as far as I was concerned, a 'Don't remind me' sketch. It was my idea, I wrote it and it wasn't funny. It was made even less memorable for being the first and only time I ever wrote a swear word into a script. It wasn't a full-blown 'put the sheet over the canary' swear word; it was one of the milder ones you wouldn't be surprised to hear on *Songs of Praise* if the vicar dropped the chalice on his foot. If a Welsh vicar dropped a chalice on his foot he might well come out with a 37-letter swear word, not that I know any Welsh swear words, apart from Llanbuggerit.

The naughty word in the sketch came when Eric told his dad,

George A., he was leaving, and his dad rejoiced by saying, 'Hoo-bloody-ray.'

The piece didn't work because the audience, and I'm sure the viewers at home, could not and would not accept these 'all of a sudden' parents. They were an intrusion on what had always been an almost sacred relationship. The audience was far too busy sulking and being indignant to laugh at intended funny bits. Audiences can be like that sometimes – especially wet audiences.

If your audience has been in a queue and the rain has been coming down like park railings, you've got a wet audience and you've got a night of damp misery ahead. The worst thing is when you see steam rising from them: it shrinks the jokes. It's not as if you can make it up to them by giving them their money back, because they got in for nothing. One night I was doing a not very good warm-up and said, 'You got in for nothing and you get what you pay for.' I thought they were going to lynch me. Incidentally that was the last time I was allowed in front of an audience.

The sausage roll continued to wobble on the shelf.

Inspiration came after Stafford. I know a lot of people who've been inspired after Stafford. I sat up and wrote in a wobbly hand on a serviette, 'BR connoisseurs'.

It wasn't long before Eric and Ern became the connoisseurs and their first bit of connoisseuring came when they explained to one of our favourite character actors, Alan Cuthbertson, the delights of the British Rail sausage. Eric looked lovingly at the sausage:

Eric. This is a truly remarkable sausage.
Ern. I would say British Rail?
Eric. I agree. British Rail – 1957?
Alan. It is indeed British Rail 1957.
Ern. Only sausage of its kind in the world. Exquisite British Rail workmanship.

Eric.   Remarkable because when the train goes into a
            tunnel the sausage lights up.

Nocturnal inspiration also visited Ernest Maxin when he was
wrestling with what to do with 'The Stripper' routine. It came
to him in the early hours when he quickly sat up in bed and
cried, 'I've got it!' His wife pretended to be asleep. It was a
divining moment, a bit like Archimedes when he jumped up in
the bath and shouted 'Eureka!' I think that's Greek for 'Ahhh!
This water's hot.'

Ernest, in pyjamas and dressing gown as he danced, hopped
and skipped around the kitchen: Diddly-Dadilly-Diddllly as he
opened cupboards and the fridge door, making the light come
on. Pom-Pam-Pim-Pum and slicing a loaf with a cleaver.
Breaking eggs in to a bowl. Crish-Crash-Crush.

The next morning his wife found him stretched out on the
floor and covered with chopped grapefruit, sausages and toast.
I like Ernest, but I wouldn't fancy him, not even with grapefruit, sausages and toast.

I wonder if his dad ever said to him, 'When are you going to
get a proper job?' How many times have we been asked that
question, those of us who have chosen this profession to earn a
crust? I wonder if Mrs Beethoven ever said to her lad, 'Ludwig,
son. What's that tune you're whistling? It's what? It's your
Third Symphony, the *Eroica*? Have you got nothing better to
do? When are you going to get a proper job?'

Or, 'Pablo! Will you stop drawing those pictures of people
with three ears, one eye and big holes in their stomachs. I don't
give a toss if it is your blue period – I'm not feeling all that
overjoyed myself. Just shift yourself and go and get a proper
job.'

My parents asked that question. And Lilly Benson wasn't
convinced when I went for my cigarettes and told her of my
ambition. 'Twenty, Lil.'

'You said something else before that.'

'I said I was going to be a scriptwriter.'

'What's a scriptwriter when he's at home?'

'Writes jokes.'

'For a living?'

'Yeah. That's what I'm going to do.'

'You couldn't leave a note for the milkman. Soft sod.'

'Charlie Chester's paid me half a crown for one of my jokes.'

'Charlie Chester? Which joke?'

I recited the Hopalong Cassidy, ten-gallon-nappy gag.

'He paid you half a crown for that?'

'Yeah.'

'He must have more money than sense.'

'I've sent some of my jokes to Bob Monkhouse and he said I've got a talent.'

'You've got a voice but that doesn't make you Frank Sinatra. Take your ciggies and sod off.'

That encounter took place forty-odd years ago. Do you know what would make me really happy, make me feel proud, make me feel I had made a mark? If one day a young and ambitious lad were to go for his paper or his cigarettes from Lil, and she were to say to him, 'You'll never guess who was here last week.'

'Who?'

'Eddie Braben.'

'Wow! Did you know him?'

'Yes. He was a soft sod.'

That would be the ultimate, the supreme accolade. The award to end all awards.

*

When Ern read for the first time this line in a sketch, which had him mistakenly thinking he was going to the USA to become

Bob Hope's head writer, I don't think I've ever seen him so enthusiastic:

Eric. You're joking.

Ern. Of course he lives in America! I'll have to leave you in this country, and I'll go and live in Hollywood in a big house with lots of shirts. And I'll have a big car with a button what you press to make the roof go up.

Eric. You're joking.

Ern. I'm not joking! I've never been more serious in my life.

What was the mythical substance of a silly comedy sketch was in reality Ern's dream of being not just a song-and-dance man, but a Hollywood star song-and-dance man. He read that line and sparked with a schoolboy's enthusiasm. 'God! That is so right! Hollywood! I used to watch those films with Mickey Rooney in them or Donald O'Connor, and they always lived in a big house with a white picket fence. They always had big bedrooms and when they opened the sliding doors of their wardrobe it would be packed with suits, shirts and shoes – and they always had a beautiful girl sitting in a car with a button what you press to make the roof go up. Off they'd go for a soda with lots of ice cream.'

This was the dream of a young man living in austere postwar Britain. It was a dream he never let go of. If Ern had his way, and this is just my opinion, I think he would have been very happy if the shows had all been one long Hollywood-style musical with perhaps a couple of comedy routines in between. How he loved those lavish, Maxin musical numbers. He went for them with tremendous vigour and vitality that proved he really was a song-and-dance man.

Sadly for Ern, like the sketch, Hollywood didn't happen. Bob Hope didn't want him to be his head writer. The telegram was from a Bob Pope, he wanted him as a head waiter. America wasn't to be for any of us; they weren't overkeen on our comedy anyway. The reason for this was, according to the real-life Bob Hope, as quoted in Graham McCann's brilliant biog of Eric and Ern, *Morecambe and Wise*, 'Eric Morecambe talks too quickly.' My own theory is not that Eric Morecambe spoke too quickly – the Americans *think* too slowly. I didn't mean that in a vindictive way, but in an honest way. Not every American citizen lives in fast-moving, high-flying New York, and not every American sailor can dance like Gene Kelly. I'm not quite sure what that means, but it sounds good. Ern was a dancer in the Gene Kelly style; he tapped the steps out with some vigour – the man to send for if you're having trouble with cockroaches.

Of the two, Eric was the better mover: he was the one who looked as though he was on castors.

They could dance, they could sing and they were funny. Not a bad mix.

Ann Without An 'e'

Eric and Ern were always appreciative of the talents of others. 'We feel comfortable with her and we can rely on her to deliver the lines to perfection. She never gives us any of that temperament bit.' Eric and Ern talking about their leading lady of so many shows: Ann Hamilton – Ann of a thousand sketches. Always there, never obtrusive, a gossamer actress who appeared in over sixty Morecambe and Wise shows. In fact, if Ann wasn't in a show I'd think I was in the wrong studio. Ann suffered the merciless Morecambe onslaught when she was Desdemona to Glenda Jackson's Cleopatra.

Eric. Desdemona? You look more like Des O'Connor.

It didn't get any better when she appeared as a sexy waitress serving tea:

Ann. Two lumps?
Eric. I had noticed.

Even worse, in a sketch set in the future as Eric's careworn wife. Both living in near poverty following Eric's break-up with Ern:

Eric. You're not dusting that mantelpiece are you? I've planted potatoes in there! What a dump! Where's the television set?

Ann. Men came from the rental firm and took it back.
Eric. Any other good news?
Ann. The doctor says I'm going to have another one.
Eric. I decide whether or not we have another telly, not the doctor.
Ann. Doctor says I'm going to have another baby.
Eric. Just what we needed; we've only got six: three sets of twins in four years.
Ann. I can't help it.
Eric. I've only got to look at you and it's a new pram.
Ann. Pansy.
Eric. Pansy?
Ann. The baby – I think I'll call it Pansy.
Eric. It might not be a boy.

Ann was the prissy shop assistant in the Mothercare-type shop – a small deposit and nine months to pay. It was a bit of a come-down for Ann after being the Queen of France the previous week. (Mr Previous! That could have been another name for André!)

Ern asking Eric not to embarrass him as he'd never been in this sort of shop before. The embarrassment, the for-real embarrassment belonged to Eric when he tripped on a word, and it was 'word' he tripped over:

Ann. Yes?
Eric. If it wasn't for that word, this shop would have to close down.

He stumbled on 'word'; he hesitated for a split second. 'I knew the line,' he explains, 'It's just that for some reason "word" got stuck.' If you get a chance to see this sketch again it's worth it just to watch as Ern tries to hold back a chuckle at his partner's mistake.

Talk about embarrassment. When John Ammonds told me

at the end of a day's rehearsal that they were going to block out my sketch first thing next morning I thought he meant they were going to get rid of it. My logic was that if you blocked something you stopped it. Not being well up on theatrical terminology I didn't know it meant sorting out moves and positions, stuff like that. That's the problem with living in the countryside – you do lose touch and your head's full of jolly robins. Something wrong with that?

I Don't Think
You've Heard This One . . .

L ife in the outback is a blessing when you're stressed out, when you're frustrated and feeling angry and your head is full of 'Grrrr'; you know what I mean. Like the cartoon characters in the comics: when they're angry you see a balloon and it's full of 'Grrrr'. That 'Grrrr' was showing in my balloon because I could feel it coming on again – that awful block writers like I are get from time to time, or, in my case, far too often. I'm determined it's not going to get the better of me; I won't be pulling at what's left of my silver hair or gnashing my teeth. Do you know, I've got so many hollow teeth I talk with an echo? I have the perfect antidote to writer's block, the perfect antidote to anything that makes you go, 'Grrrr.'

If you live in the city you probably reach for the falling-down water or go for a stroll and breathe in some fresh diesel fumes. I also take a stroll; only, I'm able to walk down the lane outside our bungalow, and a delightful walk it truly is. Very peaceful, a very Vaughan Williams 'Lark ascending' walk – perfect if you've got 'Grrrr'.

The town of Pwllheli, just four miles from our home, is a pretty little seaside and market town, extremely popular with holidaymakers and day trippers from what used to be Butlin's holiday camp.

We were in town just a week ago when a car pulled up at the lights with all its windows open and the radio going full blast with a 'Boom! Boom! Boom! Boom!' No music I or any other startled passer-by could hear. Just 'Boom! Boom! Boom! Boom!'

I went over to the car, shoved my head through the open window and yelled to the driver, 'Can you turn that up!'

'What?'

'Can you turn that up!'

'Up?'

'Yes. They can't hear it in Grimsby.'

The lights changed to green and he drove off, waving two of his fingers.

One thing absolutely vital to a country walk is a stout stick.

I've had my stout blackthorn stick for more than twenty years and it's clocked a few miles. In another six months I'll be able to use it as a toothpick. I'd be lost on a walk without my stick, even though my ferrule's knackered. It's all right to say 'ferrule' – I've looked it up. I don't expect you to do this, but I never ever go on a walk without my mouth organ. My wife bought it for me last Christmas and it's got a button what you press to make the notes change, and it helps to banish the 'Grrrr'.

With hand on heart I can honestly say I don't often lose my temper, but when I do, just watch out – I could karate chop a jelly baby.

'Good morning cows.' I really do talk to the cows in the surrounding fields. I ask them 'What's it like being a cow? Don't you get fed up eating grass all day and every day?' I never mention udders, because that's personal. They are such placid and contented beasts and you really can absorb it from them. I love it when they amble across to me at the gate and start to snuffle my sleeve and my pockets. Isn't snuffle a great word? Cows have such a satisfying smell: it's a sort of sweetly warm and earthy smell, with a dash of *The Archers* sig music. Believe me, it really is good therapy to talk to cows. Lots of farmers I know talk to their cows, and if you could see their wives you wouldn't blame them.

(That's well and truly screwed up my good relationship with the local farming community.)

I have tried talking to sheeps, but they're not interested. As soon as I start talking to sheeps, they leg it very fast – they're antisocial animals. They run away from me whenever I say, 'Mint sauce.'

On one such walk I met our nearest neighbour (I say 'nearest neighbour' even though you'd have to get four buses to reach her front door). She's a dog lady. I like dogs, but I'm not all that keen on those very small hairy dogs that scurry around like clockwork floorcloths. This lady neighbour had three of them, and as we stood there talking about nothing in particular I suddenly felt my right foot getting warm. I couldn't kick the little bugger over the hedge or I would have lost a good neighbour as well as the local farming community. I just had to make sure that future walks didn't happen when she was walking the mini monsters.

We used to have a vicious-looking Alsatian called Nellie. Nellie was the gentlest and softest dog in the world. It took me a long time but I taught Nellie to sit when I said, 'Stand,' to stand when I said, 'Sit,' and to run away when I said, 'Heel.' She was the most adorable dog we ever had – and the most confused.

I turned right at the very small crossroads about half a mile from home, almost like Scalextric crossroads, and into a one-car width and very leafy lane: this was my usual spot for a mouth-organ solo. I'm the first to admit that when it comes to playing the mouth organ I'm no Larry and Adler. I just blow away and enjoy what comes out – nobody else does (which is why I always chose to play at this particular venue).

Appropriately for a walk in the country I had selected to open my recital with 'Old MacDonald had a farm'. It was either that or the only other tune I know, 'Polly Wolly Doodle'. Now 'Polly Wolly' is a tricky one to play on a country walk, particularly if you're aged. The problem is that the lane is slightly uphill, and 'Polly Wolly Doodle' is more suck than blow and I'm gasping for breath after a couple of bars. 'Old MacDonald' is the best on this walk because you don't have to suck until you get 'Ee-aye-ee-aye-oh'.

There I was huffing and puffing away to 'Old Mac', half walking, half skipping, and thrashing my stick around like a baton, when I heard something behind me – voices! I turned and was a little bit taken aback when I saw a youngish couple wearing the full hiking gear – they were half singing, half laughing and skipping along to 'Old MacDonald'. They both stopped and the woman said, 'We couldn't do this in Carshalton.'

Which isn't true; you could do it in Carshalton. You could do it anywhere, but you wouldn't, because you're adults living in a city. It was the man in the red and yellow tartan shirt who spoke next.

'Do you live here?'

'Yes.'

'Are you retired?'

'No. I'm the village idiot.'

They both laughed and I went home without a 'Grrrr' in the world.

I thought I had got rid of all my 'Grrrr' until I switched on the telly at teatime and saw a TV presenter wearing third-generation denims and hosting a pop show. He was one of those presenters, and there's an army of them, who can't say two words unless one of them is 'fantastic' – currently the most overused adjective in the English language. It takes the number one spot in the top twenty 'Grrrr' list.

Gillian Reynolds, friend, journalist and broadcaster, has a 'Grrrr' word: 'awesome'. This is an excellent 'Grrrr' word and worth a slot in the top twenty, if only because of its popularity with football commentators: 'They were *awesome* on the attack' or, 'He was *awesome* going down the flank.' This one is my favourite: 'When the referee blew up after ninety minutes it was *awesome*.' I'll bet it was! Bits of referee all over the pitch. 'Ref! I've found your left ear.' Another good one is, 'It was *awesome* as he went down the middle with the ball inside him.' How can they not smile?

'Awesome' is now established in the 'Grrrr' list, as is this next word, because of its enormous popularity with very young people. It's a new entry at number three, and it is 'Gross'. When mums across the nation ask their children what they had for lunch that day at school, they all get the same answer: 'It was gross.' My own grandchildren are very fond of the word. Whenever I tie them to chairs and put a Morecambe and Wise video on they say, 'Grandad! That is gross!' I think they would rather be force-fed broccoli. But they haven't seen the best bit yet. 'Hang on a minute. Just watch now. This is the really funny bit. Watch this when Eric brings the vent doll on – it's ten feet tall! Ha! Ha! Ha! Just look at that!' They look. 'Grandad, that is really, really gross!' I sigh a 'what's the use' sigh and give them back their *Spiderman* DVD. I shuffle out of the door, a tired and sad old man. 'Where are you going, grandad?' 'Oh, I'm just going to make a couple of alterations to my will.' Now, how's that for gross, kids?

The TV presenter on the teatime show was introducing a singer who had a new single out, and in doing so said 'Fantastic' at least twelve times in ten minutes. The show was fantastic, the audience was fantastic, the new single was fantastic and the singer was fantastic. The singer with the new release came on and pulled tongues. I'm not sure who he was: I couldn't see much of him because of all the dry ice being used. He looked like he was singing in a very busy fish and chip shop. When I heard him sing I think his name might well have been Bud E. Ell.

The Parkinson Interview
to Plug This Book: Take Three

Parky. I really don't see the point in putting myself through all this aggravation for a third time. I'll just say that the book will be out next week; then we can all go home.

Me. You didn't talk to Harry Potter like that when you interviewed him about his book.

Parky. I've never interviewed Harry Potter and he hasn't written a book.

Me. He flamin' well has.

Parky. He flamin' well hasn't.

Me. That just shows how much you know. Harry Potter wrote that book about a lad who wanted to be a wizard.

Parky. Which lad?

Me. J.K. Rowlings.

Parky. This gets worse! J.K. Rowlings is a woman!

Me. That's his fault.

Parky. Harry Potter books are proper books; yours is dire.

Me. That's nice.

Parky. Reading your book is like walking uphill wearing cast-iron wellies.

Me. Oh, really? You wouldn't speak to me like that if

I was the man what wrote *The Lion, the Witch and the Dressing Table.*

Parky. This is getting out of hand. I can only take so much. I'm an OAP, for God's sake!

Me. Crying like that isn't going to help. Here; blow.

Parky. I've got my own hankie! Nearly fifty years I've been in this rotten business and I've never had to suffer like this. It's a bloody nightmare; it really is.

Me. You're a grumpy old bugger.

Parky. Sod off!

Me. Do you happen to know a woman called Lilly Benson?

Ad-Lib?

'Do you ever help Ernie Wise when he's writing plays for the show?'

That question puzzled me until I realised that viewers don't look at credits at the end of a show, and who can blame them? Credits just go on and on and they can be so boring. When a programme finishes on the telly it's 'put the kettle on' time, and who gives a toss about who did what anyway?

That's understandable, but when you're just starting out as a writer and you've got you first proper job with a BBC contract and it states quite clearly that your name will be on the credits, even though you're bottom of a list of six other names, you can't wait to see you name, it's more important than the seven pounds and seven shillings. When I was given my first ever credit for a show that happened so long ago I can't remember what it was called, I was so excited at seeing my name that I cut it out of the credits in the *Radio Times* and kept it in an envelope for months. Sometimes reading the credits can be more fun than the programme that went before them. It's not unusual to see anything from fifty to a hundred highly skilled people doing an amazing range of jobs, jobs with the most peculiar titles.

A good basis for a sketch. Eric coming home from the Labour Exchange to a nagging Ann Hamilton's wife:

Eric. I've been offered a job with a big film company.
Ann. A film company? What kind of a job?
Eric. Best boy.
Ann. Best boy. What do you have to do?
Eric. I was too frightened to ask. I could have been a Dolly Pusher.
Ann. Why didn't you?
Eric. I hardly know the woman. I didn't fancy being a Focus Puller either.
Ann. Why not?
Eric. I might give myself a hernia.

They went through comedy routines with the smooth precision of Astaire and Rogers. Each had total confidence in the other, so important to Eric because a line was going to come to him during a routine, a line that wasn't written by me, that was never spoken in the weeks of rehearsal. The adrenaline would be flowing at speed because this was for real, the actual performance in front of the red-lit cameras and a very live audience.

Eric would throw in that extra unrehearsed line, knowing his partner wouldn't panic, wouldn't hesitate or lose his place. He'd carry on and it really would look as though they were making it up as they went along.

'Hang on a minute. They didn't make it up as they went along.' Pointless, me crying for justice – it really did look as though they were making it up on the hoof.

Ern was quite brilliant at staying cool and on course when the unexpected happened, and this knowledge gave Eric the confidence he needed to enable him to do the ad-libs. Here's a good example.

Eric makes a mistake with his line; then rectifies it with an excellent ad-lib:

Eric. I've just seen Lord Hill walking along the powers of
corridor.
Ern. Don't you mean the corridors of power?
Eric. He was walking backwards.

All credit to Ern. He knew Eric had fluffed the corridor line,
so he quickly changed his line to give Eric a chance to get
back.

'How do you manage to keep your pace in a routine when
this happens?' A question I once put to Ern and the answer was
an interesting one. 'We've been together for forty and more
years and I can sense when he's going to ad-lib – I can see it in
his eyes.'

I think I knew what he meant; the eyes can tell you so much.
Since that conversation I've watched a performer saying one
thing while his or her eyes have been saying another.

I once saw a mixture of shock and disbelief in the eyes of
my singing idol Frank Sinatra when he walked on to the
stage of the Liverpool Empire and was welcomed by seventy
people in the stalls – it *was* seventy because I counted them.
Frank looked around the theatre and said, quite audibly,
'Holy Jeeze.' At that time his career was on a downward
spiral because of his alleged association with the American
underworld. But he was still a great singer.

The following night I stood at the stage door to try to get
this great performer's autograph. He appeared very briefly in
the doorway, shook his head at my request and got very
quickly into a waiting car. The famous blue eyes didn't look
very happy. The man on the stage door told me Sinatra
didn't have a dressing room – he just went straight on, and
straight off.

Or look at the eyes of Des O'Connor when, unseen by Eric
and Ern, he's standing behind them as he's insulted something
fierce. Ern has bought Eric a Des LP record for Christmas.

Eric. If you want me to be a gonner, give me an LP by Des O'Connor.

Ern. Just look at that nose! It's like Concorde coming out of the hanger.

Eric. Where did you buy this LP?

Ern. Boots.

Eric. Did you need a prescription?

Ern. I got it from the poison counter.

*

Three pairs of eyes and they're all sparkling with fun. The look of unquestioning trust you see in the eyes of your children, and they really do look at you wide-eyed when you tell them something that's pure make-believe, something I indulge in quite often.

'Where is the fairy's house, Grandad?'

'Erm. . . . At the bottom of the lane.'

'And will the fairy really leave me a special treat?'

'Fairies always, always leave special treats.'

'Can we go and see, Grandad?'

'OK.'

Now, I've got to stall for a few minutes here to allow her who sleeps on my right-hand side five minutes to get down the lane and plant the packet of milk chocolate buttons in the long grass at the side of the small cast-iron cover of a water main. Unbeknown by the Water Board this is also the house of a fairy squatter.

So that it would be more acceptable, and look more like the residence of our local fairy, I sneaked out one afternoon and painted the metal cover blue and yellow. Better give her who sleeps on my right-hand side ten minutes – she's no Paula Radcliffe.

It might be Thomas, Ella, Billy or Alice, but the look of delight in their eyes when they find their treats in the long

grass is unmistakeable and a great joy. How very charming –
or is it?

Maybe when there's no grown-ups about they have a meeting (meetings are the in-thing now). Perhaps they have secret
meetings we don't know about to discuss strategy.

'Right, gang, now listen up. This is the scenario – we go
along with this fairy's house routine. OK? Yeah, I know
banging on the roof is a bit naff. So what? Look, if we
play our cards right it could mean a new bike each. Play it
cool.'

I wonder if I'll still be doing this in twenty years' time? By
then I'll probably be leaving a six-pack of lager.

*

The mischievous gleam in Eric's eyes when Ern tries to explain
to him about the hardships of being a writer. You know he
won't undermine his writing capabilities, but you also know
he's going to have fun:

Ern.   It's not easy being a writer.
Eric. I know that. What time did you almost collapse into
       bed last night?
Ern.   Half past nine.
Eric. The human body won't stand that kind of
       punishment.
Ern.   It's a strain, but I enjoy it, in a masochistic way.
Eric. Only a writer could come up with a word like that.
Ern.   Masochistic?
Eric. No way.
Ern.   It's the price us authors have to pay for fame.
Eric. There was another Ernest who was a famous writer
       – Ernest Hemingway.
Ern.   New to me. I don't know the name.
Eric. *For Whom the Bell Tolls.*

166

Ern. I didn't hear anything.
Eric. Probably needs a new battery.

They may be performing to millions and they are acting, but you know that it's from the heart because you can see it in the eyes.

Star Bust

'Well,' I wondered, 'am I going to do this or not?' Yes, I most definitely was, and it was the biggest mistake of all the mistakes in all the world I have ever made. I was stepping out in front of an audience, in front of an array of TV cameras (I suppose two is an array), and I was 'starring' actually and for real 'starring' in my own TV series, and it was so bad it's an embarrassment to write about it. How I ever allowed myself to be conned into this awful project I know not, nor do I understand this abysmal happening – this was Cringe Time TV at its peak.

The one and only good thing about it was that it was only shown on BBC North-West, which meant, fortunately for me, that the posse would be much smaller.

It was only watched by close family and friends. After the first transmission the friends dropped out of the viewing figures, to be followed quickly by my once-close family, with the exception of her who sleeps on my right (and she only went because the WI shuts down during the summer months).

Incidentally, I did say to her once, 'Why don't you and the other members at your WI pose for one of those nude calendars? That lady who's president this year could be June, July and August.' That's not a bad line and I might use it if ever I write a book. Back to my brief encounter with TV fame.

The show was called (and I really am squirming as I write this; I'm having to grip the pen tightly to urge it forward) *Ready, Eddie Go*. After the first five minutes of the first show I was more than ready to go anywhere. I won't tell you who else was in it or who produced it as they might still be around and be trying to earn a few bob.

It was a time when being seen on TV meant you were instantly recognisable – God help me! People were staring at me in the street, and not with any great joy. Not staring, but pointing and saying, 'Oh! It's him off the telly. I do like him.' Not a chance. They'd point at me and seemed to be saying, 'That's him! That's the man who stole that 98-year-old pensioner's handbag.'

My nearly uncle, Billy Matchett, once said to me, 'You can always tell when a comedian's in trouble – he looks down at his feet.' During the six weeks that series endured I got to know my feet extremely well, and I can tell you my left foot is one thousandth of an inch wider than the right foot.

What is star quality? It's something I haven't got, but I know a woman who has . . . Rehearsal time in Studio 8 at the Centre and I think I found part of the answer. I was talking to Glenda Jackson before she went on to run through a flat sketch with Eric and Ern, and as we both came from Merseyside we were talking about Liverpool and her hometown, Hoylake. During the conversation, and forgive me for this, Glenda, I was looking at her and thinking. 'What's so special about you? You don't look like a star. In fact you look quite ordinary, like any woman that might have lived in our street or sat opposite me on the bus.'

Then she was called on to the set – and it happened.

The second she stepped in front of the camera the woman who had looked quite ordinary, who might have been any woman who had lived in our street or sat opposite me on the bus, that woman became a star. In front of the camera, and the star magic switched on automatically from within: it sparkled and beamed from her. It lit up her face and her eyes and there was something in her voice that hadn't been there before – she moved differently. If I had asked her later how it happened, she would probably have said, 'How did what happen?'

Ern. What makes a star?
Eric. Have you got a mirror?

What Makes a Star. That was the title of a BBC talent spotting programme broadcast on the then Light Programme, later Radio Two, in 1896 – it seems now like 1896. It was years before Doddy, or Eric and Ern. I went on that programme and incredibly I won! The reason why I went on was to get as wide an audience as possible to listen to my jokes, professional comedians in particular. I was very lucky when I went on *What Makes a Star*, as one of the panel of judges was Charlie Chester. To this day I can remember the joke I started with in my five-minute spot: 'I've had it officially from the BBC that I've had it officially from the BBC.' It was the first joke and I shall remember it forever and forever because the audience clapped. I'm almost ashamed to admit that I used that joke many, very many, times later, even Eric did it when he was doing a sort of *This is Your Life* on Ernie.

After my stunning performance Charlie Chester said he liked my jokes and would I send some to him. This I gladly did and hence the now world famous 'Hopalong Cassidy' joke. Do you want to hear it again? No? OK.

*

October 1974, and Hughie Green, the most famous talent spotter of them all with his long-running *Opportunity Knocks* on ITV, as the guest on the Morecambe and Wise show. Grrrr! To explain why Hughie merits a 'Grrrr!' we have to go back twenty years to the David Lewis Theatre in Liverpool, which was where Hughie was holding auditions for his popular TV talent show – and guess who was on next?

When I first walked into that theatre (actually it was a hall that was part of a men's hostel) I was surprised to see every seat taken, not by members of the public who had come to watch, as I thought – these were contestants! There must have been about three hundred young hopefuls, all waiting to top the bill at the London Palladium, of whom two hundred and ninety nine were singers.

After my stunning performance in *What Makes a Star* I was so very confident when my turn came, and I let Hughie have it with my proven big laugh and applause-winning first joke: 'I've had it officially from ITV [note the clever twist!] that I've had it officially from ITV.' The big laugh and the round of applause didn't happen – I was less than scintillating.

What did happen was that Hughie Green, later to become Huge Groan, waved his open right hand back and forth and said, 'Thank you. Thank you. Next!'

I came off the stage and passed the table at which sat a shirt-sleeved and harassed looking Hughie and a female assistant who looked like she'd just been told she'd have to watch *Emmerdale* for the rest of her life.

How could I possibly walk away without comment? I mean, in less than twenty seconds he'd wrecked a very promising career. Fair play, I had to say something. As I reached the table I paused just long enough to say, 'By, the way – I can only do the all-winners show.'

I left in a tantrum – that's another foreign car.

Almost a score of years on and Hughie had arrived for his first rehearsal with Eric and Ern. They both knew about my last encounter with Hughie. I'd told them what I intended doing and they didn't object. Hughie hadn't met me as yet. I was at the back of the room eagerly waiting for his first line. What that first line was I cannot remember (it was a few thousand first lines ago), but I do remember what I said when Hughie spoke his first line. I'd waited a long time to say, 'Thank you! Thank you! Next!' Huge looked puzzled when he saw me waving my open right hand back and forth. I had to have another little go: 'Thank you, son. Next!' Hughie was wearing a, 'What have I done?' expression. We were all laughing and Ern explained to him why. Hughie smiled as he shook my hand and said, 'No hard feelings?' Certainly not, I replied as I smashed a chair over his head. No, I would never do that, as I have more respect for BBC property. In the BBC Club later, Hughie offered to buy me a drink. I don't, so he treated me to a coffee and a jumbo sausage bap instead.

Home Truths

It was a rare event, the family gathered around the dining table for a meal, and it was the chef's speciality, beef casserole with dumplings. If that wasn't enough, there were also broccoli, carrots and new potatoes. Not enough room to get the veg on the plate, so it was in three separate dishes and you just dived in as you went along. There was also a large loaf to be cut up and used to help beef on to the fork or soak up the gravy. As always the food was mouth-blisteringly hot, a good thing because it meant we could talk while we waited for it to cool down – from the clouds of steam coming from the enormous dish, that would take about two days. I was surprised the wallpaper didn't fall off.

I was hoping nobody would ask about the book. I'd been working long hours on it and a break was more than welcome.

'How's the book coming along?' This was from Graham, and I could have dropped a hot dumpling in his lap.

'OK.'

'Only OK? If it's only OK you won't sell many.'

'I've still got a lot of work to do on it.'

Then I remembered an incident from his young life that would stop him asking about the book.

'I'm going to write about something that happened when you were seven, that time when you walked in your sleep.'

'Dad, you wouldn't.'

Graham was anxious; Jane and Clare wanted to know more.

'Did he really walk in his sleep?' asked Jane.

'Yes, he did.'

'Dad, you wouldn't dare.'

Dee was smiling because she remembered. 'There's no harm in your sister hearing the story.'

'But you wouldn't put it in the book?'

I told him I wouldn't if he didn't want me to. I told the story to Jane and Clare: 'One night, Graham went walkabout in his sleep. He came downstairs, dragged a chair along the hall to the telephone table, stood on the chair. We were watching him and making sure he didn't fall. He climbed on to the chair and had a pee all over the Yellow Pages.

'But you won't put that in the book?' asked a still not convinced Graham, as he reached for the broccoli.

'Of course it won't go in the book.' I hoped he was reassured. During that cooling-down period Jane had a very good re-collection.

'You'll have to write about the night when Clare and I slept in the summer house.'

'Oh yes!' Clare remembered the incident with some delight.

'No!' Deidree also remembered with very little delight the summer-house saga: she was a key player and didn't want it to be known to the countless dozens who might buy the book.

'I didn't think it was funny.'

'Mum, don't be mean,' pleaded Jane.

'It was funny,' said Clare.

'What was?' This was something Graham didn't know about. The steam from the casserole was still rising as I wiped my specs on a napkin and recalled the incident. All that steam! You could send signals to Geronimo.

The story as it was.

It was a very hot August evening when Jane and Clare asked

174

if they could spend the night in the summer house at the bottom of the garden. Jane would have been about ten, and Clare six years her junior. They wanted to know if they could come back into the house if they got scared during the night. 'Of course you can come back in,' said Mum. Clare had a good question: 'How will we be able to tell you if we're scared? We'll be right at the bottom of the garden.'

It was then I had an idea, and because of it this is now part of our family history. 'I'll tie a piece of string around your mum's big toe. The string will go through our bedroom window, down the garden and into the summer house. If you get scared, just pull on the string.'

'Just a minute!' Dee wasn't too keen. 'Why my toe? What's wrong with tying it round your big toe?'

'Ah,' I replied.

'Ah, what?' She was agitated.

'Because,' I said, as I scrabbled desperately for an acceptable reason. 'Because, erm, I'm furthest away from the window.'

'So what? We can change sides and you can come and sleep over here.'

I wasn't too keen on that idea. Quite suddenly, I was inspired and knew I'd win the day because she is a very superstitious lady.

'It's supposed to be bad luck for a married couple to change sides.'

That was quite brilliant.

'Oh,' she looked puzzled. 'I didn't know that.'

'Yes! it's in the *Thesaurus of Superstitions*. Do you still want to change sides?' There was a pause long enough for me to tie the string around the big toe of her right foot. I threw the ball of string out of the window to Jane who unrolled it and went with it into the summer house.

It was half past one in the morning when a cat frightened the girls and they both pulled very hard on the string.

'Ahhh!'

I quickly switched the bedside light on to see Dee's right leg shooting in and out of the bed.

'Cut the string! Cut the flaming string!'

There was laughter all around the table and the casserole was ready to be demolished.

As Dee was loading my plate, she said, 'You won't put that in the book, will you?'

I squeezed her hand and said, 'You have my word as a gentleman.'

She smiled and gave me an extra dumpling.

Studio 8

S tudio 8 was deserted, a vast aircraft hanger of a building when empty. Performers, technicians and production staff were all upstairs with the nose bag on and I was sitting on the settee of a rather splendid room that would come to life the following night, when four hundred people would be laughing and cheering, on their feet shouting, 'Author! Author!' There should be a question mark there somewhere. I was having a quiet ponder and making notes in an exercise book of things to do for the next show, like 'Grow a beard, emigrate, give my wrong name and run away.' As I looked around it was a bit eerie and difficult to believe this was the Ealing Studios of television, a place that had seen legendary performers and oceans of laughter – let's hope the tide would be in tomorrow night.

Somebody had come. I heard footsteps, looked up and saw the lady who was to be our very special guest the next night, Dame Flora Robson. Why she was always cast as hard-bitten queens and sombre spinsters I couldn't understand, as she had a lovely smile and the softest, bluest of eyes. Mind you, at this point of course, I hadn't yet seen Dame Flora triumph on the show and I was nervous as hell.

'Hello.' She said this very gently and I sensed a problem – she wants a rewrite. She didn't like that bit where Eric as the butler offers Ern a drink:

Eric. Would you care for a quick snort, my Lord?
Ern. Oh God.
Flora. Yes, a little please. That's plenty.
Eric. It's all you're going to get – it's the eighty-three.
Flora. Eighty-three?
Eric. Eighty-three bottles for fifteen and nine.

If she's happy with that, it must be when she declines Eric's offer of a refill, places her hand over the top of the pint glass he has given her and he pours the drink all over her hand (I'm sure it was brown ale). Or could it be when he says, 'Dame Flora; I always use your margarine.' (I think I've already mentioned how worried I was about the margarine joke.) Whatever the reason, how could I possibly refuse a rewrite to a lady who had starred in films with Ingrid Bergman, Charlton Heston, Laurence Olivier. An impressive and lengthy list.

I've written for Laurence Olivier, and made him do a Chinese accent – how's that for cheek?

She didn't want a rewrite; in fact she said she liked the words and was having a most enjoyable time. (And of course, she went on to deliver a superb performance that I still remember fondly.)

What Dame Flora did want was the answer to a question.

'I heard somebody calling your name this afternoon and I was wondering, are you any relation to Lady Braebourne?'

Sadly I had to disappoint both of us by saying I wasn't. The names sounded the same but the spelling was different. It might have been Lady Brabourne or Lady Brabin; either way it wasn't my name.

Quite honestly I would have been overjoyed to have been related to any member of the aristocracy regardless of how they spelt their names – I'm not proud. I've read a lot of

P.G. Wodehouse, and living the life of a Bertie Wooster would have been dashed topping – wouldn't you know?

I couldn't wait to hear what my mother's response would be when I told her what Dame Flora Robson had asked me. It was better than I expected.

'You know that we've got Dame Flora on the show tomorrow? I was talking to her this afternoon and she wanted to know if I was any relation to Lady Braebourne.'

'Who?'

'Lady Braebourne.'

'Good God almighty! Listen, soft lad, when you see Dame Flora tell her that Lady Braebourne has just got in from the launderette and she's got a pan of scouse on for your father's tea.'

'Mum, you're not coming with me to the Palace when I get my OBE.'

'Chance will be a fine thing. You'll get the OBE when Nelson get his eye back.'

When I asked how my father was she said that Lord Braebourne was sitting in the chair with a packet of Maynards Wine Gums watching *A Question of Sport*. She called him Lord Braebourne for quite a long time after that telephone call – and she always called me 'soft lad'.

Ern. Dame Flora is a perfectionist, the magnificent costume that she wore in my play . . . very regal that was.

Eric. Genuine article too. You don't see them on the Shopping Channel.

Ern. It was a proper regal frock of the period.

Eric. Six hours she was in the launderette with that lot.

I wonder if she saw my mother? Dame Flora must really have enjoyed being in Ern's play, and trying to keep up with Eric when he started to ad-lib, because a week or so later she sent this charming letter:

Dear Eric and Ernie,

I have become famous again. Everyone stops me in the street and says, 'What is it like to act with Eric and Ernie?' I say, 'Lovely, they are so thoughtful for one's comfort, but I wish they would learn their lines! I never know what they are going to say next!'

Actually, with the live audience, I heard dialogue I'd never heard before, away on my right, and I thought, 'We'll be running out of time', so, I let out a yell – 'WHAT are we going to do about Phillip of Spain?' Without a moment's pause we were back on our script, and Ernie's Shakespearian masterpiece was continued.

I have retired now, but the cheques from faraway places, such as China, Singapore, New Zealand, etc., are still arriving. So thank you.

By the way, The Queen Mother is your fan.

Go on and prosper, and bring us pleasure. We love you.

Glenda Jackson also wrote a letter, perhaps not as gentle as Dame Flora's. But what else would you expect from a lady who once said in a speech during a debate in Parliament, 'The reason why the opposition is so inept is because they don't have policies like what I have got.' She went on to say that Eric and Ernie were both very good professionals and that they treated all their guests alike – very badly. She ended by saying she would be more than delighted to appear in another Ernie Wise play if matron would allow her out on her own from Wrinkle Lodge, Home for Retired Folk, Eastbourne near England. There was a PS: Would it be a waste of time asking for payment? Yes, I know it will be a waste of time so why am I bothering? Ruggish!

Peter Cushing was another ex-guest who was less than overjoyed with the financial arrangements for his appearances, which prompted the following:

Dear Mr Morecambe and Wise,

Despite many appearances singing and dancing in your revue, I am still in desperate need of my original fee. At current rates of interest you now owe me £3.65p plus VAT – vexed actors tax. Please do not send me another cheque. I was unable to cash your last cheque as we do not as yet have a branch of The Noddy Bank of Toyland here in Whitsable near England.

This is my 75th letter.

Yours hopefully,

P.C.

Praying for Cash

After conducting the 'Grieg piano concerto' by Grieg, with Eric as soloist, André Previn wrote, after a period of convalescence, that it took him several months to break the Morecambe and Wise-inspired habit of standing on the rostrum in front of the London Symphony Orchestra, jumping in the air and shouting, 'A-one, a-two!' Do you know what I think? I think, in fact I'm quite certain, that given the opportunity they would all do it again – and for nothing.

If I had the opportunity would I do it all again? I'll have to sleep on that one.

Leaning against a wall in the attractive village of Tremadog just fifteen miles from my home, a sign reads, 'Delicious Welsh Maid ice cream on sale here'. Further up the wall of this very Welsh stone building, another sign reads, 'Lawrence of Arabia was born in this house 1888.'

In the summertime tourists flock here in their thousands – which is no surprise, as it is delicious ice cream . . .

I've slept on it. If I had the opportunity to write the Morecambe and Wise shows, would I? First reaction was, no I wouldn't, for fear I might not be able to deliver – and I couldn't live with that possibility. If I didn't write them somebody else might; they might also do a better job and I couldn't live with that either.

This is all based on the assumption that I can climb aboard Mr Wells's magnificent time machine and go back to 1969 with the knowledge and the experience I have now. I'd have to do them all again – if I didn't, there'd be so much I'd miss. Eric picking up my script for the fist time and saying, 'Did you write this or will it get laughs?' Ern also reading for the first time. He wasn't smiling as he looked at me over the top of the specs he always wore when reading, and said, 'I do like this.' Then he read aloud, and I remember this moment: 'Tomorrow I leave for France, which is just outside Paris.' Eric said, 'That's funny.' Ern was looking very serious: he always took funny lines apart to examine them, find out any problems. But he was happy with this one: 'It's not a belly laugh.' Eric was in very quickly: 'I'll have it if you're not keen.' Ern explained, 'It's not a big laugh line but it's so right for my character. I'm saying a funny line; I don't know that what I'm saying is funny or silly; that's why it's so right for me. Yes, I like that very much.' Then he went and spoilt it all by saying, 'I'd like a lot more of them.' I'd miss creating Ern's character and proving that he was more than just a straight man.

More than Eric or Ern's reaction, I would miss my own glee. That's a very underused word and it describes exactly how I felt when I first heard the funny line that had been manufactured, I know not how, inside my head. I laughed because I was hearing it for the very first time – nobody else had heard it until I typed it out on paper, took it to London and gave it to two men who would stand in front of a TV camera and tell it to millions of people, who might laugh.

No, I couldn't wait that long; I had to tell someone. Once I was so eager, so enthusiastic about a line, that I tried it out on our window cleaner. It was this one:

Glenda. But you've go to let me appear in Ern's play! My
name's in the *Radio Times*!

Eric. They advertise garden sheds in the *Radio Times*
but they're not in the show.

I knew that line was in with a chance because his ladder
wobbled. The poor man was so surprised, he just gave an
embarrassed smile and asked for a bucket of water. The reason
why I remember that incident so clearly is because our window
cleaner had a very bad stammer and it took him ages to say
'bucket'. Whenever I came up with a line that gave me a tingle I
would rush downstairs in search of the woman who sleeps on
my right and say, 'You've got to listen to this!' I wonder how
many times I've said that since 1969?

If I think of a funny line now I don't rush downstairs. We live
in a bungalow, so I rush along the hall instead. But the
command hasn't changed: 'You've got to listen to this!' She
can't listen to this because she's gone to the shops. I can't tell it
to my children when they come home from school because they
are now on their way to schools to pick up their own children.
I'm certainly not going to tell my children's children because
they are at an age when they speak honestly, and the last joke I
told them was summed up quite brutally: 'Gross, Grandad.'
How they love that word.

Over the forty-plus years, and when I've been the only one in
the house, I've tried out new jokes on four different breeds of
dogs and a cat. The cat would always turn its back on me and
walk out with its tail sticking straight up – was that an opinion?

Grrrrrr!

No two ways about it: it was a revolting-looking dog. And I like dogs. In yapping order we have had furniture legs chewed by Roger, Nellie, Amy, Benjie, Poppy, Joe, Dotty, Peg and Bonnie, and that's a lot of Winalot.

This dog I'm telling you about now, I just could not take to it, try as I did. It was a shapeless, hairy, slow-moving black hulk on the end of a length of rope and held by an aged person – more aged than me, so he was pushing it a bit.

He looked exactly the way you would expect someone who owned such a Heinz 57 dog to look: slow moving, overweight and a cigarette burnt so far down he must have had asbestos lips. They lived together in the smallest house I have ever seen, just two rooms and a solitary chimney pot that never smoked (not even when it was minus 50), poking up through the branches of an enormous oak. The house was at the bottom of a track that nobody ever went down, with the exception of go-anywhere Mormons. When they did venture down it was not long before they were back on the main road and wiping the dog poo off their shining black shoes in the long grass.

If I was out walking and talking to cows and sheeps, or trying to keep up with a Red Admiral butterfly, and I saw him and his bloody dog coming towards me I'd do a very quick about-turn and head for home. Out of luck this time, as I

turned the bend in the lane they were just yards from me. If you
think I'm being unkind to this old man and his dog, I must tell
you that the animal had flabby slobber chops, which it liked to
wipe on clean and neat-looking trousers. And as my trousers
were the cleanest and neatest-looking trousers in the area I had
to do some nifty side-stepping.

I slowed my walking down to half a mile an hour so as not to
exhaust the dog, or him.

'I hear that you write.' He huffed and puffed this question.

'Yes.'

That was it for about fifty yards.

'What do you write? Books?'

'No.'

The bloody dog was sniffing around my trouser bottoms.

'What do you write?'

'Get to hell out of it!

'Eh?'

'Oh, erm . . . Television comedy.'

'I haven't got television; I listen to the wireless.'

*You haven't got a life either, but that's not my fault, and keep
a tight hold of that rope.* There was slobber on my good shoes
and I was doing what the Mormons do in the long grass.

'Who do you write comedy for?'

I really could have done without this 'Happy Hour' – even
with a normal human being it would have been painful. Just
look at my good shoes!

'Who does your comedy?'

'Morecambe and Wise.'

'Saw them once at my sister's; didn't like them.'

'What where they doing at your sister's?'

'What?'

I lied when I told him it had been nice talking to him; then
quickened my step and headed for home. I have this picture of
him in his small house with the dog at his feet as he listens to

Sunday Half Hour, Your Hundred Best Tunes and the shipping forecast.

*

Home alone and any one of our dogs would have shown respect as I spoke aloud a line to see if it sounded right. It was a bit like trying out a new recipe. Did it need a few more words? Were there too many words? Did it have a rhythm? All very important, in the final outcome. When you're telling a joke you're telling a story. All jokes have a beginning, a middle and an end, like a rather small play, and this applies to the shortest of jokes. As far as I can remember, this is the shortest joke I have written, just seven words: 'I've got three children, one of each.' I promise that's a joke; it did get laughs and still does. Short as it is, it has a beginning, middle and an end.

To try to make sure I've slotted all the words together correctly, I speak the line aloud and our dogs have been very respectful – or were they being very tolerant? Perhaps they were gazing up at me in the hope that amongst that jumble of words they might hear something of interest, such as 'Walkies' or 'Biscuit' or 'Leg of Postman'.

They didn't find much to interest them when I recited the following for the very first time:

> They went to Spain, but never again
> The men there drove her crackers,
> They stood beneath her window at night
> Shaking their maracas.

Eric relished the words of those schoolboy, mischievous poems. I was with him in his dressing room when he was going through that rhyme for the first time. He read it, chuckled and then read it again for effect. He paused after, 'The men there drove her crackers', looked in the mirror and said, 'I want an expression for when I get to the end of that line.' What he wanted was a look of mock surprise at what he was reading; he wanted a pause to give the audience time to anticipate the line they thought was coming, but it never did and that's what made it funny. If it had happened the way the audience thought it was going to happen it wouldn't have been schoolboy mischievous: it would have been very adult and not at all funny. That word 'innocence' springs to mind.

Eric with head and shoulders through the curtains as he asks Ern to introduce him as 'Uncle Eric', because he's going to do something for the kiddies:

> **Eric.** I'm Uncle Eric, you see.
> **Ern.** You want me to introduce you as Uncle Eric?
> **Eric.** Who's got a little friend.
> **Ern.** And it'll pop out?
> **Eric.** [*looking puzzled at this.*] Well, I hadn't rehearsed that bit.

André Previn once said, after a period of convalescence, 'What I liked so very much was that he never told a dirty joke. He could make an innocent line so filthy – yet when you examined it there was nothing in it.'

Away from the cameras there was never a dirty joke, never a four-letter word. 'Bloody', 'bugger' and 'sod it', that was as bad as it ever got. I was there and it's a fact.

*

Endearing. Yes, I'll have that word, as it describes perfectly the film I was watching on TV.

> **Ern.** What's on the television, Eric?
> **Eric.** A bowl of fruit and an ash tray. [*Laughing*] A bowl of fruit and an ash tray!

It was a black and white Hollywood musical called *Lady Be Good*. It was made in 1941 and I was watching the whirling, twirling Eleanor Powell with the same fascination I felt when I saw the film as a very young boy. How could she spin faster than a top and smile? She kept her top hat on as well. Great stuff, Eleanor. Fred Astaire said of Eleanor, 'She can put 'em down like a man.'

Children Graham, Jane and Clare came in; they'd been for a walk with their brats, who were now in the garden trying to decide which flowers to trample on. I pointed to the screen.

'She was the best tap dancer of ever and ever.'

'Who was?' asked Clare.

'A real star. Eleanor Powell.'

'Don't know her,' said Clare, and picked up a magazine.

I tried to get some bells ringing: 'She was married to Glenn Ford.'

'Glenn Ford? Never heard of him.' This from Jane who's reasonably intelligent.

'Nor me,' said Graham, shaking his head. He is clever, supposed to be: he's a teacher.

God help us!

'I give in. I'll see you all later.'

'Where are you going?'

'I'm going to take the dinosaur for a walk.'

I was deep in despair – what had I done wrong that my own children had reached maturity not knowing who Eleanor and Glenn were?

It was just as well that I didn't mention Gene Autry, Cavan O'Connor, Zasu Pitts, the Merry Macs, the *Topical Times*, Will Hay, Gilbert Harding, Rinso, Inspector Hornleigh, Hutch, Buck Jones, Gillie Potter, Mansion Polish, the Ovaltineys, Collinson and Breen, Big Bill Campbell, Mrs Ginochie, Nosmo King, Stanelli, the *Daily Sketch*, Pansy Potter, Raymond Glendenning, Drene Shampoo, Dick Barton and Kolyno's Dental Fixative.

That little lot would have given them something to puzzle over.

As I walked I was listening to a rather nifty little radio I had treated myself to for being good (that's what I told myself when I paid fifteen pounds for it), and it fitted rather snugly into the top pocket of my jacket. I would have stopped and passed the time of day with the cows, but they were a couple of hundred yards away on the other side of the field. That made me think: had they spotted me coming down the lane and passed the word: 'Here comes that soft old bugger from the bungalow. Let's go, girls; he might start chatting us up again'? No. No. Cows wouldn't do that.

I must have had the radio tuned to a wrinkly programme because Doris Day was singing, 'It's Magic'. It was magical to me when I first heard her sing it in the film (they're called 'movies' now) *Romance on the High Seas*. I don't remember who Doris had as her leading man, but with a title like that it should have been Popeye the Sailor. It was a rotten film, but I went to see it three times in one week during 1948 at a cinema in Caterham just to hear that lovely lady sing 'It's Magic'. As I was washing pots, pans and dishes in the cookhouse at RAF Kenley at the time, my six in the morning until four in the afternoon shift allowed me the luxury of frequent visits to the pictures. Apart from Doris singing that great song, the other reason why I remember that film so vividly was the couple who came and sat next to me. They were just about to settle into snoggin' mode, when they paused, sniffed the air like a couple of prarie dogs and then went and found shelter under another bush.

The cookhouse bouquet was resilient, but it's not too bad now – I can visit our local cinema with some confidence. Incidentally our local Pwllheli cinema must surely be the only cinema in the UK where you have to go up three flights of stairs to get to the stalls. I call them the John Buchan steps, as there are thirty-nine of them: I've counted them and they really do take you up to the stalls. It's a cosy little cinema and we've become quite friendly with the lady who plays the piano during the feature films.

There's a film that will unpleasantly haunt me for the rest of my days. It's called *Up the Front*. In my opinion this is one of the most wretched, unfunny films of all time, and I should know, as I was in part responsible for it.

It came about because in 1972 Eric and Ern decided to take almost the whole of that year off so they could concentrate solely on the Christmas show. Too long a period for me to be doing nothing, which is why I was quite pleased when the phone call invited me to a meeting at Ned Sherrin's London town house to talk about a comedy film. The star was Frankie Howerd, and how could any comedy writer resist the opportunity of writing for this really talented funny man? Also to do their careers no good at all in that film were Zsa Zsa Gabor, Stanley Holloway and Dora Bryan.

Ned and Frankie were present at that meeting along with two or three others whose names and faces are long since forgotten. What I will never forget from that day is The Man in the White Suit (I've given him capital letters because he was most impressive). He stood discreetly at the back of the room, partially out of sight yet able to see everything and everyone, rather like an *Upstairs, Downstairs* Hudson, alert and ever ready to pamper our whims. My whims were not in need of a pamper, least of all from a man wearing a white suit – and why was he looking at me like that? I very soon found out. I was smoking and flicking the ash into a small saucer-shaped ash tray on a table at the side of my chair. When I got to the end of the ciggie and started to stub it out I heard a gasp and he swooped swiftly and silently like a snowy owl and scooped the saucer away from this Liverpool moron who didn't know a Ming Dynasty saucer when he saw one. Anyway, it was some kind of Far Eastern dynasty and quite valuable. In fairness I must say that Ned was smiling, but his knuckles were white.

What came out of that meeting really surprised me: I was to return home with the film script some other poor devil had sweated blood to write, and make it fun, or funnier. That must have been a kick in the teeth for the original writer – I know I wouldn't have been overjoyed. Ned and Frankie felt the script needed stronger laugh lines. This was 'The Boys Feel . . .' all over again; only, this time it was somebody else's turn.

'I'm sure you'll do a very good job – I've always admired your work and you are the best in the country at writing one-liners.' This was Frankie speaking. Good man, Frankie, I've always liked you.

However, experience has taught me that in the beginning there are always Songs of Praise. The biggest surprise of all came when they told me how much they were going to pay me. Who said, 'When are you going to get a proper job?' I wanted to rush to Lilly Benson's wooden newspaper emporium to tell her.

'Two thousand pounds, Lil.'

'How much?'

'Two thousand.'

'They must have more bloody money than sense.'

I couldn't believe it either. The meeting came to an end and there was a taxi waiting to take me to Euston Station.

'Do you mind if I share your taxi? I've got to go to the office and it's on the way.' Frankie Howerd climbed in and sat next to me. I liked Frankie very much. I didn't get to know him very well but he was always very courteous. This much I remember from our conversation on the way to jolly Euston Station.

'Have you ever thought of leaving Liverpool and moving to London? You would be able to mix and exchange ideas with fellow writers.'

'Never given it a thought.'

We had arrived at Euston Station.

When I got home I telephoned Ern: he'd asked me to let him know how the meeting went.

'They're going to pay me two thousand pounds.'

'That's not enough.'

'I'm happy with that figure.'

'You're underselling yourself and you should get more. You're in a very strong position – make the most of it while you can.'

'Two thousand isn't bad.'

'I could get you more.'

'Really?'

'Do you want me to try?'

Ern was always a very good business negotiator; I wasn't. Two days later he called me back.

'I've got you four thousand.'

'How much?'

'Four thousand pounds.'

'You'll have to take a percentage.'

'No. You've done a lot for me. This is my way of saying thanks.'

When we met at the Centre some months later he wouldn't even discuss the deal. This is the first time I have ever told this story.

*

Working on another writer's script wasn't easy and I felt like a burglar going through somebody else's house. The plot of this First World War comedy revolved around Frankie having a map tattooed on his bum, with various characters wanting to get their hands on it. Clever, eh?

I'm going to be as brief as possible because it's something I'm not overproud of. I went through that script many times and added scores, perhaps a hundred one-liners. I saw the film when it came out and watched in shocked disbelief – only one of my jokes made it to the final film. Now am I the best in the business or what?

I wonder if anyone has ever been paid four thousand pounds for one joke?

Laff List

The following are just a few of my favourite comedy moments. Extremely difficult to compile this laff list as there have been so very many of them, and aren't I very fortunate to have had so many laughter-filled experiences? I've had one or two miserable moments as well, but you won't find them between these covers.

My best bits are not necessarily in order of laughter merit and not necessarily even funny or in chronological order, with the exception of my dad's joke, which for obvious reasons has to be placed at number one.

He told me this joke when I was of an age when I could understand and laugh at a joke. I was about eight, and hope still to be smiling at this one when there's a 'y' in the end of 'eight'. This was my initiation joke.

'Did you hear the one about the man with a hump on his back?'

'No, Dad. What happened to him?'

'He fell over and he rocked himself to sleep trying to get up.'

I had to wait until I was ten before he told me my first naughty joke.

'We're going on holiday next month.'

'Where to, Dad?'

'We're going to feathers.'

'Where's feathers?'

'Around the duck's bum.'

I laughed at that joke more in pride than anything else – I was grown up now because my dad had told me a naughty joke.

It should be compulsory for all parents to make their children laugh at least once a day.

I'm not sure whether William Shakespeare wrote that or me. I think it must have been me, as it's written with a biro.

*

'I'll get you for that,' a catchphrase used exclusively by Eric and me in a series of private silly events that lasted throughout our relationship. It first started one morning at the reception desk at the TV Centre.

Eric had just collected his dressing-room key, and the two girls behind the desk were laughing – he couldn't leave reception without going out on a laugh. I doubt very much if he could walk out of a lift or a telephone kiosk without going out on a laugh, and quite right. It was the way he was; any other way and he wouldn't be the comedian he was. I deliberately hold back from using the word 'genius'. Neither of us liked it and felt it was overused, except in Ern's case.

Eric saw me as he turned from the reception desk and called as I was about to disappear down the corridor.

'Have you got a minute? I've got something to show you. This is a knockout.'

'What is?'

'Follow me.'

We went out of reception, across the road and stopped side by side on the top step of the BBC car park. He pointed.

'What do you think?'

'About what?'

'I'll show you.'

We went down the steps. Eric stopped and stood proudly at the side of a Rolls-Royce.

'Be honest.'

'Yours?'

'What do you think?'

I walked slowly around it and then said, 'You must have had a hell of a job getting it out of the Corn Flakes packet.'

There was a short silence before he said very quietly, 'I'll get you for that.'

He got me for that and a great many other silly jokes we played on each other.

He got me for that Rolls-Royce jibe about two weeks later.

Rehearsal had finished for the day in the enormous Studio 8. I was going out of one door in the empty studio and Eric was standing by another door at the extreme opposite end. He called, 'Something I forgot to ask you. Have you got a minute?' There should have been a bus service to the other end of that studio.

When I finally reached him, which seemed to take forever as it had been a very long day, I said, 'What?' As soon as I asked that question I knew I'd made a mistake. There was an impish look in his eyes as he said, 'How are you keeping?' A fifty-yard hike and he's asking about my welfare! He knew how I was: we'd been working together for the past week.

He clamped his hand over his mouth to stifle a laugh, before a quick exit. I'll get him for that.

He very much enjoyed embarrassing people in a gentle way. We were having a meal out at some function, when the waitress appeared at Eric's chair with the coffee. 'Coffee, sir?' He smiled, nodded and the waitress asked, and I knew he was up to something because he had that 'butter wouldn't melt' look. The waitress asked, 'Black or white, sir?' He said, 'Yes, please.' The puzzled waitress asked, 'Black or white coffee, sir?' His so innocent smile as he asked, 'What other colours have you got?' You didn't have to be a star to get the treatment.

It was because this was a natural trait with him that it worked so well in the show. When Richard Baker announced himself rather formally as 'Baker', Eric casually replied, 'A large sliced and two small browns.' This got a good response from the audience as it was said to a man who was the epitome of BBC correctness. This is what the audience laughed at, rather than the man. It was always what the guests represented that was deflated, not the guests.

Shirley Bassey got a foretaste even before she stood in front of a camera. She was coming from her room to the studio to run through her famous 'Diamonds Are Forever' number at the final rehearsal and was wearing a dazzling glittering full-length gown. When Eric saw her he laughed and said, 'You look like a Brillo pad.' Shirley laughed as well; then kneed him in the groin. That didn't happen, of course. The reason why I've said that is because I had a nagging feeling that one day he was going to say something like that to someone minus a sense of humour – then watch out.

A lady viewer from Birmingham is on my laff list for the letter she sent me, in which I was severely reprimanded for being thoughtless and totally irresponsible. This slap on the wrist was administered because of a quickie in the show in which Ern put a note in the empty milk bottle on the front step, went back inside and closed the door. Eric, as his next-door neighbour appeared, took the note from the milk bottle, wrote on it, placed it back in the bottle and then went into his house. The following morning Ern came out to discover one hundred bottles of milk on his front step and along the path. The lady who wrote to me did not think this funny. Even less funny were the ten bottles of milk waiting for her on the doorstep that morning, and she only ever had one pint a day.

The letter could have been signed 'Mrs D. Mented'.

And now for Eric's most embarrassing and most dangerous trick.

This is the one that could really have got him clobbered; it has caused a lot of unsuspecting females a great deal of embarrassment (I've seen it happen on many occasions). For maximum effect it's best carried out when there are plenty of folk around. This is how I saw it.

We were walking along a corridor when a young girl from one of the production offices stopped for a brief chat. OK up to then. She said a cheery goodbye and walked off. When she was about five yards away Eric called after her, 'And don't forget your promise.'

The look of puzzled embarrassment on the girl's face when she stopped and turned around, the look of the faces of all the other people who had stopped to look around. Quite honestly, it was painful to watch. I said to him on more than one occasion, 'You'll come unstuck one day.' His usual reply was, 'A man needs a hobby.'

Prime Minister Margaret Thatcher was visiting Nottingham and was scheduled to make a visit to Central Television Studios. I was also paying a visit to the same studios and was doing the warm-up prior to the *Jimmy Cricket Show*. I was doing all the usual rubbish: 'The microphones overhead are very sensitive; try not to snore too loudly. We had a good audience last week, a religious audience. The show had only been on for five minutes and they were all praying for the end.'

And so it went on for about ten minutes. Then I told the audience Mrs Thatcher was visiting the studios and might well call in on us.

I had completely forgotten all of this until Jimmy quite recently reminded me and I was surprised. 'Did I really say that?' Yes, I really did say that and this is what I said to the audience: 'If Mrs Thatcher does come in here, as a mark of respect would you all please stand and sing, 'The old grey mare she ain't what she used to be'.

I'm told the Prime Minister did hear about this and that there was a quick reshuffle of the New Year's honours list outside Make-up. If she'd had a pair of scissors with her she would have made me a Dame.

An associate producer who was working on the show didn't take kindly to this and said I should have shown more respect for the office of the Prime Minister. I apologised and bit his arm. I was quite surprised that anyone involved with comedy didn't know that most humour is based on disrespect for authority and those who apply it.

This was a fact perfectly illustrated to me some years earlier in Liverpool, a prime location for showing little respect for authority.

It happened one day as I was walking past a tenement block and saw written on a wall the following legend, obviously written following a papal visit in the North-West. It read, 'God Bless Our Pope'. Nothing wrong with that sentiment. However, when I went past a few days later I saw that somebody had added a 'y' and an 'e' to the end of 'Pope'. Even the parish priest laughed, and it's well worth a place in the laff list. It's true to say that without disregard for authority and those who apply it we would have been short of laughs in the Morecambe and Wise shows.

'Hello, vicar. Still on the one-day week?'

Lots of letters about lack of respect for a member of the clergy – not one from a member of the clergy. When I say 'lots of letters' I mean no more than six. If we got more than six letters of complaint about anything we did, it was never repeated.

I'm putting this idea on the laff list because it makes me laugh. The ideas for quiz shows that are just that little bit different are still occurring and begging for consideration from any TV company willing to take a gamble, something they ask members of the public to do every week. Incidentally (and this is something that motivates my 'Grrrr' factor), why do TV companies always ask viewers to phone in with their verdict at the end of a programme? This happens quite often on talent shows. Why? I take it the companies putting them on are all more than financially solvent, so why can't they foot the bill for their own programme? They take the profits after all.

It seems every time I switch the TV on I'm told calls should cost me no more than sixty pence, or whatever the charge is. If not a telephone call, then I'm being invited to forward-slash somebody with a stroke dot com – whatever that means.

And that's better out than in. A little bit of a grump now and then does you the world of good.

Now, back to this quiz show with a difference. It's specially tailored for all those very many people who never win anything. It's designed for those of us who aren't very bright, who can't boast a retinue of A levels, for the sort of person who would have to phone a friend when the presenter asks, 'How are you?' The sort of contestant who thinks 'backgammon' is the rear end of a pig, that 'Sherlock Holmes' is a block of high rise flats, that you spell 'circle' with an 's', that 'Pearl Harbour' is a blues singer.

If your IQ is up to this standard, then you could quite easily and without any difficulty whatsoever be an eager contestant when the TV host introduces the brand new quiz show with 'Hi, guys! And welcome to *Thick as a Plank*.'

Wild 'Woo! Woo! Woo! Woo!' whoops from the specially invited *Thick as a Plank* studio audience.

And watching at home are about ten million *Thick as a Plank* viewers.

Don't even consider applying to take part in this TV quiz unless you are quite monumentally and positively thick. To enter for the top money prize you will need to have a handful of diplomas in thickology and a letter from your GP stating that if you had a brain you would be brain dead. I'm quite certain there won't be any shortage of contestants as the money to be won is quite staggering! The show has started, the host has said, 'Hi, guys! Welcome to *Thick as a Plank*,' and he's given you one hundred thousand pounds cash in your hand before a question has been asked. Not bad, eh? One hundred thousand pounds cash in your hand – now for the difficult bit. Every time you give a wrong answer you have to hand back ten thousand – you've got one hundred thousand and there are twenty questions to be answered, so be very careful. If you really do think 'backgammon' is the rear end of a pig, then you are in serious trouble, and you could well finish up owing the TV company a considerable sum.

At the end of the show, as contestants are being scraped of the pavement six floors below, captions will invite you to phone in if you wish to take part. You will be advised that telephone calls will cost twenty pounds a minute and should last no longer than forty-five minutes, or you can e-mail at
 servesyoubloodywellright.meatpiehead@thickasaplank/uk

*

It was my ninety-sixth birthday. I felt ninety-six, as I'd just finished writing a Christmas show. The woman who sleeps on my right-hand side was also sharing this day with me – our birthdays both fall on the same thirty-first day of October, Duck Apple night and a maiden name of Cox. A coincidence that often brings a smile.

'Great! Thank you! It's something I've always wanted!' And it was something I had always wanted, a very neat and very compact dictaphone.

'Now you won't have to wake Mum up at all hours when you switch the bedside light on and start making notes.'

This was said to me by my ugly daughter – that should give

them both something to argue about. The ugly one is on the right; now watch them change places. It is a fact that I do wake up at night, switch the light on, sit on the edge of the bed and write down some very clever and original thoughts that will have countless millions helpless with laughter. Unfortunately when I read those middle-of-the-night thoughts in the cold light of day they are pathetic, not in any way clever, original or funny.

I'm tickled various shades of pink with the dictaphone. Now I can be like Dick Powell, Humphrey Bogart, Robert Mitchum, James Garner – I can be the next ace detective, Phillip Marlowe. If I wait until they've all gone I can close the door. I switch the birthday present to record and it's fun! Trilby hat on the back of my head and gazing out at the New York skyline. My turn to be Phillip.

'My name is Marlowe, Phillip Marlowe, private eye. I got my other eye on the National Health.'

I was enjoying this.

'Down below I saw Velma standing on the corner of ninth and twelfth. She's a big girl.' What other Phillip Marlowe one-liners did I know? How about, 'The Salvation Army band was playing down by the empty warehouse. It's an unusual hymn.'

And what about my favourite Phillip Marlowe one-liner of ever and ever, 'I could hear Velma in the outer office. She opened the door with a smile: it's a good trick and not many people can do it.'

It would be criminal to leave this one out: 'Velma was like no other dame I'd ever met. She was tall and walked with a Welsh accent.'

And I'm rather keen on this one: 'When she smiled it was like looking at tombstones through a gap in a hedge.'

I suppose this one is OK: 'She had a big spread in the country; it looked like she'd brought it with her.'

And there was more flattery to follow: 'Velma was different from other dames. She was tall, slim, with shoulder-length ears.' Followed by: 'She had that hungry look, she had a face like a pizza. She had get-out-of-bed eyes.'

The dictaphone was worth its weight in Uncle Joe's Mint Balls, the most used aid I had, apart from Tipp-Ex and Bisodol. Many middle-of-the-night ideas did expand and eventually arrive on the TV screen.

It was two thirty in the morning when she on my right side sat up in bed rather quickly.

'What centurion?'

'Pardon?'

'You said centurion.'

'Oh, it's for a joke.'

'A centurion at half past two in the morning isn't funny.'

'You never know your luck.'

There was a slight 'Grrrr', a tug of the duvet and she was asleep before I could try out my fresh joke. Ern was a soldier of Rome:

Ern. I'm a centurion.
Eric. You're all talk, you are.

That gem of a gadget proved invaluable on more than one occasion. I was working on an idea for an opening spot with Eric as the quiz king of Great Britain. Once I'd got the idea I could finish an opening spot in a day, but this one was sticking. Deep into the night I woke up and spoke two names into the tiny machine: Flash Gordon, Joan Collins. It worked. Eric wasn't the quiz king he claimed to be and was very reluctant to answer Ern's questions. What followed was sparked off by Flash and Joan:

Ern. I'll ask you a question.
Eric. Good Lord! Is that the time?
Ern. Never mind the time.
Eric. I've just remembered: I've got to take the wife out.

Ern. That can wait.

Eric. But she's been in the oven since yesterday.

Ern. Here is a question. Who invented the zip?

Eric. Flash Gordon.

Ern. Correct. Name a famous adventure playground.

Eric. Joan Collins.

As the world slept and some of its inhabitants snored, I pressed 'record' and said, 'Pavarotti, North-West.' I knew what I wanted to do with that short phrase and wrote the thought up the next morning for a sketch in *Jimmy's Cricket Team* on BBC Radio 2. It was the most laugh-filled sketch I have ever written for radio. Wonderful, wonderful radio – this was a comedy routine I could never do on television. The idea was that opera star Luciano Pavarotti had arrived in the UK (which is not far from Great Britain, England).

Jimmy interviewed him prior to his tour. The great singer was played quite brilliantly by the vastly experienced Peter Goodwright. Pavarotti had to be played with a very heavy Northern accent. Peter did that and so much more:

Jimmy.   It's a great honour to have you with us, Signor Pavarotti. You're no doubt looking forward to your tour of our country.

Pavarotti. 'Appen.

That one word was greeted with a roar, a really massive laugh that took us all by surprise – and it got better.

Jimmy.   And you will be singing with the London Symphony Orchestra at the Royal Albert Hall, Signor Pavarotti?

Pavarotti. British Legion, Accrington.

Jimmy.   British Legion, Accrington? What about the London Symphony Orchestra?

Pavarotti.	Have you seen the size of the British Legion, Accrington?
Jimmy.	But a great singer such as yourself needs the London Symphony Orchestra.
Pavarotti.	Nellie Clegwell, accordion.
Jimmy.	Nellie Clegwell, accordion!
Pavarotti.	'Appen.
Jimmy.	We're all looking forward to hearing you sing that beautiful aria so closely associated with you, known and loved the world over. I'm sure you know the one that I mean, Signor Pavarotti?
Pavarotti.	'Appen. Mess on doormat.

That was arguably the biggest laugh I ever got in my life. After that we might as well have packed up and gone home. A greatly treasured radio moment.

Glorious, magic-box radio, so much that I could do with you and did. I have done the Eurovision Falling Downstairs contest, the fascinating sound of a hen laying the Band of the Royal Marines, a distressed climber, mobile phone in one hand while hanging by fingertips of his other hand on the summit of Snowdon. Two elderly and not very competent members of Mountain Rescue try to get help as they try to summon a helicopter by looking through the Yellow Pages.

'Edwards and Sons Undertakers, erm . . . Earnshaw's DIY . . . Enid's Wool Shop. It's no use, I can't find 'elicopter anywhere in this book. Have you put the kettle on, Archie? Have a look in the tin and see if there's any digestives left.'

I was extremely fortunate, I was able to grab hold of the coat-tails of radio comedy before it disappeared forever. Why has it disappeared?

I've just looked from cover to cover of the now inappropriately named *Radio Times*. This issue has 148 pages, 18 of them devoted to radio – and these squashed down at the back of the periodical by pages that have nothing to do with radio or its times.

As a listener and lover of radio comedy I found the following quite staggering, almost sinister, because I didn't know how it happened. In seven days of broadcasting on the nation's most listened-to station, BBC Radio 2, there is just one solitary hour of comedy. One hour in one hundred and sixty eight hours of broadcasting.

'Is that gross, Grandad?'

'It's not cool, son.'

Now here's the really frightening bit. If you're a potential Tony Hancock, Frankie Howerd, Ted Ray, Bob Monkhouse, Ray Galton and Alan Simpson, Ken Dodd, Spike Milligan, Peter Sellers, Frank Muir, Denis Norden, Eric Sykes, Kenneth Horne or Al Read, then not only are you out of luck; you are very much out of favour as well. The awful thing is that there are equally richly gifted people out there waiting to prove themselves, and it's not going to happen for them. We need laughter and we desperately need the comedy talents that can give it to us, but they're being ignored. Not to worry, I've left a message on my dictaphone to have a word with somebody in authority with a string vest.

TV or not TV

'Why don't you like the sketch?' Eric was puzzled. 'You wrote it; now you don't like it. What's the problem?' A similar question from Ern after they had both read the sketch for the third time. Everything I ever wrote for them was read and read again; then discussed in great detail. The sketch I was having doubts about was set in the future, a departure for us. Eric and Ern had split up and while Ern had make a successful career as a businessman, or so it appeared, an out-of-work Eric was living a life of misery and poverty and was married to childhood sweetheart Ada Bailey, who was now a nagging wife. Eric looked again at page one and smiled: 'There are some good lines in this. Ann Hamilton was Eric's nagging wife.

Ann. Why don't you go back on the telly with Mighty Mouse and make some money.
Eric. I've told you once: I've got me pride. [*Sips tea*] They all think I've got it made. [*Sips tea again*] Make another pot of that tea and I'll do the doors with it.
Ann. The rent's due today.
Eric. Listen, when the rent man knocks you . . .
Ann. When he knocks I am not going to shout, 'They've gone on their holidays.'

Misgivings had to be spoken of now: casting doubt on whether the sketch was funny or not by the time it got to the rehearsal stage would only have destroyed confidence. So I'd better put my case now.

'I know it's only make-believe, but even make-believe has to be acceptable, and I don't think the audience will accept this. They wouldn't like the idea of Eric and Ern being separated. They won't accept a wife, because she had split up the two men they care so much about. It's too real. It hasn't got the cosy feel of a flat sketch or a bed sketch or any of the comedy situations you've both been in. Yes, I know I wrote it – now I wish I hadn't.'

Ern as ever was so practical: 'Let's sleep on it. We'll think again tomorrow. Incidentally I love this line.' He pointed halfway down page five.

It was when an affluent-looking Ern arrived and looked in dismay at the squalor in which his former partner was living:

Ern. It's, erm . . . nice little place.
Eric. Only temporary, Ern; only temporary.
Ann. Any minute now it'll fall down.

Before we all slept on it they were both trying to convince me that my own work was funny. Ern showed me a page and said it would be a shame to lose it:

Eric. My dear, I think I can hear Rupert crying.
Ern. Rupert?
Eric. Our youngest girl.

At this point Ada goes to attend to the baby, leaving Eric and Ern together for the first time in ten years.

Ern. Well then, Eric?
Eric. Well then, Ern?
Ern. How long is it now?
Eric. How long is what now?

That night we all slept on it, if you'll pardon the expression. The following morning we reassembled and they decided they would do it. A waste of time trying to persuade them otherwise.

When the sketch was performed in front of an audience it took them a while to come to terms with what was happening. There were laughs, quite a few, but not laughed with any great conviction. I suppose what I'm trying to say is that the laughs would have sounded better had it been a flat sketch. There would have been heartier, much warmer laughter.

When that particular show was over I left in a tizz – that's another foreign car. As I've said before, I was never keen to take them out of their natural habitat; neither was I interested in writing a film, not after my previous experiences with that medium. When early in the 1980s they did ask me if I would be interested in writing a film for them I said I would 'if'.

'If what?' Almost a joint question.

'Can I tell you tomorrow?' They said I could – and I did.

'I would, if I could write a ninety-minute-plus film that took place in the bed and the flat.'

They both wanted to know what the plot was.

'It starts off with you both in bed.'

Ern. It's cold.
Eric. Minus seven, last night.
Ern. Minus seven?
Eric. Snow White slept on her own.

'If it was a film,' I went on, 'you could get away with thirty minutes in the bed quite easily.'

'What happens next,' Ern wanted to know. Trust him to make life difficult.

'You both hear noises from the living room. Someone has broken in and you're being turned over, as they say. You catch the burglar, a very timid villain, and after a while it turns out that Eric went to Milverton Street School with him. Ern doesn't know him. Even though he went to the same school their paths never crossed because Eric and the miscreant were in class 4C. Ern was in class 1A and didn't mix with those who had a doughnut between the ears.'

They both wanted to know what the tag was. Typical of all comedians, always wanting to know what the tag was, always making life difficult.

'The tag is, and it's a very good tag: I get lots of money and you both win an Academy Award.'

They gave me a 'This boy's a fool' look; then started talking about doing a summer season in Great Yarmouth. I still think that, given ninety minutes plus and in those situations, I could have given them a quite decent film.

Unlike my film idea, there were some routines they got enthusiastic about after reading just a couple of lines. I found this happened when the routine I had shown them was inspired by the real-life variety acts I had seen and they had worked with. If they hadn't appeared on the same bill as 'The Lannons', then I'm quite sure they must have known or worked with a very similar act, 'The Lannons – Mum and Dad'.

That's how they appeared in the programme when I first saw them at the Pivvie, an affectionate shortening for the Pavilon Theatre in Liverpool, and that same Friday night Lilly Benson was sitting a few rows in front of me in the stalls. I was going to hear about this on Monday night.

The Lannons – Mum and Dad, were the first act on and played accordions of diminishing sizes, did a clog dance and finished their act by playing 'The Bells of St Mary's' on hand bells. They got a great ovation because we felt sorry for them and they were probably worse off than we were.

I never forgot the hand bells.

Eric, wearing the obligatory ill-fitting evening dress (this one belonged to a magician, which was why feathers kept floating out from it), stood proudly beside a table on which stood the hand bells, nodded to the camera and his top hat on a spring wobbled from side to side. Just where the wobbly hat gag came from I really have no idea, but he used it whenever the opportunity presented itself. Ern looked at the bells; then at Eric:

Ern. Are you going to play a round?
Eric. Not tonight, the wife's in.

At Ern's request Eric agrees to play 'The Bells of St Mary's'. He picks up one hand bell after another, gives them a shake, but there's no sound from them. Eric makes the bell sounds himself as he shakes them:

Eric. Ding-dong-ding-dong-ding-ding—
Ern. Hold it! Hold it! You're making that sound yourself! Those bells haven't got any clappers in them!
Eric. Of course they haven't! You fool! If they had clappers in you wouldn't be able to hear me going ding-dong-ding . . .

For me that was one of the funniest front-of-curtain routines we ever did – I would even place it above the dialogue with André Previn prior to the 'Grieg piano concerto'. Besides, I had a lot more in common with the Lannons than I had with Grieg, and Wigan's a lot closer to our house than Norway.

The same theatre, the same night and screaming on to the stage came a troupe of Eastern acrobats who called themselves 'The Six Amazing Abduls', or something really Eastern. They bounced and hurled themselves around the stage, leapt over one another, all the while shouting very loudly, 'Hi-Hup!' Lilly looked around at me while shaking her head. She wasn't smitten by the Abduls. I certainly was: I never forgot them and used them every week in my radio series as 'The Four Herberts'. All they ever did was shout, 'Hi-Hup!'

Recalling those many wonderous nights in the variety theatres, I feel sorry for those who have never sat in a Woodbine-
and-orange-peel-scented auditorium and have missed glorious
performers such as Freddie Bamburger and Pam. Freddie, quite
immaculate in white tie and tails, and the so very sophisticated
and elegant Pam in tight-fitting evening dress. This memorable
line from Freddie, who was seated at the grand piano: 'Now a
song dedicated to my mother-in-law, entitled "You're the
Cream in my Coffee" – you old cow.'

Freddie was the inspiration behind so many of the 'quickies'
that we did with Eric and Ern in evening dress and at the piano.

Monday night and I went for my cigarettes. I had a feeling
that Lil wasn't going to give the acrobats a gold star or even a
VG.

'Did you enjoy the show on Friday, Lil?'

'Those acrobats got on my nerves, hi-huppin' all over the
stage. I never have liked acrobats.'

'They're only trying to earn a crust; can't be many variety
theatres in Egypt.'

She looked puzzled. 'Egypt? They came into the pub when I
went for a drink after the show. They were all Geordies.'

My surprise turned to pride when she said, 'Billy Matchett
was very funny. I liked that joke about the Ink Spots.'

Swamped now with pride, I had to tell her. 'He's my
uncle.'

'Billy Matchett, your uncle?'

'Yeah.'

'Oh aye, and Ingrid Bergman's my sister. Here's your ciggies.
Sod off.'

I was about to step off the pavement when she called me
back. Had I forgotten my change? No, I hadn't.

'The acrobats I met in the pub.'

'What about them?'

'One of them is a poof.'

Lil would have made a very good Miss Marple, if only she could stop telling people to sod off.

Leslie Welch, 'The Memory Man'. It was he who motivated me to write an opening that saw Eric as 'Professor Memory'. In 1950 Leslie Welch had had me spellbound when I sat in the stalls of the Walham Green Empire, as he answered a barrage of sporting questions from a packed house – and he got every question right. Just as well, because if he gave you a wrong answer he gave you one pound. The wallet stayed closed that Saturday night. I'd been looking forward to my weekend pass from cookhouse duties so I could see Leslie Welch in the flesh. Heard him a lot on the radio. Even more eagerly I was looking forward to seeing Alicia in the flesh. She was billed as 'The Beautiful Alicia, with her daring and provocative seasonal poses.' I was nineteen, four rows from the front and had excellent eyesight.

Alicia's first daring and provocative seasonal pose was as Spring, standing against a pantomime backcloth of the countryside and holding a large bunch of daffodils. With an effort I could just about see her bare left elbow. It was the same seasonal cover-up as Summer with a sun hat that the Band of the Royal Marines could have stood behind without notice. For Autumn Alicia held very daintily an oak leaf the size of a bin lid. Winter came, and I'd lost interest now anyway. For the record, as Winter Alicia clutched a muff that would have served well as a hearth rug. I saw more of her after the show when she was going back to her digs – both ankles.

Leslie Welch was just as brilliant at answering the questions from the audience as he had been when I first heard him on the radio. Two decades later when I was in dire need of an opening spot, I remembered that night at the Walham Green Empire. Suppose Leslie didn't know the answer to any of the questions? I had the opening spot.

Ern introduced Eric as Professor Memory. He was again

wearing the ill-fitting evening dress, this time minus the trousers. He was Professor Memory.

Ern. Good evening, Professor.
Eric. Good morning.
Ern. Professor Memory.
Eric. Oh yes.
Ern. Can you tell me . . .
Eric. Oh yes.
Ern. Can you tell me, Professor Memory, can you tell me who won the FA Cup in 1950?
Eric. Oh yes.
Ern. Well?
Eric. The FA Cup in 1950 was won by, erm . . . in 1950 it was won.
Ern. Who by, Professor?
Eric. Oh yes, erm . . . it was won by, erm . . .
Ern [*coughs the name 'Arsenal'*]. Excuse me, I have a bad chest.
Eric. Chester! Chester won the FA Cup in 1950!

After that opening was first shown, if you coughed in a public place it wasn't unusual for a voice to respond with 'Arsenal!'

*

All those wondrous nights of sheer delight spent in variety theatres and watching almost mesmerised performers who I had booked weeks in advance to see. Jimmy James, how he made me ache with laughter, Max Wall and his very funny walk, magical Frank Sinatra, despite the audience, or lack of one. Billy Cotton, especially when I thought he had handed my dad a bag of sweets and had said, 'Give these to your Eddie.' The dazzling, flawless Nicholas Brothers as they finished their dance routine by landing in eye-watering splits that had every man in the audience going, 'Ooh!'

I have a much-treasured memory of meeting these two gifted gentlemen when they appeared on *Des O'Connor Tonight*.

It is a long and glorious list of excellence, and perhaps my fondest memory is of all those performers who never made it to the top: maybe, like me, a great many people went to see you and not the top-of-the-bill star.

Your diverse talents brought me so much pleasure, so much joy, and so very much inspiration.

By the way, Alicia had beautiful eyes.

Some More New Lines What I Wrote

An idea I've had for some time has been running wild in my head with nowhere to go. I often have a fantasy that I'm asked to write a brand new Morecambe and Wise show. It will sadly always remain a fantasy, but it doesn't stop me from thinking what that show might be like, and it wouldn't matter if nobody ever saw it on TV, – it would be great fun to do. If I did, the following idea that has been pleading to be put on paper would be in that show.

Like fingerprints, no two walks are alike: nobody walks like you and nobody walks like me, and that's a fact. It's also a fact that every celebrity, every star performer, has his or her very own and instantly recognisable walk. If you couldn't see his face but could see him walk it would only take a matter of seconds for you to say, 'That's Bruce Forsyth.'

It was this thought, the realisation that no two walks are alike, that led to this routine. And I'm really delighted to have put it on paper for the very first time:

Ern. Tonight, ladies and gentlemen, I'm going to do something quite unique, unusual and astonishing.
Eric. A new joke.
Ern. No.

Eric. No. We did it last year. The one about the vegetarian cannibal who only ate greengrocers.

Ern. No.

Eric. No. It didn't get a laugh when we did it last year.

Ern. For the first time ever in Great Britain or this country, stars and their walks. Thank you.

Eric. Stars and their walks? You've kept that one to yourself.

Ern. Every international star celebrity who is also famous has a walk that is instantly recognisable.

Eric. Ern, that is a knockout idea! Do a star's walk now! Do one.

Ern. Very well.

> *Does the slow, languid and slightly menacing walk of John Wayne*

Eric. Ern, that is brilliant! Only one person in the world walks like that.

Ern. You could tell who it was supposed to be from the walk?

Eric. We all could.

Ern. And you knew it was John Wayne?

Eric. Oh. I thought it was Dale Winton.

Ern. Dale doesn't walk like that!

Eric. He might, on one of his bad days. Do another one.

Ern. Right. Who's this?

> *Does quick and very short Ronnie Corbett steps*

Eric. No. Give me a clue.

Ern. He's smaller than me.

Eric. Nobody's smaller than you!

Ern. Ronnie Corbett! You knew it was Ronnie Corbett!

Eric. Of course I did. On his way to bungee jump off a mushroom. Do one more.

Ern. Let me think. I'll try and think of an easy one, instantly recognisable.

Walks a couple of paces as he thinks

Eric. John Inman! That is brilliant, Ern! That is the best John . . .

Ern. I wasn't doing a star's walk! I wasn't doing John Inman.

Eric. No wonder the milkman calls you 'Chunky'. Give me an easy one.

Ern. I'll do the walk of the most famous, the most talented and the most loved star ever to appear on the show. Ready?

Eric. I'm bound to get this one.

Ern. Watch.

Struts and swaggers with pride

Eric. Sorry.

Ern. I'll do it again.

Struts and swaggers

Eric. No idea.

Ern. Me.

Eric. Watch this walk.

Ern. Whose walk?

Eric. Me going off to the bar.

Interestingly with that routine the roles could have been reversed and it still would have worked. If Eric had done the stars and their walks, Ern could have had the funny lines and Eric would have got the sympathy laugh:

Eric. I'll do one of my star walks.

Eric does the very obvious James Cagney walk

Ern. I've no idea who that was supposed to be.

Eric. It was flamin' obvious who it was supposed to be! Everyone knows that walk!

Ern. I don't.

Eric. The audience knows – ask them.

Ern. Be a pity to wake them up.

On a number of occasions we had looked at a comedy routine and discussed the possibility of changing the funny lines from Eric to Ern; as with the stars walk idea it would have worked, proving that this was a comedy double act where the so-called straight man could also do the funny lines. To the best of my knowledge only Laurel and Hardy had the same inter-changeable relationship.

Walk Watch

It was very interesting doing a couple of hours' research for the walks idea; in fact it was most pleasant sitting at the window table of the delightful town-centre tea rooms with the exotic and evocative name, 'The Blue Moon'. Now, with a name like that you might well expect a Humphrey Bogart lookalike to greet you as you went in with, 'Here's looking at you kid. The carrot cake is very good.' Or, 'We also do a hill of beans on toast.'

I settled back and watched with much interest as a continual flow of locals and holidaymakers passed by the window. The locals were quite easy to pick out, as they walked with a Welsh accent. Lots of people with weight problems, the fatty bum-bum brigade, and from careful observation they all have a very similar walk. Obviously it's not a sprightly step: it's a plodding tread on flat feet and stiff legs. They never bend their knees, never lift the legs up. It's a rolling walk from side to side with each step, as this helps to evenly distribute the weight. They were also a bit of a hazard, as slim people had to step off the pavement and into the road to overtake them.

One lady waddled past the window, causing an eclipse of my carrot cake. She was excessive and inspired this: 'If she was the only one in the Royal Albert Hall it would be full.'

Now that is a great walk! That is a beauty! I've got to make a note of that one. I'm sharing the table with the woman who sleeps on my right-hand side. She's wearing a cream-coloured hat with a wide brim; she's looking at me all dewy eyed and saying, 'Oh Rick, have you forgotten what happened in Paris?'

What she's really saying is, 'One of these days you'll go too far and land yourself in trouble.'

It's true that I had been doing a lot of staring at some of the walks. It's also true that some of the walkers had stared back with an expression that said, 'Who do you think you're looking at?' I was going to have to be more discreet.

The walk I wanted to make a note of was the copyright of a wrinkly, about my age, a recycled teenager, and he was going at a merry trot using a walking stick, but it was the way he was using the walking stick that captivated me – if you can become captivated by an old age pensioner with a walking stick.

As he was walking he appeared to put the stick down too far in front of him and he had to quicken his step to catch up with it. It was hysterical, a gem of a walk. I wanted to see more, so I went and stood in the doorway so I could watch his progress up the street. He was still trying to catch up with his stick, which seemed to have a life of its own as it went weaving in and out of folk on a crowded pavement. It would have been perfect had he shouted, 'Come back here, you bugger!' I returned to the table and what was left of the carrot cake, had a nibble; then made an observation. 'Do you know I haven't seen one bandy-legged person all day?' There used to be lots of bandy people when I was young.'

'Will you keep your voice down!'

It's true there were lots of bandy people when I was a boy – perhaps they trained to be bandy by sleeping with their legs wrapped around a barrel. I was careful not to say this out loud. In my youth we had a neighbour who was bandy and my mother used to say of him, 'He'd never stop a pig in a back entry.' If she saw someone with large feet she'd ask, 'I wonder if he has to pay ground rent?'

I finished my carrot cake and pocketed my notes on 'assorted walks'. It's a pastime I can highly recommend. We reached our car in time to see a traffic warden slipping an invitation under the wiper blade of a vehicle that had overstayed its welcome. As he went predatory-like down the line of parked conveyances, I couldn't help but notice that he had an evil walk.

*

How many words are there in a ballpoint pen?

If you straightened them out and laid them end to end, how far would they reach? From here to Clacton? To Rome? Even Hawaii? Follow the ball-point road; it's bound to reach somewhere, even if it's only two hundred and seventy-fifth in the bestseller list.

How many full stops are there in a bottle of ink?

Does anyone still buy ink?

'What's a fountain pen, Dad?'

'What did you wrap in blotting paper, Dad?'

Where have all the bandy people gone?

'Miss, can I have a new nib? This one blots.'

'No you can't have a new nib [1940]. Don't you know there's a war on?'

'Can I give the milk out, miss?'

'What's a nib, Dad? Does it bite, Dad?'

Where have all the bandy people gone?

Even More New Lines What I Wrote

T he idea of writing an entirely new Morecambe and Wise
show is a pleasant one, as I don't give myself any deadlines
to agonise over and everything I write is so original, so
brilliantly funny that I can take the rest of the week off prior
to collecting, from her most Gracious Majesty, the award for
being 'The Best Comedy Writer in the World . . . ever!' for a
record twelfth time.

The 'stars and their walks' idea I'm quite sure would have
worked, because they loved doing visual comedy. And because
of the subject there would have been just cause for 'additional
material by' because Eric did a very good Cary Grant walk, and
Ern's Ebenezer Scrooge walk was quite breathtaking. They
would, of course, have put a lot of extra ideas of their own into
this idea, and I can picture them in the room trying out star
walks I had overlooked. They would have made it very funny,
as they did with the wide assortment of shop sketches I wrote. If
Eric was reading a script for the first time and he came to a shop
sketch he'd smile and say, 'I enjoy doing these.'

This particular shopping spree saw Eric as the customer in
the electrical goods shop: he wanted to buy a calculator. This
idea came to me just days before, when I really did go and buy a
calculator (I just wanted to make sure the BBC weren't over-
paying me).

Anyway, I'm getting in the way of Eric, who's just entered the electrical goods shop to purchase a calculator. Ern is the assistant. Oh, and I'm going to take this opportunity to release some new lines I've been aching to share:

Ern. Good afternoon, sir.

Eric. The weatherman said this has been the wettest month since 1896.

Ern. Really?

Eric. Surprised me because he doesn't look that old.

Ern. How can I help you?

Eric. You could pay off my mortgage? Perhaps cure my wife of her drinking problem?

Ern. Sir, I am a purveyor of electrical goods.

Eric. And do you by any chance purvey calculators?

Ern. We are specialists.

Eric. Then I need go no further.

Ern. Rest assured.

Eric. I don't want a mattress.

Ern. Sir, we have been selling calculators for more than five hundred years.

Eric. Speaks volumes for the strength of your batteries.

Ern. Indeed, sir.

Eric. Do the calculators that you purvey vary in price or do they cost different amounts?

Ern. Well, they vary in price but some do cost different amounts.

Eric. Inclusive of those excellent batteries that last for five hundred years?

Ern. Most definitely inclusive, sir.

Eric. You see, I don't want to come back to you in four hundred years' time and complain that the batteries have run out.

Ern. In that unlikely event, sir, should you come back

here with such a complaint in four hundred years time and I'm out at lunch, one of my assistants will attend to you.

Eric. The very old assistant?

Ern. Very probably, sir. Would you like to try one of our calculators, sir?

Eric. Thank you.

Picks up the calculator and speaks the numbers aloud as he punches them in

Eric. That is amazing. Three thousand one hundred and twenty.

Ern. Three thousand one hundred and twenty what, sir?

Eric. It's got nothing to do with you.

I may not hear those new lines spoken but it's still good to see them on paper. The epicentre of all shop sketch mirthquakes happened when Eric took his wife to buy her a ring. Ern was the ever-patient assistant as she tried the ring on only to find it didn't fit her finger:

Ern. We can have it made larger.

Eric. If you can make her finger larger then I've got a little job that you can do for me.

That was very much a typical Eric Morecambe line, not like the calculator sketch when the dialogue was what they both called 'A little off centre!' They also admitted that had they read dialogue like that before I started writing for them they would never have considered it, as it was not their style. It was a comedy linguistic tool I was able to use only when they were two characters in a shop and not 'Eric and Ern', as in a stand-up spot or bed/flat sketch.

I'm going to have to find a shop sketch for the next show – a barber's shop sketch? We never did one because it's difficult to act cutting someone's hair, and who'll be the barber? I'm going to give that one a lot of thought.

On Stage

S ummer 2000, the phone went. I managed to stop it with my foot. It was David Pugh, one of the most successful impresarios in the country, or so he kept telling me. A man of many parts held together by six and a half yards of sticky tape.

He was calling me from London, which is not far from Great Britain. He wanted to come and talk to me about his latest project, and when he told me what it was I almost dropped the phone.

'It's a play based on the comedy of Morecambe and Wise.'

Surely he wasn't being serious? A play about Eric and Ern? Never! Nobody could possible do a play about those two! It was unthinkable! Even worse, it was close to being blasphemous. Who could even consider putting two men on stage pretending to be Morecambe and Wise. It would never ever work and the public just would not accept, would never ever accept, anyone trying to take the place of Morecambe and Wise. This was a project destined for certain disaster and I wanted no part of it.

'I've got to come up to Liverpool on Tuesday. How about if I called to see you at your house in Wales on Tuesday afternoon? I really would like to know what you think about the idea.'

'Certainly, David. I'll be more than happy to talk to you about it.'

He was so enthusiastic I just didn't have the heart to tell him what I really thought of his ridiculous idea.

'You know whereabouts I am?'

'I think so.'

Just to be on the safe side, so he wouldn't get lost in all the greenery, I gave him directions: 'Turn left at Bryn Terfel, and we're the first on the right past Aled Jones.'

I didn't have the heart to tell him that although the title *The Play What I Wrote* was familiar to me, it sounded like a stupid title for a comedy play. The biggest surprise was Kenneth Branagh directing – I was going to have to mark his card as well! David Pugh was coming all the way from London to see me about an idea that was never going to work. Never mind, the fresh air will do him good.

Four days later, when David arrived at our hilltop house, he collapsed in a heap from his pack mule. He was helped indoors by the local policeman and a Sherpa who had guided him for the last twenty-five gruelling miles. After a bowl of reindeer soup and a good night's sleep in the barn, David was his old familiar self – yuck!

'Optimistic' would greatly underrate the enthusiasm he so obviously felt as he handed me a copy of *The Play What I Wrote*. It had been written by and would be performed by the highly talented Sean Foley and Hamish McCann, and making this a very gifted trio was Toby Jones. Toby is the most impressive character/comedy actor I have seen for a very long time.

I read the work, added my four pennyworth and still didn't think much of its chances. All the doubts I had and kept secret about *The Play What I Wrote* were blown sky high, appropriately on 5 November 2001, at Wyndham's Theatre in London's West End. The building really did tremble that night as the audience roared with glorious laughter. They stood and cheered and clapped and quite a few shed a tear as they sang 'Bring Me Sunshine'.

During the interval the theatre was like the Kop at Anfield. The woman who sleeps on my right-hand side was arm in arm with Norma Farnes. Norma looks after the business side of things and makes absolutely certain that nobody, but nobody pays me too much money, and she's done a superb job. In all the years she has been looking after me not one person has got away with paying me too much. You're not dealing with a mug here. Thanks, Norma. In a crowded bar you couldn't have a better woman by your side than Norma, she has the most vicious elbows I have ever seen and she gets to the bar like a – well – like a woman with vicious elbows. She should have a licence for them.

The place was full of very famous celebrities who were also quite well known. I saw Ned Sherrin and thought, 'God! He's going to ask for his money back for that film.' He didn't see me, so I came out from under the table.

Dee was having a great time star-spotting. There aren't very many celebrities where we live, not counting Mrs Thomas, who got a first for her dried arrangements when she stood too close to the radiator at the WI.

I'd never seen so many famous celebrities who were also quite well known, stars of stage and Job Centre.

She tugged at my sleeve: 'There's wotsisname from *East-enders* – he got shot last week.'

If he was wearing that suit I'm not surprised. I wish I had the nerve to wear it. It was a large check suit and I remembered what Eric said every time he saw someone wearing a check suit: 'I've got six down, but I'm not sure about four across.'

Dee was having a great time: 'He's in *Emmerdale*. He was in intensive care after that car crash.'

'Oh! Isn't she in *Coronation Street*?'

Just answer yes to that question and you've got to be right.

'Yes, she was. Remember her?'

'No.'

'Yes you do. She got run over by a lorry outside the shops.'

It went on like this for the duration of the interval, and all I can say is, if you're thinking of a career in television get yourself a job on *Songs of Praise* – you'll live longer.

The Play What I Wrote played to sell-out audiences in the West End for almost three years. It was hugely successful on tour and is, as I write. It did better, much better in New York than I thought it would. Picked up a few Olivier Awards as well.

What do I know?

OK. I got it a bit wrong.

Before I go any further, I've got to tell you what I think is a very interesting little titbit: Did you know that the first Women's Institute was founded in 1915 at . . .

Llanfairpwllgwyngyllgogerychwyrndrobwllllantysiliogo-gogoch.

Get that right and you deserve to win a million.

I'm very proud that I can say that place name – not very often, as it brings me out in a rash.

Buy a ticket to that station and it will take two of you to carry it.

Roughly translated that place name means, 'Why does it always take you longer to find your front door key when it's pouring with rain than it does when the sun is shining?'

But I've turned off the main road again. Back to the play.

The sun had never shone so brightly as it did in Covent Garden on the morning of 6 November, following the opening night of *The Play What I Wrote*. Now for what the papers say.

The critics gave it acclaim by the bucketful – some said they ached with laughter, while others agreed it was the funniest show they had seen for many West End years.

I'm always going to remember that morning after, because the bed in our hotel room was covered with the sixty-eight newspapers I had bought at six o'clock that morning.

We both sat reading the reviews and it was all rather jolly because I'd seen them doing exactly the same in so many Hollywood musical films. 'Dee, baby! We made it!'

'Were you famous after that, Grandad?'

'I most certainly was, Thomas.'

'How famous, Grandad?'

'How famous? Well, everywhere I went people were crowding around my Zimmer frame asking for my autograph.'

'You must have been really famous, Grandad.'

Well, I was a bit of a celebrity, if only for a few hours on the morning of 6 November 2001.

The opening night brought back a world that had been full of golden memories, and not only to me.

Nobody was more surprised than I was at the audience reaction at that opening night performance, more so when I saw how young some of them were – surely they would have been in bed when our shows were on? I was.

When the curtain went up I could sense the apprehension. What's this all about?

What are they trying to do? They're not a bit like Eric and Ernie.

That's what was so clever about the idea: they weren't supposed to be. Had they tried to be like them the whole concept would have died in minutes. What they saw were two men who very cleverly and very skilfully reminded them of what Eric and Ernie did, what they said, how they said it and how they moved. They never said, 'We're trying to be like them.' And it didn't take the audience long to accept and appreciate what they were doing.

Everything Sean and Hamish did was welcomed with open arms, becoming even wider smiles, becoming laughter. It was laughter that made ribs ache and happy eyes water. As I sat and watched and listened I was tempted to ask in a whisper, 'What do you think of it so far?'

The longer the show went on the more obvious it was just how much the audience loved Morecambe and Wise, how much they needed to laugh at what they did and said. It didn't matter that they'd seen and heard it all before a hundred times.

I remember something Sean said to me after a perfomance: 'I'll swear to God that they expect Morecambe and Wise to walk out on to the stage.'

Maybe they did, but this was as close as they were ever going to get and they made the most of every glorious minute.

I was so proud to be a part of it.

Ern. I feel really tired today.
Eric. I'm not surprised. What time did you get to bed last night?
Ern. It must have been well gone nine o'clock.
Eric. The human body won't take that kind of punishment, Ern.

How very true that was.

After the jollifications of the previous night I did not effervesce; I didn't get to bed until half past eleven, and that's the truth. I had to take early retirement because I'd been given a glass of champagne and the obligatory sip had gone straight to my head and made me feel dizzy. That's the way it has always been: I just cannot take alcohol, not even a tiny sip.

The day after the night before and I had to do TV, radio and newspaper interviews, and the prospect was not blissful. One interview every six months with the *People's Friend* I could manage, but not ten, one after the other, and not when the first one was at eight o'clock in the morning. Now I fully appreciate why Bob Hope was so grumpy all those years ago when I met him at the Savoy Hotel. He had done more than twenty interviews that day, the first at six o'clock in the morning and he had every reason to look clapped out when he saw me parked on his sofa.

He sat next to me in American, noticed the small mono-grammed 'M' on my jacket and asked. 'What's the "M" for? "Michigan"?' I corrected him: 'Merseyside.' He said, 'I've been there,' and I had the nerve to reply, 'We've all got to go there sometime.' It was a line I used when any place in the world was mentioned. There was just the faint hint of a smile from the great man. The hint of a smile from Bob Hope! I was happy with that, ecstatic would describe it much better.

It was the one and only time in my professional career that I was ever in awe of a truly great star – a Hollywood star. I used to see him at the pictures.

'Bob Hope's on at the Gaumont.'

'What in?'

The Road to Llanfairpwllgwyngyllgogerychwyrndrobwll-lantysiliogogogoch.

I'll bet that was in Cinemascope.

It was two o'clock in the afternoon. I was about to face my fifth interview of the day and was feeling tired, hungry and fed up with the now same questions and I didn't want to be a celebrity anymore.

Normally, and a lot of people will vouch for this, I'm an amiable, extremely tolerant man with a merry disposition. 'Oh, you mean the grey-haired gentleman who lives just over the crossroads? I know him very well, such a gentle and charming man. Always got a cheery greeting and a kind word.'

That's me they're talking about. If some film company wanted to do a remake of *Miracle on 34th Street* I'd be first choice to play the part of Father Christmas. However, it doesn't take much to turn me into a narky old bugger.

I can't remember her name, so I'm going to call her Nellie Bladder – it suits the kind of person she was, and she did manage to turn me into a narky old bugger. She was a young TV reporter who was obviously trying to make a name for herself – her questions made that very clear. She was looking for something that wasn't there; if it wasn't, she'd put it there. The questions I objected to came in the middle of the TV interview and were meant to catch me off guard. That brought the narky old bugger to life – she must have thought I'd fallen off the back of a turnip cart. The warning light started to flicker when she started to ask questions about ill health. I refused to answer those questions, explaining that ill health wasn't a happy subject and that it didn't make people smile – unless it happened to Adolf Hitler. It didn't take her long to get down to what she really wanted.

'What was Eric Morecambe like in real life?'

'Tall, with glasses.'

'Did they ever argue?'

'Only when they were together.'

'I mean, did they ever have rows, bust-ups?'

'Yes, they did once have a bust-up and it's something I've never spoken about before.'

Her little face lit up and she almost shivered with excitement and anticipation as she sat at the side of the camera with the red eye.

She was going to hear the truth for the first time! The truth about a bust-up between Morecambe and Wise!

'What happened?' She asked this question quietly, as though she didn't want to frighten me away. I wasn't going anywhere.

I told her.

'Ern was like a man possessed, like a wild man as he hurled himself at Eric. His clenched fist smashed into his face with such a ferocity that I could hear the crunch of bone. There was blood everywhere . . . .'

I continued this story narrative until the TV crew started to laugh and she ordered, 'Cut!' It was never screened.

After the final interview all I wanted was sausage, egg and chips and a taxi to Euston Station.

On the way I asked the driver to stop so I could get out at Wyndham's Theatre: I wanted to see my name lit up on the posters. It's something that will never happen again.

The euphoria of the West End experience had me quite bewildered; it came at a time when I was quite happy to concede that my day, and it had been a very long and pleasant day, had gone. I'd been there, done that, got the truss. I had accepted that I was clapped out, written out, knackered and ready to join the bowls club, when along comes *The Play What I Wrote*, and audiences are laughing at lines I had written when they were at school (maybe some of them hadn't even been born). And that's why I was bewildered, greatly puzzled that I could get this kind of reaction from a generation I thought I had nothing in common with – they even spoke a new language that made me feel like an alien.

'Get this down your neck' (have a drink).

'It hacks me off big time' (I'm fed up).

'Chill out, man' (relax).

'I'm up for it' (eager).

'The bottom line is' (finally).

'Get out of my face' (sod off).

There I was, all set and looking forward to membership of the bowls club, something I'd promised myself I would do ever since I saw the bowls championships on afternoon TV, very civilised. Nobody had his shirt pulled; they used hankies to blow their noses and nobody called anyone else a wanker.

These much-looked-forward-to treats would now have to be 'Put on hold' (wait) as I was still getting laughs.

'You could be another George Bernard Priestley.'

'Shaw.'

'Positive.'

And that really did get a very respectable laugh at a time when I thought those days had long gone. No, this generation, they're pretty cool, man – big time. Perhaps the time hadn't come for me to shove the quill back in the duck's bum.

It's good to be back home in Wellieland where I am now a bit of a celebrity, or as much of a celebrity as they'll ever let you be in Wellieland. This welcome home from a neighbour who had just walked into our kitchen:

'Saw you on the telly.'

'Oh, yes.'

'Did you have to wear that jacket?'

And before I can defend that terrible insult to my very best mustard coloured corduroy jacket, I am completely disarmed by the follow-up question.

'Do you want anything from the shops?'

'You can get us half a dozen donkey eggs.'

I had to come back at him with something. I had to remind him that he was crossing ad-libs with a man whose name is up in lights in London's West End. You're not dealing with a mug, here, sunshine.

The quill can remain adjacent for a little longer, as there are a couple of ideas I want to try and make something of before I become fossilized.

Have you ever sneezed when you're eating crisps? Everybody gets some.

*

My first ever visit to the watering hole favoured by showbiz folk, the Ivy, was memorable. No disrespect intended to the Ivy, but it took me back to my RAF days and the NAFFI. If you don't know what NAFFI means, then ask your grandad. If he doesn't know . . . the dinosaur's wagging its tail. Walkies!

It was dimly lit, but I could still see at a nearby table a couple of men who were dressed as women (don't see that many of them where I live). We do have a lot of women who dress just like men but that's only when they're muckin' out and it's a necessity – I hope.

Elbows Farnes explained they had just come off stage after appearing in a West End show. I understood now: 'They're Transistors.'

Elbows corrected me: 'Transvestites.'

I chanced a quick look at them again: 'They might as well be transistors – they're on a different wavelength to me.' I don't see anything alluring about a six-foot woman in need of a shave.

'Excuse me.'

This was to the waiter, who had put my bread roll on the paper table cloth and I hadn't been given a side plate.

'You haven't given me a side plate.'

Elbows explained that you don't get side plates anymore.

'No side plate?' I'm puzzled. 'Have they done away with side plates? Is this something to do with the Common Market? What kind of a place is this? Paper tablecloth, no side plates, big hairy men with frocks on.' I'll just have a bowl of soup, and the next train back to Wellieland!

Wellieland

I've been going through the dictionary looking at all the words that up to now I haven't used. 'Sombre.' I don't even like the look of that adjective. Nor do I have any use for things serious, grave, dark or gloomy.

'Contrapuntal.' I've never used that word either, and wouldn't think of mentioning contrapuntal because I've never been there.

'Electropalatography.' Haven't written about electropalatography simply because I'd use up half a ballpoint writing it down. Not only that, but electropalatography means: 'the study of the way the tongue makes contact with the roof of the mouth when you're talking or having a bit of dinner.' How's that for riveting?

Anyway, if you were serious about making a study of electropalatography you'd go home at night covered with gravy and bits of mash and two veg.

'Environmentally friendly.' Just come across that one on page 424 of my Chambers, and it sounds OK. Without checking, I think 'environmentally friendly' means you're quite happy to do it in a field.

Now, where was I up to? Oh, yes.

Back home in the High Street. Something nice and cosy about 'the High Street'. It seems every town has one, and it always makes me think of that film *On the Town* – the scene where Gene Kelly and Vera Ellen discover they both come from the same small town and they go into a nostalgic song-and-dance routine. Gene Kelly? Vera Ellen? Oh, you haven't? That dinosaur's getting plenty of exercise. There was a good cosmopolitan selection of eating places in the High Street that could act as hides so that I could carry out research into the eating habits of the human male. There was a Chinese takeaway, an Indian takeaway and an Irish bring-it-back.

I was ensconced (I like that word), at a most convenient corner table with a good view of all the other diners, twenty in all. I ordered a ham and mushroom omelette, brought to me by a cheery waitress who had a strip of white plastic pinned over her left boob and it said 'Brenda'. I decided not to ask her what the other one was called.

I didn't have to wait very long before I saw something worthy of a quick note on my pad, and I must admit this is something that has happened to me more than once. He was lifting up a wedge of potato to his mouth, it was almost there when it fell from the fork and landed with a little splash in the gravy, leaving a nice brown stain on his cream shirt. His wife, so obviously his wife because only a wife could give a man looks like that, was not ecstatic.

Brenda reappeared. I didn't tell her that I'd christened her other one Sylvia.

'I enjoyed the omelette. Thank you.'

'It's a pleasure. Would you like coffee?'

I was so glad she'd asked me that question because I remembered Eric's, 'What other colours have you got?'

She smiled. 'Black or white?'

'Yes please.'

She laughed. She didn't have to. I was going to leave a tip anyway.

I liked Brenda. She was very polite, always cheerful and she had the biggest and brownest eyes I had ever seen – like two tins of treacle with the lids off. What I liked even more about her was that when she placed my coffee on the table she didn't say, 'There you go.'

Over the next couple of days I noted a lady, obviously a very busy lady. She came smartly in and said to my friend Bren, 'I've only got a couple of minutes, so I thought I'd just nip in and grab a coffee.' This I had to see, someone who was going to grab coffee. How do you do that without spilling it? She didn't grab it: she sipped it rather daintily.

There was the man who ate with his mouth open. It was like looking through the porthole of washing machine on slow spin.

Another male diner, and it seemed it was always the men who needed to improve on their table manners. This man was a 'Phoopher' – he blew on his food. What a terrible habit!

I watched fascinated as he blew twice on every mouthful. 'Phoo! Phoo!'

I couldn't understand, as he blew twice, one every mouthful. 'Phoo! Phoo!'

I was puzzled because he was eating salad.

Believe me, I'm not having a go at any of these good people – far from it. The truth is, without them I'd have to get the proper job I was advised to get very many years ago.

Tea TV Centre

As I sit here having a ponder and half a Kit Kat, I can't help thinking that if I wrote down every single detail of my fourteen years with Morecombe and Wise, you might need help in lifting the book down from the shelf. So I'll trim it down slightly.

I was with Ern in the tea area outside Studio 8. This was just minutes before rehearsing the 'Health Food Shop' sketch with that gifted character actor, Frank Williams, famous as the vicar in *Dad's Army*. We were discussing the merits of health foods and how they were allegedly helpful for a wide range of ailments. Ern asked, 'I know you don't drink, so what helps you relax?'

'Delius.' Which was quite true: I loved his music; it did help me unwind.

He looked thoughtful when I said this, and as long as I live I shall never forget what he said next; it was pure Ernie Wise.

'Is that powder or liquid?'

There's a warm smile every time I recall that line. I could never have written it.

In the sketch Ern returned from doing the shopping. Eric wasn't too happy when he saw what was in the shopping bags – Ern had been to the health food shop. Eric took a packet of cereal from the bag and looked at it suspiciously:

Eric. What's this muck?

Ern. That's not muck. That's good healthy food that is –
muesli.

Eric. Muesli? What's muesli? [*Reads aloud from the
packet*] May contain sawdust?

Ern. It doesn't say that. Good food that is. From now on
it's healthy eating!

Eric. I'm all for that. Sausage, egg, bacon, black pudding
and fried bread.

Ern. That's not healthy eating!

Eric. It is if you leave the window open. You can't get
healthier than that, sunbeam.

Ern. You can please yourself. From now on I'm going to
keep myself in good trim.

Eric. You sound like a wick.

Ern wasn't a fitness fanatic but he did look after himself. He
didn't smoke, drank little, was an excellent swimmer, played a
lot of tennis and was a very good cricketer. Eric joked that Ern
was a natural-born cricketer, as he had two short legs. He also
said his partner was a very good weightlifter and got a lot of
practice using his wallet.

*

I've been working on that idea I had (in fact it's coming along
better than I expected), the one about the boy who wants to be
a wizard. It does have possibilities and I might use it for my
next book. At the moment I'm having a slight problem trying to
think of a name for the boy, a name readers will remember. I
had thought of Tommy Watson but I don't think that's quite
right. Anyway, I'll see how it goes. It's just that sometimes an
idea like this can be a nice little earner. I just thought I'd bring
you up to speed (let you know what's happening).

Reading a brand new comedy routine is like trying on a new suit: more often than not it doesn't fit and has to be altered. Over the many going-for-laughter years I've had quite a number of comedy routines I've had to take back and alter because they didn't fit.

Usually I could tell by their faces if it was going to be an alteration job. They'd both have a look that said, 'It's a bit tight under the arms. Can you do something about it?' It was good that they did complain when it didn't feel right – alterations made a difference.

From memory, the badly fitting comedy suit, the one that caused me more frustration than anything I have ever written, was a sketch about a tea planter in some Eastern country. It was a nightmare.

June Whitfield was the guest in November 1974, and comedy actresses don't come any better than this gifted lady. When I'd finished writing the sketch I knew it wasn't right (unusual for me as I'm one of my biggest fans), but I had to hold both hands up and admit it was rather short of merriment.

Had I needed confirmation I only had to look at the expressions on the faces of Eric and Ern when they read it for the first time: they could have been sitting on broken glass.

They both said, 'It's not right.'

I said, 'It's dire.'

John said, 'It needs alteration.'

Six attempts before I got that suit to fit. I wasn't present for the recording of that show – my mum sent a note to say I had a bad cough.

Occasionally the suit fitted to perfection first time of reading. When this happened we all knew we had something special.

This happened when I told them about an idea I had, not even written at that stage, and I'd called it 'The Connoisseurs'.

I explained to them, 'There are connoisseurs of wine and works of art – suppose you were both connoisseurs of chips? You only have to look at a chip, sniff it, nibble it slightly and immediately you know where the fish and chip shop is, you know the name of the chipster. . .'

'Great.' Eric was on to this idea with some enthusiasm: 'We've got to do that. We could even have a little sniff of the vinegar and tell them what year it was bottled.' Ern was equally keen. It wasn't very often that he came up with a line, but he did on this occasion: 'We could also tell just by feeling the chips that they were made from King Edwards.' Eric was on his feet and rubbing his hands: 'Knockout idea. We'd know that the fish and chip shop was in Tarryasson Street and served by Ada Bailey.' Ern was inspired: 'The south side of Tarryasson Street; makes it sound more like a vineyard.'

Between them they'd just about written the sketch before I'd left the room to enquire about redundancy payment.

This underlines the problem I've got with my fantasy show: there isn't anyone with sufficient experience or comedy knowledge to be able to say to me, 'This doesn't fit right – it's a bit short of merriment. I think you had better take it away and make a few alterations.'

I don't think I could trust myself to do that. I'd be inclined to give me an easy ride. How about if *you* did it? I mean, you're reading this, so you're in a good position to say, 'This is not funny. Take it back and make a few alterations.' I have a great deal of experience in the comedy world, and if you say it's lacking in merriment that's good enough for me. I accept and respect that. Not that it will make the slightest difference, because as you're reading this I'll be cruising in my luxury yacht off a sun-drenched-and-draped-in-palm-trees exotic Caribbean island where I've just bought a luxury villa with the royalties I've made from this book – so you can say what you like.

It's also possible I might be stacking trolleys at the Spar supermarket in Pwllheli.

I rather like hearing nice things being said about myself – don't we all? But it really does pain when a piece of comedy I've worked so hard and lovingly on gets binned as rubbish. You know, I take it into a meeting and nobody likes it at all. I imagine it's the sort of feeling you would get if somebody looked at your new baby and said, 'Eagh! Isn't he ugly!'

My Fantasy

Smitten, really taken with the idea of a make-believe Morecambe and Wise show, and I don't want anyone to be able to say, 'Eagh! Isn't he ugly!' I can have anyone I like on this fantasy show, any star in the whole wide world. It will last for at least six hours – have to, as it's the only way I'll be able to fit all my favourites in. I'm like a little boy in a sweet shop.

Can I have, er . . . can I have, erm . . . John Wayne? Of course I can have John Wayne; it's my fantasy. John wouldn't have to do much, just walk on the way that only John Wayne can. He'll just amble on and say, 'The Hell I will.' Then ride off into the Shepherd's Bush sunset.

Now I'm buying British and Ken Dodd's on next – I'm enjoying this. Ken Dodd comes on and all the audience have got sticks and I shout, 'Charge!!' Now they can get their own back for all the last buses and trains he's caused them to miss. Maybe some have had their horses clamped. Doddy! You've taken up two of my six hours! Gerroff! It's time for the Nicholas Brothers! Just look at those two gentlemen dance: 'Rat-a-tap-a-rat-a-tap-rat-a-tap-a . . .' Wow! Their legs are just a blur. Sensational! Now I've got a problem with the running order. I can't put the Lannons' 'Mum and Dad' on after the Nicholas Brothers. Mum and Dad do a clog dance and they couldn't follow those two gentlemen; they can play their accordions. They'll be a sensation and finish up on the Royal Variety Show, no more than they deserve. It would be my affectionate nod of appreciation to all those performers who never topped the bill in the variety theatres but gave me so much pleasure. They were many and varied: the jugglers, the plate-spinners, the magicians, the man on the one-wheel bike, the tightrope walker, the contortionists, the acrobats, the ventriloquists, the little fat man who played the xylophone. Just a moment – I haven't got a singer. I've got to have a singer in my fantasy show. The trouble is, there are so many really good singers to choose from. Who shall I go for?

Ern. Des O'Connor.
Eric. You mean they still haven't found a cure?
Ern. He opened in his one-man show last night.
Eric. There were three of them in the show but only one man in the audience. Outside the theatre twenty-pound tickets were changing hands for one pound fifty. The seats nearest to the exits were the first to go.
Ern. Does he sing in the show?
Eric. Oh yes, but there is a health warning inside the programme.

The very least I can do is give the singing spot to Des, after all the taunts and jibes and ridicule he's had to endure over the years.

A flat sketch; I've got to have a flat sketch – always my favourite spot in the show. This one starts off with Ern on the phone to his publisher. This is fun!

Ern. Yes, I know that you have a deadline for publication. You must appreciate that I didn't start writing the book until after lunch and it won't be finished for at least another three quarters of an hour . . . Pardon? . . . The trilogy? I've got another four to do. Goodbye.

Eric. Was that someone important or was it the director general of the BBC?

Ern. It was my publisher.

Eric. Publisher? That man is a joke! He's only ever published one book and that was a first aid manual – and it was withdrawn.

Ern. That first aid manual is a standard work.

Eric. Standard work? 'What to do if you break your leg: hop.' That was a lot of help.

Ern. He's a proper publisher he is.

Eric. Rubbish.

Ern. He publishes Thomas Hardy.

Eric. *Tess of the D'Urbervilles?*

Ern. No, Thomas Hardy. Thomas Hardy sent him a fax this afternoon.

Eric. I didn't realise he was that good. What did he want?

Ern. He's keen to publish the book what I wrote.

Eric. The one that you wrote coming up in the lift?

Ern. We are on the fourth floor.

Eric. What's the book about?

Ern. It's a romantic love story. It tells of a woman who falls in love with a naval architect.

Eric. He makes the belly buttons for teddy bears.

Ern. No. They meet while they're on a skiing holiday. He takes her in his arms and murmurs, 'I never expected to meet such a beautiful woman here in Felixstowe.'

Eric. In Felixstowe?

Ern. Yes.

Eric. On a skiing holiday?

Ern. What's wrong with that?

Eric. Well, if they're waiting for the snow to cover the mountain slopes in Felixstowe, they'll have plenty of time for a touch of the 'Hello folks and how about the holidaymakers?'

Ern. How dare you imply that my work is untoward!

Eric. It's not like you. That's torrid that is.

Ern. I don't write torrid!

Eric. He's taken her in his arms. The next thing you know he'll be touching her bare elbows.

Ern. There won't be any unnecessary fumbling and grappling in my play.

Eric. I should hope not. They don't like that kind of thing before the watershed. Come to think of it, they won't be all that keen on it in Maidenhead.

Ern. As a writer I do fully appreciate that I have a responsibility to my public.

Eric. Is he still working at Chester Zoo?

Ern. I've no idea.

Eric. I thought you would have known. He always sends you a Christmas card and a piece of fruitcake, in a little cardboard box with mistletoe on it: 'To Ern. Merry Christmas from Cyril.' He never forgets you.

Ern. All I know is that I don't write naughties. There's no place in any of my work for S–E–C–K–S.

Eric. It's not in your nature. You are and always have been a man of substance, a man of integrity and great wisdom.

Ern. I have standards.

Eric. You finish writing your book. The last book you wrote was very heavy; I could hardly lift it.

Ern. I used a lot of long words.

Eric. That explains it. How many more chapters have you got to write?

Ern. Seventeen.

Eric. It's only eight o'clock. If you're in a hurry you could take the lift.

Ern. I'll finish it in my own time, if I'm not interrupted.

Eric. You won't be. If Thomas Hardy rings I'll tell him you're busy.

Ern. Good. Is there one or two e's in skiing?

Eric. I'll make a cup of tea, Ern.

I don't think I would have had a problem with that comedy suit: it would have fitted first time.

Yes I am getting carried away by all this, and it must seem like a childish dream, but childish dreams aren't just for children. I have them all the time.

There's got to be a place in this show for Wilson, Kepel and Betty, had they still been performing when we were doing our shows they would have appeared more than once. Eric and Ern loved them. Remember the sand dance with Glenda Jackson in 'Antony and Cleopatra?' Jerry Lewis told me he liked Wilson, Kepel and Betty. He seems to have a liking for all things Egyptian. 'I like that big guy; he wears a fez and keeps getting all his tricks wrong.' We know who you mean, Jerry. A word of advice – don't try to follow him. I first saw the original sand dancers, Wilson, Kepel and Betty when they were appearing at the Palace Theatre in Manchester. Uncle Billy Matchett was on the same bill and he told a very true and very funny story about this glorious act.

They had been booked to play a season in Las Vegas, not far from America. It was their first ever visit to this internationally famous resort and it was the early 1950s. It was a dream-come-true booking. Being the meticulous performers they were, they left nothing to chance. When they were appearing at the Palace Theatre Uncle Billy told me that they always arrived at least an hour before curtain up and made totally certain that their costumes were pressed and laid out, and that their props were ready and in good working order.

When the time came for their departure to Las Vegas nothing was overlooked, nothing left to chance. Fastidious as ever they even took their own sand. They took a small sack of sand to Las Vegas! Can you imagine how the American customs official must have reacted to that. I don't think he would have seen the funny side: American customs officials aren't noted for having a sense of humour. I once did a joke at the airport in Florida when a customs officer asked me, 'Have you anything to declare?' I replied, rather wittily I thought, 'Snow White's Lee Marvin's mother.' From the look on his face you would have thought I had just removed the pin from a hand grenade.

Florida was made for me, the most glorious and fun-filled two weeks I can ever remember. We went with our daughter Clare in 1993 and I remember this advice from Eric before I left: 'Whatever you do, don't go to Disneyworld.' When I asked him why not he replied, 'They might not let you out.'

We got a nasty shock on the first night at our Florida Hotel. I opened the door of our ground-floor room and there, just yards away on the lawn, was an alligator. It wasn't a Walt Disney alligator, it was a bite yer leg off real one. I rang reception to inform them about this unexpected and unwanted visitor and complained as only the British can when there's something serious to complain about. 'Hello. I'm awfully sorry to be a nuisance. I wonder if you can help me. There's an alligator outside our front door.'

I have to say that Americans aren't the fastest-thinking creatures on two legs, and they don't improve the further south you go. By the time you get to Florida you could have problems with communication.

'Alligator, sir?'

This was the girl at reception who was answering my gentle plea for help.

'Yes, an alligator.'

'Right. Just one moment, sir.'

There was a long pause while hopefully she sought out the alligator ranger who was going to rescue us. Skippy would have rescued us.

'Sir. Keep your door closed and don't go outside.'

'We had considered that. There's not much chance of it coming in here, not at these prices.'

The following year we played it safe and went to Scarborough.

That really was a very pleasant holiday. When it rained, it didn't rain continuously, I remember that it did stop for twenty minutes on the Thursday. When it did rain there was always the Spa Pavilion, where you could listen to the music of Max Jaffa and the Palm Court Orchestra. We walked in the rain.

My most treasured memory of Scarborough will always be of the happy British holidaymakers sitting in deckchairs in fog so thick you couldn't see the end of your stick of rock.

I did go into the Spa Pavilion and listened to the music of Max Jaffa, just a couple of segments. From which came this:

'Doctor, will my son be able to play the violin again?'

'Yes. We've just grafted on another chin.'

I'd fallen in love with Whitby, home of that great sailor, navigator and supreme adventurer, Captain James Cook. In February of 1770 he steered his ship, HMS *Endeavour*, along the western coast of Australia, where he spotted Rolf Harris, and Captain James Cook did a very nifty three-point turn for Portsmouth.

Home, James, and don't spare the mainsail.

We enjoyed Scarborough so much that we went back the following year.

In moments of blissful nostalgia I play my autographed Max Jaffa CD.

*

It's Ammonds for the comedy and Maxin for the musical number in my dream show, although this would be a wonderful opportunity to get my own back on John for an incident that happened many years ago when he was a radio producer at the BBC, Manchester. I've never spoken of this to John: if he's reading this, then he's finding out for the first time.

It must have been in the early sixties. Not yet a full-time writer, I was trying for a comedy foothold and John was producing a radio series for North Country comedian Ken Platt: 'I'll not take my coat off; I'm not stoppin.' This was a time when a comedian felt semi-naked without a catchphrase. Ken Platt didn't stop for me, because John read the script I'd sent him, and in a very courteous way John wrote to me telling me to get lost. Not the first to tell me to do that.

Then there were the comedians I sent material to: they either didn't reply, despite the s.a.e., or wrote to say, 'We don't accept outside material.' In many cases this did not stop them from using some of my jokes, which was, to put it mildly, rather annoying. This was at a time when I needed all the help I could get (not much of it about), which is why I'm rather pleased to relate this little happening in about 1970 or 1971.

'Excuse me,' she said as I was walking along Eaton Road, not far from my West Derby home in Liverpool. It was rather pleasant being accosted by this lady. She was elderly, very good looking, make-up applied to perfection and was a snappy dresser.

'Are you Eddie Braben?'

'Most of the time.' That wasn't an ad-lib, just a stock answer to that question to make whoever was asking think, 'Wow! He's quick.'

'I hope you don't mind me stopping you in the street like this. My daughter wants to be a comedy writer.'

'Good. We need all the laughs we can get. How can I help?'

'Could you spare just half an hour to give her some advice?'

'Glad to.'

'Are you still living in Honeysgreen Lane?'

'Yes. Number 45. How about tomorrow, three o'clock?'

'Thank you very much.'

The following afternoon her daughter did come to see me. Young, slim, blonde and totally scatty. She really did sweep into our living room. She was barefoot, wearing a kaftan and had probably just come from hugging an oak tree that was about to be demolished, or she might even have been trying to sabotage the Knotty Ash hunt. She was certainly different, a one-off, not your typical housewife. We talked about comedy, she asked a lot of questions and I did my best to give her a lot of answers. Carla Lane thanked me and went off home to write *The Liver Birds* with Myra Taylor. Carla went on to even greater success with her massively popular TV series set in Liverpool, *Bread*.

Today, if I walk down the lane from our home and look out across Cardigan Bay, I can see St Tudwal's Island. Carla bought it some ten years ago, not to use as a place to live or as a holiday retreat – she bought it to safeguard the residents, rare species of sheep and goats and assorted cattle.

Maybe, perhaps, who knows? If it hadn't been for me that afternoon there might not have been a *Liver Birds* and we might not have had any *Bread*. I also like to think I might even have helped to save that very rare bird, the St Tudwal's seagull. It's got three legs and a wheel. Good for you, Carla. A fine lady of comedy and committed animal lover.

Sometimes young writers trying to get a start in this business can be a nuisance, a real pain, despite the sympathy and understanding I have for them. Not so long ago I was getting letters almost every day asking for help and advice, people even asking to come and see me. Not a chance. The material was quite dull and there wasn't a laugh in it. Eventually I did write and tell him, as gently as possible, he was wasting his time. Can't remember his name, J.K. Somebody.

*

'He didn't do much, did he?

'Who didn't do much?'

'The little one. The tall one with the glasses, he was a hoot.'

'The little one wasn't?'

'Not really. No. I mean, I'm laughing now just thinking about the tall one with the glasses. He'd just have to stand there, not say a word and you'd start laughing.'

'Not say a word? God I hope not. I've got a wife and three children. It could be four, I haven't been home since this morning.'

'I mean, the tall one with the glasses, he was a hoot. He could make you laugh if he just read the telephone directory.'

'I'm not sure about that. Perhaps by the time he got to, T. Ellis and Sons, Bakers and Confectioners, you might be reaching for the "off" button.'

'But the little one, he never really did much.'

'I've had conversations similar to that more than once over the years and it is all so very unfair because he was a gifted performer. But the little one always did get overlooked, and not just because of his size. The truth is, we remember more the man who made us laugh than the man who set up the laugh in the first place.

No books written about the little one without the glasses. Now then, perhaps I should write a book about him? Yes, I'd call it *Life after Snow White*. He'd like the title. There isn't a statue of him in his hometown with a plaque at the base inscribed to the one without the glasses – little Ern. He'd be seen in a suitable pose, pen in one hand and his wallet in the other.

255

There was a line I wrote for Eric in a routine where Ern had to go off for about ten seconds to fetch a prop. As he was leaving, Eric called after him, 'Don't be too long: I get a cold draught all down one side.'

Little did I realise how much truth there was in that line; it said so much about the closeness of their relationship. 'Don't be too long: I get a cold draught all down one side.'

Commenting later on that line, as we did with almost every line that had been done in a show, Eric said he was aware there was a space, an uncomfortable emptiness when Ern wasn't there. 'I'm fine. I'm OK for about two minutes. After that it doesn't feel right.' I knew exactly what he meant; I'd watched them very closely over many years. There was nobody to turn to for reaction or, more importantly, for reassurance if things weren't going well. Perhaps a line I'd written didn't get the expected laugh. I could almost see them mentally holding one another up.

Offstage they could manage without each other, as they had family and various interests to occupy their valuable leisure time. In the studio, the rehearsal room or the variety theatre that was very different. The following has happened when I've gone in to Eric's room.

'Have you seen Ernie?'

'He's in the gallery talking to the soundman. Do you want him?'

'No, no. Nothing important.'

This has happened in Ern's room.

'Is Eric around?'

'He's at the tea machine. Did you want him?'

'No. I'll talk to him later.'

Each one looking for the other half of himself. It got to the stage where I felt reassured when I saw them together. If I was going up to the BBC Club with Eric he'd bang on Ern's dressing-room door.

'Ern.'

'Hello!'

'I'm just going for a sandwich with Eddie.'

'Right!'

They were welded together.

'Don't be too long: I get a cold draught all down one side.'

Top that, Sunshine . . .
And I'm Still Trying To

There was a harsh 'Chack-chack-chack' coming from the field next to our bungalow. The fieldfares had arrived. Thirty or forty of them swooped low over the bramble hedge and settled before moving across the field, almost like sheep grazing for breakfast. It was a competition between Eric and me as to who would see the fieldfares and the redwings first. He won every year because he cheated: if I said I'd seen them on the nineteenth he'd seen them on the sixteenth and I had to buy the tea.

I'm watching the fieldfares now and remembering how he said he'd seen them and that meant time to record the Christmas show. I must confess I do miss the tingle of excitement that was part of that time of year, and the stress and the anxiety.

No doubt there will be repeats that I shall watch and think, as I always do, 'Did that really happen? Was I really a part of all that?'

How then could I have been so closely involved and not have appreciated it?'

Possibly because I was too close.

Anyway, I'm cheered by the fact that I can still dream, which is what I'm doing with 'The Barber's Shop' sketch.

Ern is the barber. He is looking rather forlorn as he looks

upon his empty shop. His face lights up with a welcoming smile when Eric enters:

Ern. Good morning, sir.
Eric. If you've got a rush on I could call back.
Ern. That won't be necessary, sir.
Eric. Would you like me to make an appointment for next week?
Ern. I can fit you in now, sir.

I am now reasonably aware of what would and wouldn't work for them and I know they would have paused at this point and Eric would have said, 'I like that "Got a rush on – make an appointment" line. It flowed well. We've done it before and we know it works.'

He'd be letting me know I had written that line in the past in a different sketch. Had it been ten years before, one of them would have remembered it. They wouldn't let me get away with anything.

Ern. How would you like your hair, sir?
Eric. Not too much off the top.
Ern. That shouldn't be too difficult.
Eric. Pardon?
Ern. I was about to say that I haven't seen you in here before, sir.
Eric. When was that?
Ern. About a month ago.
Eric. Yes, I think it must have been about a month ago when I wasn't here last.
Ern. I thought so: I never forget a face. Are you from these parts, sir?
Eric. No. I live locally.
　　　　They both pause and look rather puzzled after
　　　　that little exchange. A 'What was all that about'
　　　　look . . .

Eric. I need to look my best tonight; I'm taking my wife out to dinner, our wedding anniversary.

Ern. Congratulations, sir.

Eric. Received a very nice telegram from the British Boxing Board of Control. Twenty years to the day, married at All Souls, next to the shoe factory.

Ern. Twenty years is a long time, sir.

Eric. Forty years is twice as long.

Ern. Little ones?

Eric. It's not her fault.

Ern. How long have you been living in these parts, sir?

Eric. All day. I've just bought a home here.

Ern. Of modern design, sir?

Eric. Walk-in bathroom.

Ern. The 'in thing' now, sir. All done, sir. Would you care to have an appointment for your next visit?

Eric. In case you're not here?

Ern. Exactly.

> *Both look very puzzled into camera*

Ern would have reservations about that sketch. I just know he would. Always practical, always looking for the tripwire. Eric would be all for doing it because of the one-liners. Not so, Ern.

'I'll tell you why I don't think it'll work.'

'Why won't it work, Ern? Tell me now before I kick the legs from under you.'

'In the first place it would look phoney because I'm not a barber and I wouldn't know how to "act" cutting hair. Also . . .'

I'd now have my head in my hands. 'He's got an "also".'

'Also, if someone's having a haircut you've got to see hair being cut.'

So practical and so true that I wouldn't be able to offer a defence. But wait! I'd found a way around all of his objections.

We could do it! On good old radio! It would work better on that medium of the imagination – just get the FX man to do the scissors snipping away and you could watch as much or as little hair as you liked falling to the floor. Ern wouldn't have to pretend to be cutting Eric's hair: all he'd have to do was hold and read the script. Wonderful radio.

Eric enjoyed radio. He said he liked it because he didn't have to get shaved or wear a tie. They both had very good 'radio voices'. Eric's delivery on radio reminded me so much of Tommy Handley, Ted Ray and Bob Hope.

Sally Army Saturday

Christmas 1987, I was standing outside Woolworth's in Liverpool Church Street holding a plastic bucket, collecting for the Salvation Army. It was Saturday morning and the street in the city centre was a river of shoppers, a heaving mass of jocular humanity, and how they gave! It seems that everyone, regardless of religious beliefs, has a warm spot for the Salvation Army, more so at Christmas. 'God bless you, lad.' This was a very old gent as he dropped ten pence into my bucket. 'I'll never forget the Salvation Army. Always there with a cuppa.' From his age he must have been talking about the First World War and I felt like a cheat for accepting his praise, for 'always being there with a cuppa'. I wasn't even born then. The city council had granted us two hours, a prime two hours at the best collection point in the city. There were other charitable organisations, almost in a queue to take over from us, each allocated two hours. My plastic bucket had been generously filled, then emptied more than once, and my arm ached beautifully. At the end of my two hours Major Ray Ebdon, boss man of the Walton Corps of the Sally Army, looked very pleased as he told me the total. 'Well over two hundred pounds.' Two hundred pounds in small change in one bucket, in two hours. There were three other buckets on duty that morning as well as mine and it was a wonderful experience. Ray Ebdon hadn't finished with me just yet. 'How would you like to be our Father Christmas next week?'

Seven days later Father Christmas arrived at the Walton Citadel after touring the surrounding streets in an open-top Citroën, and how I loved every minute of it. Mums out shopping were holding their children up: 'Wave to Father Christmas.' This was special!

I arrived at the hall to more cheering children. Ray showed me to my Winter Wonderland Grotto and I spent the afternoon shaking tiny hands and handing out presents. After a wash and a change back to my usual clothing I was enjoying a cup of coffee with Ray and his wife, Joyce, when a small boy, still clutching the crayons and crayoning book I had given him earlier, said, 'You're not the real Father Christmas.' The cheek of the brat! I thought I was very convincing in my Santa outfit and my much practised 'Ho-Ho-Ho!'

'I didn't say I was the real Father Christmas.'

'You pretended you were.'

'What makes you think that it was me?'

'Because you've got the same ring on your finger and the same shoes.'

That boy is now head of Interpol, the FBI and Scotland Yard Special Branch.

We're not an overreligious family, although I always say grace before meals, and it's always the same prayer of gratitude: 'For what we are about to receive, oh Lord, we thank thee for making the manager of Tesco look the other way!'

When I told Ray Ebdon this he laughed and even included it in one of his sermons, which were always fun and mercifully short.

That's what we liked about the Sally Army: it made religion a three-letter word, f – u – n. Its songs were lively and happy, and they were sung by jolly people with smiley, shiny faces. Its band was always cheerful, a 'Rumpty-Tumpty-Rumpty' band. Some

Sunday mornings I'd march with them. 'You're worse than a child,' said she who sleeps on my right-hand side. That was true. I enjoyed marching with them even though I couldn't play an instrument. I did try playing the tambourine but it hurt my mouth. It was just a privilege to be part of that joyful organisation. How very pleasant to be with people who only want to give. Treasured memories of one of the most gratifying times in my life.

Recalling that episode has put me in such a happy mood that I need to play some jolly music before I write the next bit.

Ten minutes later. The jolly music was Charles Penrose singing, 'The Laughing Policeman'. It made me laugh when I was in my first childhood and it brings a smile even now.

The following year, 1987, following a visit to Alder Hey Children's Hospital, just five hundred yards from my home, I decided I wanted to try to raise some much-needed funds for the leukaemia ward. I was offered, free of charge, a stall at the weekend antiques fair that was being held at the much-visited Albert Dock – couldn't be better. The Albert Dock got thousand of visitors every Saturday and Sunday, I couldn't help but make a lot of money for the cause. My biggest problem was finding something that would sell, something different. After a lot of thought I decided to frame part of my cigarette card collection and picked out what I thought were the most colourful and most interesting sets. The cards were framed beautifully for me and at cost price by a highly skilled frame maker, Alan Roberts.

Alan, a tall, friendly man, always wore a gentle smile and a John Lennon hat. He had a unit at the Brunswick Dock and we became good friends. Alan lived in the same Dingle area where I had misspent my childhood and he was a very interesting character.

At that time, he was supplementing his income as a club

entertainer and also as an extra in *Coronation Street*. I very often saw Alan sipping a pint in the Rovers Return.

Alan also framed for me some very old reproduction tobacco advertisement posters and they really were attractive. He liked them so much that he bought one from me, took it with him to Granada and that poster can still be seen to this day hanging on the wall of the bar in the Rovers. It's an advertisement for Bulwark's Tobacco, and shows an old sea dog, wearing oil-skins and a sou'wester. The TV company made a contribution to the cause. I was actually watching an episode one night, when a customer in the bar accidentally knocked the frame with his elbow and I went, 'Ooh!'

First Saturday at the antiques fair and the whole family helped me set up the stall and it's thirty-odd framed sets. We were ready for business, but sadly there wasn't any business. It was heartbreaking. It had taken weeks to set up and the public just weren't interested in my framed cigarette cards. Lots of 'Oh, I used to collect them when I was a child,' but nobody wanted to buy them now that they were adults. From memory I sold two frames that day and went home sadly with twenty-eight pounds. It was painfully obvious that framed cigarette cards were not popular, the price didn't help. Ten pounds for the cheapest frame was asking a lot and I should have realized at the outset that nobody coming for an afternoon out with the family was looking to part with a tenner on a luxury item. So, what could I tempt them with? There had to be something they were interested in and would be happy to buy at an affordable price. What were they interested in? When the answer finally came I was annoyed with myself for not thinking of it in the first place – football. Here I was in the heart of a soccer-crazy city and if I could find footballing items and memorabilia at a reasonable price, then I should do a lot better than twenty-eight pounds.

Liverpool and Everton Football Clubs could not have been

more helpful when I told them of the charity I was collecting for. At Anfield, Ken Addison, the charming man in charge of marketing, supplied me with colour photos of the players, all autographed. He also let me have over two hundred coloured posters showing famous Liverpool players past and present. Prominent was a great action shot of one of the most exciting footballers I have ever seen, Billy Liddell. I'd known Bill for a number of years and when I asked him if he'd come down to the Albert Dock the following Sunday he agreed without hesitation. It gave the day a great boost when the *Liverpool Echo* ran a story on the charity, adding that Billy would be autographing photos – that did it. The following Sunday afternoon the antiques fair, held in a shed that was a former dockside warehouse, had never seen so many people. There came a great multitude of fathers who were saying to their sons, 'That's him! That's the great Billy Liddell. Get him to sign your poster. Good lad, Billy!' One very excited customer said, 'Remember me, Billy?'

Billy didn't remember him; the fan reminded him.

'I was standing on the Kop and I threw the ball to you when you went to take a corner.'

There were twenty thousand standing on the Kop that Saturday and every other Saturday when they were playing at home.

At the end of a momentous day Bill's arm was aching and I was overjoyed because we'd taken two hundred a fifty pounds.

An elderly Everton fan asked me if I had any cards at all of Dixie Dean, Everton's brilliant sixty-goals-in-one-season centre forward.

I took a Dixie card from a set, had that one card framed in blue and gold and he gave me seventy pounds for the charity. In all we managed to raise just on two and a half thousand pounds.

In my early teens Billy was my soccer hero, I'd cut dozens of action photos of him from the sports pages and they were plastered all over my bedroom wall. And at one time I even tried parting my hair in the middle the way he did. That was when my mother said to me, 'You and your Billy "bloody" Liddell. Tell him to get a clean shift and I'll keep him!'

Twenty years later he became a very dear friend and his wife, Phyllis, godmother to our daughter Clare.

Blank Screen

*I plant words on paper in the hope that they will
blossom into laughter*
(William Shakespeare, *Parkinson*, BBC, 1612)

All I could see before me were blank sheets of paper,
glaring, dazzling sheets of foolscap defying me to place
a word on them, daring me to put a word on to the virgin
parchment, and I couldn't. All the meaningful words, all the
funny phrases and the brilliant one-liners, all the clever ideas
had migrated to a place where I couldn't find them. This was
desperate and probably the most bereft-of-ideas time I could
remember – it really was like chipping granite with a spoon, a
rubber spoon. My brain felt like a dumpling.

Even the TV screen I'd drawn on the wall in front of me
wasn't working, and it had been so very useful to me at other
barren times.

No tiny figures pranced to inspire me. This fun famine
couldn't have happened at a worse time (they never happen
at a good time), but this was made more head banging because
the script for the next show had to be with John Ammonds in
seven days and I hadn't progressed beyond 'Good evening
ladies and gentlemen. Welcome to the show.'

I remember Bob Monkhouse telling me that many years
ago when he was doing something like four or five shows a
week, and was close to exhaustion, he found a way out by
'fainting' during a TV show. Des O'Conner 'fainted' when he
was facing a hostile audience at the Glasgow Empire. I was

facing hostile blank papers and fainting wasn't going to do me much good.

I did think about ringing the Samaritans, but they're not much good at writing jokes. It was in despair that I rang Eric at home to explain the problem I was having, something I had never done before. I told him that nothing was happening, with only a week to the deadline – a complete comedy blank. He said, 'Where are you speaking from?'

Now I don't know why I said it, because I wasn't feeling particularly jolly – I said, 'A hole under my nose.'

He laughed, but really laughed. It was a high-pitched laugh that ended with, 'Dearie me; that was a belter! Did you just think of that now? And you're trying to tell me you've dried up? That'll be the day.'

That was it, that was the spark that lit the blue touchpaper. The show was on John's desk seven days later.

That was in 1970, a year of surprising contrasts in guest stars, and the script arrived on time for guest, Richard Greene. A familiar British actor before he went to Hollywood because his face was seen on posters and in magazines advertising Brylcreem. I was looking forward to meeting him because I remembered seeing him in *The Hound of the Baskervilles* and Basil Rathbone was Sherlock Holmes. Richard did a lot of swashbuckling in Hollywood before returning to Great Britain, which is just outside Runcorn, and he is probably best remembered as TV's Robin Hood. It was these areas of his career I wanted to ask him about, but he wasn't very forthcoming; didn't have much sense of fun either. In the sketch with Eric and Ern, Richard played the part of an international air-racing pilot, Miles Behind. Now I know I'm always biased in my favour but I thought that was funny; I do like silly names. Incidentally, I've got a 'Dr Piecrust' who will feature in an epic yet to be written. Eric and Ern also though Miles Behind was a funny name for a racing pilot and laughed whenever it cropped up in the sketch. Not so Richard.

I can remember the phone ringing at the rehearsal room and Eric saying, 'That'll be Maid Marion – you've left your tights on the bedside table.' We all laughed, but not a flicker from Richard.

After that I had it written into my contract that I wouldn't have to write for big daft outlaws who didn't have a sense of humour, and specially those who used Brylcreem. Then came the surprising contrast in guests when John Ammonds called me at home.

'Robin Day.'

'John, you're kidding me.'

'No, honestly. Robin's the guest on the next show.'

When I heard this news I had a thought that John, Eric and Ern had made a mistake in getting Robin Day. My first thoughts were of a tough, hard-talking, unrelenting TV journalist, the very last person I would have thought of as a guest in a comedy show. I was very wrong. Robin Day was a joy, a sheer delight, a full-of-fun gentleman with a secret ambition to be a song-and-dance man. Of all the guests in all the shows I was ever involved in I can't remember anyone who enjoyed the experience more than Robin Day. He happily accepted every indignity, and they were many. He even had a vase broken over his head and relished every minute. Some guests were like excited schoolchildren when they came on the show; you could see how delighted they were just by looking at their faces. There was a permanent smile, a sparkle in the eyes and an eagerness to take part that I hadn't seen on other shows I had worked on. Yes, an excited schoolboy: that's how I remember Robin. Could always tell when a guest was really enthusiastic when he, or she, said, 'Wouldn't it be funnier if I said . . .' or 'Wouldn't it be better if I did . . .' It rarely was, but I was never annoyed at their suggestions, because it showed how keen they were.

I didn't meet Robin again until July of 1999 at the unveiling of Eric's statue at Morecambe when we were sharing the same hotel with Joan and her family and also the splendid Frank Finlay, who wore a magnificent 'actor's hat'. I've always wished I had the nerve to wear one. Frank enjoyed his appearance on the show, even though he admits he had never before felt so nervous as when he was doing the front of curtains dialogue with Eric and Ern. I'm told that very quietly he whispered to Eric, 'Get me off.' Never easy for proper actors.

I was at the reception desk in the hotel asking for directions to the nearest bookshop when Robin came over and wanted to know which book I was looking for. He said, 'I'm only interested because I'm a writer like what you are.'

When I told him I was looking for a copy of his book *Speaking for Myself* he bowed his head and said, 'I'm extremely flattered.' Fifteen minutes later there was a knock at our door and there was Robin offering me a copy of his book: 'I've written a little inscription . . .' (Modesty forbids reproduction of Sir Robin's words.) It will always be a much-treasured memory of a very nice man and a bit of a rascal.

At the reception after the unveiling Robin told Joan that she had very nice legs and told the woman who sleeps on my right side that she looked, 'remarkably like Grace Kelly.'

I said to him, 'Sir Robin, you are a bit of a rascal.' He smiled. 'But I hope I'm a lovable rascal.'

*

The year 1975 would have been a very good one if it hadn't been for Bill Cotton. In fairness, the years up to that time had been more than very good, thanks to Bill, but not 1975. It all started in the foyer of the Philharmonic Hall in Liverpool, 1974. It was the interval in a concert given by the Syd Lawrence Orchestra (that's what I call a boy band), and for the first half, forty-five minutes, I had been spellbound by the big-band sound, as had a packed and very enthusiastic audience, starved so long of this great sound.

I spotted Syd in the foyer, talking to a group of fans. I hadn't seen him for many years – the last time was when he was playing lead trumpet with the BBC Northern Dance Orchestra (at that time they were the equal of the great Ted Heath Band). In those early days I saw quite a lot of Syd when I went with Doddy to Blackpool to record a very popular and prestigious radio programme of that time *Blackpool Night*. Doddy seemed to be on every other week, as were two other newcomers, Morecambe and Wise, and it was also where I first met a very young and very nervous Les Dawson, making what was then one of his first ever radio appearances. It was a great breeding ground for new comics.

My comedy idol, Dave Morris, was the resident comedian, the same man who almost twenty years earlier had told me 'not to take any wooden money' as he passed my market stall. Dave's 'straight man' was played by Joe Gladwyn. 'Do you know 'ow much 'e paid me, Eddie? 'Ow much do you think? A rotten fiver.'

This was Joe many years later when we met in the BBC Club. Fiver or not, it led to greater things for Joe when he played Norah Batty's husband in *Last of the Summer Wine*, which, by a very strange freak of fortune was, and is as I write, produced by Alan J.W. Bell. Alan's first TV job was a floor manager on our show. When John first introduced Alan to us he said, 'Alan will liaise between us.' From then on he was known, christened by Eric, as Alan Liaise.

Back to Syd in the foyer. He now had his back to me as he talked to a group of big-band fans. I tiptoed up behind him and spoke the words *Blackpool Night* compère Jack Watson used every week to introduce the programme:

> Come where the stars are shining bright.
> Be gone dull care; it's *Blackpool Night*!

Strike up the NDO! And away we go for a jolly sixty-minute romp.

Syd spun around with a look of surprised disbelief. 'Bloody Hell! Eddie!'

Our reunion didn't last long, as the bell rang to end the interval. I got a very pleasant surprise when Syd said, 'Can we play something for you in the second half?'

'Would you?'

'If I've got it in the library we'll play it for you.'

They did have it in the library and the band played 'Leave us Leap'. Always one of my big-band favourites because it's got a great drum solo. The Phil rocked and the audience went wild. It was quite a surprise when the applause died and Syd introduced me as the one who had requested that number. I went up on stage and said what a great honour it was to be standing on the stage of the famous Philharmonic Hall, and to be standing on the actual spot where Rach had his Maninoff. I also mentioned that one band member was playing the very latest trombone, the only one of its kind – it does twelve Glen Miller numbers to half a bottle of gin. Just those two gags and that gave me the idea of doing a TV pilot show with Syd and the band. I got the green light for the pilot and called it *Sweet and Sour*, a musical show with a comedy break of no more than a minute between each number. It worked at the Phil; why not on TV? It didn't work on TV. Bill Cotton looked at the tape of the pilot and didn't like it. He had a lot of experience with big bands, so I sadly had to accept his decision.

I could have kicked the legs from under him.

However, Eric and Ern liked the big-band sound and Syd and the orchestra appeared on the show just one month after the Philharmonic concert. Eric introduced them as 'D.H. Lawrence and his Arabian Orchestra', their first of two Morecambe and Wise appearances. I was very pleased, as it was the only successful guest suggestion I had ever made.

Choosing the right guest for a show was very important; a lot of time and a lot of names were put forward and carefully considered, as the guest could make or break the main sketch.

This was an area I never ventured into, except on one memorable, and for all the wrong reasons, occasion. It was a dreadful mistake and the only time it happened.

I put the name forward and everyone agreed this guest was right for the part. John checked and he was available. He was booked and we all looked forward to meeting him at rehearsal – even now I get the shakes just thinking about this. He arrived on the Monday morning with a hearty 'Good morning everyone!' Then made his way across the room to where we were all seated with our little plastic cups of tea and coffee and looking forward to the first rehearsal. It was as our guest was walking across the room that we suspected we might have a problem, as with each step he took there came a merry 'chinkle-chinkle' from inside his BOAC bag. We looked at each other in horror – it wasn't Veno's cough mixture inside that bag.

Trouble, trouble, trouble! Right here in White City.

He took his overcoat off, said, 'Excuse me for just two minutes.' Then headed 'chinkle chinkle' for the Gents. 'What are you looking at me for? Be fair; you said he was right for us when I suggested him.'

Eric was worried. 'Hell fire! He's on the falling-down water.'

That was a fact.

The astonishing thing was that he never looked drunk, he never sounded drunk, he didn't sway when he walked. He did have a fixed smile, probably because he was permanently happy. Credit where credit is due: on the night he gave a stunning performance. The only problem we had was that during the actual recording we had to stop three times so that make-up could try to restore his nose to something like a normal colour. He could have lured ships on to the rocks with that nose. Did it really matter? He gave a superb performance, he was a very nice man and he was happy and didn't give us any problems – we created them ourselves.

Always after that when we were discussing who to have as the guest, if I said, 'How about . . .' that was as far as it got before somebody said, 'Chinkle-chinkle.' Other guests, other problems; some of them rather unfortunate problems. There was the occasion when a much-respected and very distinguished guest had a troublesome tummy, what Eric described as 'a touch of the tapiocas'. It was very embarrassing for the unfortunate guest who had to leave the set at a trot quite frequently during the final dress run. There was a short break and Eric asked the now almost exhausted actor, 'Have you tried that pink stuff?' He responded very quickly because here was salvation, 'What pink stuff?' I was up in the gallery when this dialogue took place and I almost fell off the chair when Eric replied, 'Elastoplast.'

Is this coincidental? Of all the guests we ever had on the shows, the ones I got on really well with, all had one thing in common: everyone of them had a gentle voice, spoke quietly. It was the same with the people I met and became friends with outside the profession. Ordinary people with proper jobs, they all spoke gently. Lilly Benson was softly spoken even when she told me to sod off. Gentle Amy, the flower seller in St John's Market: 'I've been to see the doctor about me legs and he says that I've got very close veins'. Gordon Jackson, a quiet, unobtrusive man with a gentle voice that retained a hint of his Scottish background. Gordon was delighted to be a guest in the 1975 Christmas show. We were standing together watching a final dress rehearsal and there was a smile on his face as he watched Eric and Ern rehearse their opening spot. He turned to me and said, 'I'm so pleased to be a part of this.' A simple, quietly spoken statement but said with such sincerity. Another Gordon, Hannah. When she said, 'How very nice to see you. How are you?'

The answer should have been, 'Bewitched.' A velvet glove of a voice.

But it was Peter Cushing who had the gentlest of all the gentle voices and I shall always remember the last words he ever spoke to me. They came after we had both taken part in Ern's *This Is Your Life*. We were saying goodbye after the reception when he took hold of my hands and said, 'I'm older than you and I shall probably go first. When you do eventually arrive will you ask for Peter the Fisherman.'

Gypsy Jim

The piece I'm writing now could well have the heading 'Notes from the Countryside'. I'm rather taken with that because it makes me sound like a naturalist writing for some upmarket and trendy magazine aimed at people who have big houses in the country. Not too far into the country – perhaps a twenty-minute four-wheel-drive from the nearest all-night chemist. Those who like to think of themselves as gentry to the manor born.

I fancy myself as one of those writers, no late nights going for a laugh a line. Writing stuff like that, I need a different name. Nothing very earthy about the one I've got. I'd call myself Gypsy Jim; that's a good name, Gypsy Jim, with his 'Notes from the Countryside' and useful hints like 'How to Curry a Hedgehog'. And incidents like the following, even though I admit they have been coloured up a little, are based on real events that have often led to a few prime time laughs. Because they are 'of the land' Eric would have enjoyed them: there was a 'Squire Morecambe' aching to get out.

The sun came out, had a look at the weather and then went back in again.

Sandbags were stacked three high against doors and very tall men in the village, as it hadn't stopped raining for fifteen years – in reality two weeks that felt like fifteen years. I was fit to be tied down because I hadn't been able to go o'er bush and heath. In desperation I prayed to the Mountain God, sacrificed two sheep and a goat, buried a left sock (green) and the rains ceased.

If ever you're on holiday and the weather isn't too encouraging, you'll know what to do.

At wonderful last the sun put his hat on and came out to play, the words of a song I used to sing when I was five, and my very proud dad would say, 'He's going to be something special when he grows up.' There's still time yet.

Out came the sun, out came the hikers and one of them came over the stile next to our gate like a mountain goat. He jumped the last two steps and as he landed sliced the head off a wilting and defenceless nettle, just to show me how fit he was. He had a weather-beaten face, the colour of a brown paper bag, and was wearing the full hiker's uniform: boots he could have kicked a donkey into the next county with, corduroy trousers that whistled while he walked, a knapsack (and what a 'k' is doing in front of that word I'll never know), all topped off with a rather natty line in brown berets. He leant on his stout stick of hawthorn, surveyed the surroundings and me as I came out of our gate. Had I seen him first I would have done a very quick about-turn and gone back in because I know the type, meet a dozen or more every year. And even though it was mid-December there were still a few hardy types roaming unchecked – after November we usually put them to sleep with tranquilliser darts. Like a lot of city dwellers on holiday in the countryside, he felt he had to have a conversation with somebody who was 'of the land', and I was it – back home his neighbours probably couldn't get a word out of him.

He saw me and thought, *I'll have a word with this old yokel; I shall say to him, 'Good morrow, aged rustic.'* As it happened, he said nothing like that, which was just as well because if he had I would have kicked the stick from under him.

He was very pleasant and greeted me with a jovial, 'Good morning. Isn't it a beautiful day?'

I couldn't disagree.

He wanted to know what I liked about living in the country-side.

I answered him honestly.

'I enjoy the noise.'

'You like the noise?'

'Of the cows, the sheeps, horses, chickens and the occasional tractor. Noises that I can quite happily live with. Church bells sound good on a Sunday morning, even if you don't respond to the call.'

He was absorbing the view, well worth soaking up and taking home.

'You're very lucky living in a place like this.'

I couldn't disagree.

'You don't have the problems that we have in the city.'

'Like what?'

'You don't have a drugs problem.'

Again I couldn't disagree.

'Drugs aren't a problem here: old Ned in the village can get us all the crack, speed and ecstasy we need.'

He didn't smile. Surely he doesn't believe me!

'I was joking.'

'Oh.'

'His name isn't Ned; it's Charlie.'

I put a laugh on the end of it, for all the good it did. They're making city dwellers a bit thick since I was one.

He pointed his stick in the direction of the field from whence came the frantic 'gobble-gobble-gobble' of a hundred or more very nervous turkeys.

'They're making a lot of noise.'

'Well, it is getting close to Christmas and they're probably making their wills out.'

I now had a hat-trick of no smiles. One last try.

'If they get too noisy I can shut them up quite easily.'

'How do you do that?'

'I just stick my head over the hedge and shout, 'Paxo!'

He was looking at nothing in particular and I was angry with myself for trying to do jokes with people I don't know and who don't know me. Will I never learn? In fairness I don't suppose he was expecting brilliant and original one-liners and certainly not from an aged yokel with acky on his boots.

Off he went at a not-so-merry gait, and more than likely thinking that country folk aren't what they used to be. He would have been better off if he'd stayed at home and listened to the omnibus of *The Archers*.

There wasn't any jollity in his knapsack – that 'k' still doesn't look right.

He was heading towards the crossroads, and not a laugh or a smile as he passed the sign nailed to a post and placed in a field by a neighbour who has a lovely sense of fun, and who's also sick and tired of people using his field and leaving the gate open.

The sign reads, 'BEWARE OF THE BULL. IT'S GAY!' Which isn't true because all the cows are very contented.

He was almost at the crossroads. That wasn't a water mains cover; that was the fairies' house. If you stop and look in the grass you might find a packet of Maltesers. *Miserable old devil.*

I'll bet when he was a kid and his parents took him to see a pantomime, he was one of those who refused to shout, 'He's in the corner!' I'll bet when he was a kid he never went to the pictures and threw orange peel at the organist. I'll bet when he was a kid he never stuck a lump of chewing gum on to the end of a long cane and shoved it through the iron grating outside Richard's grocery shop on the corner of Monkswell Street so that he could pick up the small change that had accidentally fallen through the slats. I'll bet when he was a kid he didn't have a wee out of the back bedroom window at night, because it was too cold to go down the yard.

I could still see him. He wasn't looking back over his shoulder – he probably thought I was dotty. Miserable old devil. Didn't he know who he'd just been taking to? What a talking point that would have been when he got home.

I was tempted to shout after him, 'I'll bet you've never met the Queen! I'll bet your dad's never shook hands with the Chancellor of the Exchequer! I'll bet you've never won an award and got a kiss from a beautiful Hollywood film star! I'll bet you've never had a ride in Eric Morecambe's Rolls-Royce! I'll bet. . . .'

He'd gone.

Jolly Robins

There's a Christmas 1973 show to write and scraps of paper lie everywhere like large snowflakes. If there are fifty scraps of paper with ideas that will become words that will become comedy routines that will be acceptable and performed, then two or perhaps three at the very most will become a comedy reality. For some reason ideas last thing at night always, certainly in my case, disappear at first light. Not very often the ideas that blossom to laughter come when I'm not searching for them; I could be writing a comedy routine when a totally different idea pops up and I jot it down for later use. Always there are scraps of paper. 'Whatever you do, don't touch them!' They're spread out in no particular order across the floor as I tiptoe to the door to collect a cup of tea. Nobody dares to come in for fear of stepping on my brilliant comedy ideas – it's like crossing a minefield.

There's a yellowing and now crispy half-page torn from a notepad. I found it in a pink folder that had been stowed away at the back of the garage many years before; in fact it was next to the typewriter that had been retired in 1983. There aren't many of us around who know how to change a typewriter ribbon. On that little piece of paper I had written two words: 'Lord Ern – Ring John in the morning.'

OK, seven words; it was 'Lord Ern' I wanted.

I rang John.

'Could you get me a purple throne for Ern?'

'I get asked for them every day.'

'It must be purple. It's also very important that it's too large for him, so that when he sits in it his feet mustn't reach the floor.'

'OK. What's the idea of the throne?'

'He's been made a Lord in the New Years Honours list that Eric has typed out in the stop-press column of a newspaper.'

'That sounds good.'

*

The audience laughed when Ern sat on the throne and his little legs dangled six inches from the floor.

Eric was about to read the New Years Honours list from the *Harpenden Bugle and Advertiser*.

This was to be the opening spot of the Christmas show of that year, 1973.

Eric. A very Christmassy audience, mostly fur trappers from Maidenhead. Did you get your free BBC orange on the way in? If not you'll have to be quick – there's only one.

A very excited Ern was seated on the throne, his little feet swinging, as Eric read from the stop-press of the *Bugle and Advertiser*:

Eric. Her most Gracious Majestee bestows upon the following – To John Betjeman, a Sir Hood.

Ern. He's already got one!

Eric. He's got two now. It's like double cream. She would have given you one, only she didn't think that Knights were that short.

Ern. Just get on with it!

Eric. Her Most Gracious Majestee is pleased to bestow upon Ernest Wise, short-legged comedian, the title of Lord Ern of Peterborough!

Ern. That means that my wife is now a Lady.

Eric. That'll give you something to do on the long winter nights.

Incidentally, the 'double cream' was not in the script; that was a rather neat ad-lib. Which recalls an even better one from the 1972 Christmas show when Ern wasn't too keen on Glenda Jackson appearing in his play. He'd had enough of actors ruining his work:

Ern. They're not much good without a script.

Eric. And you're not much good with one.

For me that was one of his best ad-libs. It came without hesitation and the timing was immaculate. Good enough for Ern to applaud, and I can't remember him doing that before.

Glenda was upset at being told she wasn't needed:

Glenda. But I'm in the *Radio Times*.

Eric. They advertise garden sheds in the *Radio Times* but they're not in the show.

Ern graciously agreed to allow Glenda to appear in the show as Queen Victoria, even though she wanted out after she'd read Ern's words. There was no way out for her, as Eric had recorded her agreeing to take part. It's a nasty business.

Ern played Prince Albert in half a dozen dialects. He began in English; then moved to French, German, Italian and Spanish. He told me later that one of them had to be right. Not that it mattered, because when it was a romp there weren't any rules. He told me later that he wanted to do an Australian but that it

kept coming out as a very poor Cockney accent, and now it was
my turn to ad-lib: 'You could have taken all your clothes off
and done "Skippy the Bush Kangaroo".'

Eric laughed and rubbed his hands together between his
knees – glee.

A lot of people laughed when he appeared in that sketch as
Prime Minister Disraeli, with his usual 'Evenin' all. Sorry I'm
late.' He really liked that opening line and wanted to do it
whenever possible:

Eric.   Evenin' all. Sorry I'm late; only I was digging
              the Suez Canal when some fool filled it full of
              water.
Glenda.   Have you had your treaties ratified?
Eric.   Not only that, but they've drawn up my
              stipulations and inserted a proviso. It's a wonder
              I can walk.

That show was memorable for the dinner break (no
disrespect intended to the talented performers who took part
in it). It was the dinner break the day before the recordings
that I shall cherish. The studio was deserted and I couldn't let
this great opportunity pass by as I stood before the famous
Morecambe and Wise staircase, down which some of the
best-loved performers in the land had stepped, danced,
glided, or, in Penelope Keith's case, trod with some apprehension – she even did that with great dignity. I had to do it.
I'd always wanted to do it and I went up and down that
staircase half a dozen times, and it was great. The following
night Glenda, Eric and Ern would step down it with a lot
more style to the music of *Cabaret*.

Can you imagine that a grown man would want to prance
up and down a flight of stairs on his own because he didn't
want anyone to see him? Silly? Of course it was, and still is.
My life has been full of silly things, nonsense and make-

believe. It's something I want to do and have to do. I have to write silly things because even grown-ups like fairy stories and I try to write them: I'm one of the Brothers Grinn. Once upon a time, there were two men. One of them was tall; he wore glasses and he was always saying and doing silly things. The other man wasn't very tall, and the tall one with the glasses kept slapping him on the cheeks and straightening a wig he didn't have and saying things about his short fat hairy legs – but really they were very good friends. The smaller man (his name was Ern) was very, very good at asking questions that would make the tall one with the glasses say funny things. The tall one with the glasses was called Eric and he made a lot of people laugh. They both lived in a flat where lots of silly things happened:

Eric. I've been reading in this magazine about a Swedish dietician who's written a book on how to slim.
Ern. Is it any good?
Eric. It must be: he's been awarded the Nobelly Prize.
The Nobelly Prize! That is a knockout, Ern! That is a belter!

And I have to confess that when this blather, this piffling nonsense occurs in my head and before it goes on to paper, I laugh, chuckle or smile because I'm hearing it for the very first time. What puzzles me is how the silly thought got there in the first place? I didn't press a button, turn a switch or pull a lever – it just happened. The best answer I can come up with is that my head is full of Jolly Robins. I doubt very much if Tchaikovsky could tell you how he built the fourth bridge – he just did it. When I read this out aloud to the woman who sleeps on my right, she looked puzzled and I had to explain that it was a piece of nonsense and that Tchaikovsky didn't build the fourth bridge – if he did it would have been difficult to put it under your chin and get a tune from it. A Jolly Robin put that thought in my head as well. I'm very grateful.

*

There were twenty-five words, I placed them in the right order and had my very first joke, not 'gag' – that's too American; 'joke' sounds more cosy. It was my first piece of silly nonsense and it had been on the wireless. To this day it remains the most exciting, breathtaking moment of my life. No matter what I might have achieved professionally since that day, my first joke will always remain the one I cherish more than any other. I wanted to rush out into the street and tell anyone that my joke had been on the wireless.

When Charlie Chester did that Hopalong Casssidy joke I didn't think, *I've earned half a crown*. What I did think was *Wow I've made people laugh!* That was the magic, that was the reward and it still is – laughter. It must surely be the most beautiful sound a human being can make.

Then came the realisation that I had been given a little bit of a gift and that this was something I had to do.

Some men are born to read gas meters, lay linoleum, sell meat, repair cars, make furniture, drive trains, remove gall-stones, clean windows, rob banks, put wigs on and judge those who rob banks, make pizzas or join the army. I write silly things. What a privilege, what a glorious way to earn a living – making people laugh. Not hurting, not bruising, not causing distress, but creating laughter, and inspired to do so by so many other Brothers Grinn, the beautifully gifted ones: Ted Kavanagh, Frank Muir, Denis Norden, Spike Milligan, Eric Sykes, Johnny Speight, Ray Galton, Alan Simpson, Bob Monkhouse, Denis Goodwin. Each and every one of them a brilliantly lit comedy beacon. They laboured to produce the words; then gave them to the funny men who treated the words as if they were nuggets of gold. They knew the true value of what they had been given; they breathed a magic into the words and the nation laughed.

The End

But the laughter goes on.

PICTURE ACKNOWLEDGEMENTS

©BBC Photo Library, page 5 top.
©Bill Batchelor, page 5 bottom.
©*Liverpool Daily Post and Echo*, pages 6 top right, 8 top (photo John Davidson).
©ITV Pictures, page 2 top.
All other photographs are from the author's collection.

Every reasonable effort has been made to contact the copyright holders, but if there are any errors or omissions, Hodder & Stoughton will be pleased to insert the appropriate acknowledgement in any subsequent printing of this publication.